FOURTH EDITION

Psychology A Level Year 2

THE TEACHER'S COMPANION

Michael Griffin • Rosalind Geillis

Consultant Editor: Cara Flanagan

OXFORD
UNIVERSITY PRESS

CONTENTS

SECTION 1 General Notes 1

SECTION 2 Lesson Notes

Introduction to Lesson Notes **10**

Research Methods **11**

Issues and Debates in Psychology **20**

Relationships **27**

Gender **35**

Cognition and Development **43**

Schizophrenia **50**

Eating Behaviour **60**

Stress **68**

Aggression **77**

Forensic Psychology **86**

Addiction **98**

SECTION 3 Handouts

General handouts **107**

Research Methods **117**

Issues and Debates in Psychology **133**

Relationships **145**

Gender **159**

Cognition and Development **169**

Schizophrenia **180**

Eating Behaviour **193**

Stress **209**

Aggression **228**

Forensic Psychology **243**

Addiction **259**

AQA psychology specification

Approaching the mark scheme

Assessment objectives (AOs) are set by Ofqual to ensure consistency across different psychology specifications and exam boards. As well as defining the three AOs students are to be tested on, Ofqual also state that at least 10% of the overall qualification will contain mathematical skills equivalent to level 2 (GCSE A*–C) or above and 25–30% of the overall assessment will assess skills, knowledge and understanding in relation to research methods.

When teaching exam technique a famous quote I (RG) like to share with my students comes from the martial arts actor Bruce Lee, 'knowing is not enough, we must apply'. If students are unsure what the question is asking them to do then they will not know how to use their knowledge in a way to ensure the question is addressed in their answer. It is helpful to teach students the different AO skills they need to demonstrate and refer to these when introducing activities in lessons, attempting exam questions and giving feedback.

Applying mark schemes – the ladder approach

Choose a level

When marking a student's answer begin at the lowest level (level 1) if the student's answer meets all the criteria for this level then move to the next level.

At this second level (level 2) again consider whether the answer satisfies the criteria stated, if so, the answer climbs to level 3.

When deciding upon a level consider the overall quality of the answer rather than focusing on small areas that may not have been done so well.

Awarding a mark

Once you have identified the appropriate level take a best fit approach to identify the mark. For example, in the case of a student whose answer seems to fit into level 3 but has a few elements of level 4 their answer remains at level 3 as they have not satisfied enough of the criteria to move to level 4 but would receive a mark close to the top of the level 3 band.

Using mark schemes with students (see Handouts 1–3 for generic marking grids)

Handout 3 may provide a more visual guide to marking essays and help the student to understand instantly where they need to improve (e.g. knowledge or evaluation or use of terminology). You can draw an arrow next to each thermometer to indicate the level for each element of the essay (and also how close to the next level it is, e.g. strong level 2). The bottom of the page can then be used to justify the overall level if the different elements of the essay achieve different levels.

Self/peer assessment and teacher feedback

Handouts 5 and 6 can be used for self and peer assessment, as well as teacher feedback by simply colour coding which cells a student's answer has met for the AOs contained in the question. When marking answers encourage students to annotate AO1, AO2 and AO3 so they are able to break visualise the various components of the answer before applying the mark scheme. Students will need to be trained in how to apply the mark scheme if self and peer assessment is to be meaningful. A useful activity involves giving students a high scoring answer and a low scoring answer for the same question. Working in pairs, students annotate the answer to identify relevant AOs. They then meet with another pair to work as a group of four, comparing their annotations and using the mark scheme (or the appropriate generic mark scheme from Handouts 1 and 2) decide on the level, and possibly mark for the two answers. The teacher then shares the actual level and mark with the class explaining what elements of the question lead to the final level and mark. I (RG) would recommend buying back a few exam papers each exam series to be used in lessons.

Writing frames

When setting 16-mark extended questions students may benefit from writing frames to direct their attention to the required AOs. Each frame should be specific to the question asked and may include sentence starters to provide a guide as to what needs to be considered.

Once familiar with these questions frames can be removed however, students who struggle with literacy may prefer to continue using them.

Approaching revision

Revision records

With the move to linear examinations, creating revision notes across the course is more important than ever. Handout 4 provides a generic template for a revision record that can be used for A Level students. These can be completed as homework tasks or time can be given in lessons as a means to check progress. Completion of the record could be set as a paired task with the final record being photocopied so each student receives a copy.

The top of the handout requires students to state the topic and also the overall section and paper to help with organisation of revision notes.

Completing the six sentence summary and topic glossary provides an outline of the topic which can be used to address AO1 questions requiring students to state, identify, outline and describe research.

The final four cells encourage students to create PEEL evaluations (AO3). Aim for two strengths and two limitations as exam questions may ask students to describe two limitations for example.

Although the record covers AO1 and AO3 skills the record can be a useful tool for tackling AO2 application questions nearer the exam period. The record can also be used in revision sessions with students giving them to a peer who then asks questions to test their retention of knowledge.

Toolkit of activities and ideas

Starters and plenaries

Question Raffle – At the start or end of the lesson, ask each student to write a question related to the topic and/or lesson objectives on a piece of paper. Fold up the questions, place them in a hat and ask the students to pick out a question and answer it in front of the class.

Blankety Blank – Ever asked students to read part of a sheet or textbook and been frustrated by how little they have taken in? Try setting a time limit and warning them that they will be tested on that information shortly afterwards. Lift quotes from the text they have read and blank out keywords/variables etc. to see if they can remember what those keywords were. This activity works even better if you can create a PowerPoint which mirrors the old game show!

Odd One Out – Display four pictures, keywords or concepts on a PowerPoint or whiteboard and ask students to select which one they think is the odd one out and justify why. You can either deliberately manipulate the odd one out to test knowledge, or purposefully not include an obvious odd one out so that students can make their own links/comparisons between different things.

Quick Sentence – Very easy. Ask a student for a number between say, 20 and 40. Whatever number they select, the students must summarise the lesson in exactly that number of words. Another idea that makes your workload easier.

Jerry Springer – Explain that at the end of his shows, Jerry Springer always does a summing up. It usually starts with the phrase "So… what have we learned here today? We have learned that…." Ask the students to complete their Jerry Springer summing up of the lesson. You can then ask some students to read theirs out. Again, for those of the 'gimmick' persuasion, consider buying a humorous Jerry Springer style wig for this moment – the cheaper the better!

I have learnt that … – You and your students may be familiar with the game "My Granny went to the shops and she bought …." This plenary is a variation of that game. Students must write down one thing they have learned that lesson. Then, the teacher selects one person who must say "I have learned that …. (then whatever they have written down) ……". Then the teacher should select a second student who must state what they learnt, but also what the first person learned. And so on …! This promotes active listening in students, and if my experience is anything to go by, it can require some practice!

Pictionary – Give students a key word, theory or psychologist, and ask them to attempt to draw this in a visual form that other class members would be able to guess. This could be setup as a whole class activity, or a small group competition.

Mixed Bag – On an A4 sheet of paper write a series of plenary statements such as: "What information is important to remember from this lesson?", "What are the three key words relevant to this lesson?", "How could I have improved my work?", "How could I use the knowledge/skills from this lesson in my other subjects?", "How can I relate what we have learned in this lesson to my own life?", and "How valuable has my contribution to this lesson been and why?" Cut these questions out and ask students to pick one at random at the end of the lesson. They could then feedback their answers to the rest of the class.

Post-it® Continuum – This is particularly useful for evaluation lessons. Display a continuum on the whiteboard, e.g. low ecological validity to high ecological validity. Give each student a Post-it® note and ask them to place it on the continuum along with a justification of why they have placed it where they have. You could even introduce a continuum with both horizontal and vertical axes for a challenge! Look ahead to page 86 for an example.

Making connections – Display lots of key terms/concepts/ studies on the board. Ask the students to make three or four pairs and explain their connections. This makes a good starter to a lesson.

Assessment for learning

A B C marking – Marking and feedback has been a big focus in colleges and schools over recent years following an Ofsted emphasis. The best marking and feedback tends to engage students in dialogue and provides evidence of impact. I've seen different schools/colleges and teachers approach this in different ways. The method I (MG) prefer is very simple and genuinely has the potential to move students on in their learning. In the body of the student's answer/essay, ask three questions which you think will help them to move on in their learning and to progress their understanding. Label these questions 'A', 'B' and 'C' and the students can then use **Handout 5** as a template for their responses. With my classes, all assessed work follows this format and their work is then stored in a separate assessment folder. Examples of questions can be seen in the work below.

Match me up quickly – Taking inspiration from the 'fastest finger first' game in Who Wants to be a Millionaire… display four key terms/concepts and label them A, B, C and D. Then display the definitions and label them 1, 2, 3 and 4. As soon as the definitions are displayed, the students use their mini-whiteboards to match them up as quickly as possible and hold up their mini-whiteboards when they have finished. This is a good little game at the end of the lesson if you have a series of four/five rounds.

Did you…? – This activity can be used in a number of ways to encourage students to reflect on what needs to be included in a successful answer and can be adapted to suit questions that combine two or more assessment objectives. The checklist can be used to cover exam technique (using key terms correctly, including the correct assessment objectives in an answer, writing in PEEL paragraphs) or can relate to actual knowledge and understanding needed to answer the question. For example,

Outline and evaluate research on self-disclosure in virtual relationships. (8 marks)

Did you…	Muddled/ flawed	Basic	Reasonable	Effective
Did you select relevant research?				
Did you outline procedures accurately?				
Did you state findings accurately?				
Did you use PEEL to structure evaluations?				
Did you….				

The class could work together to create the *Did you?* table before sitting the assessment or could use a table the teacher has produced to engage in self or peer assessment before submitting their answer to be marked.

Essay Oscars – On completing an assessment provide students with a list of Oscar nominations from which they are to choose one or two they feel their answer could be awarded. This should be done before seeing teacher feedback. For example:

- Concise yet detailed writing style
- Consistent use of evaluation signposts
- PEEL used to structure evaluative comments
- Direct links made to question.
- Common words spelt correctly.
- Accurate use of specialist terminology.

Bingo – Students can place their feedback on a bingo grid so they can visualise what information was missing from their answer. For example:

Outline Bowlby's monotropic theory of attachment. (6 marks)

Showed an understanding of the evolutionary basis of attachment.	Gave examples of social releasers and explained their function.	Explained the concept of a critical period (3–6 months).
Defined the term monotropy.	Explained the concept of an internal working model and its importance in social relationships.	Showed an understanding of the continuity hypothesis.
Highlighted the difference between primary and secondary attachments.	Made a distinction between the formation of attachment and the consequences of attachment formation.	Mark awarded _____

Students read each cell of the bingo grid and tick comments that refer to aspects they have included in their answer. Alternatively students can colour code each cell of the bingo grid (green – I explained this clearly, yellow – I implied this or my comments were muddled, red – I did not mention this in my answer). Students then re-write any ambiguous areas and add missed information to form a complete answer.

Once students have identified their particular strengths they are to predict one or two areas they need to improve – seeing other students' answers may help them do this. Only when this has been done, then students are given the teacher feedback and mark. This could be on a sticker that can be stuck at the end of the assessment.

This activity helps students reflect on what they have written rather than rushing straight to the mark they were awarded as well as encouraging student ownership of assessment for learning. A variation of this could be to withhold the mark until improvements have been acted on then students can be provided with their original mark and their post-improvement mark enabling them to visualise how they have improved.

Making use of students work – Giving students an overview of how the class as a whole is working can be a useful tool when giving feedback and encouraging students to identify their own areas to improve.

1. Share aspects of the assessment that were done well by the majority of the class.

2. Highlight one or two common errors that were seen in the majority of student's answers.

3. Work through these errors by assigning students to groups with a lead learner (a student who did not make that error and asking them to share their assessment) or as a whole class by annotating a model answer or setting a 'fill in the blanks' task to form a model answer.

4. Students then revisit their assessment to reflect on what they did well (step 1) and re-write areas they need to improve (steps 2–3).

Keeping a record – Either at the front of their folder or in a section containing previous assessments students should keep a record of their assessment marks and targets to improve, along with any improved marks for re-written assessments. This record should be referred to before sitting each assessment to provide a reminder of previous targets to ensure the same mistakes are not being made and focusing students on the areas they need to address when preparing for the up-coming assessment. These records are a valuable source of information for parents' evening and when writing reports.

Objective Venn diagrams – Identify three objectives for the lesson or class task. Display a Venn diagram to the class similar to the one shown here, making sure each objective is clearly displayed. Give each student a sticky note and tell them to write their name on it and place it on the Venn diagram to show which objectives they feel they have achieved. You could also ask students to give a justification of their choice.

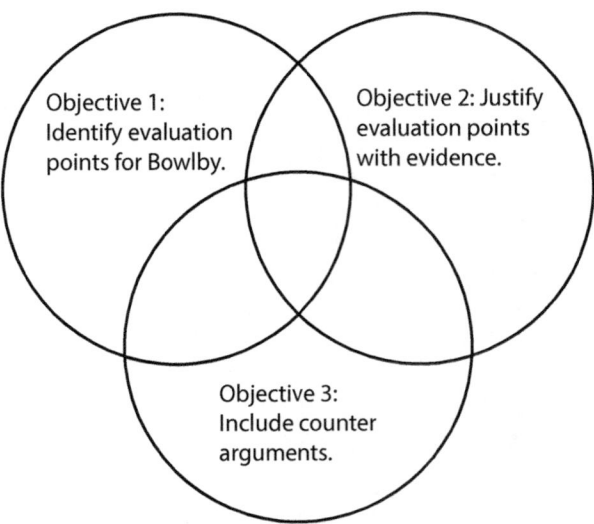

Objective 1: Identify evaluation points for Bowlby.

Objective 2: Justify evaluation points with evidence.

Objective 3: Include counter arguments.

This assessment method encourages students to reflect on their own learning and quickly demonstrates where the class is as a whole. If the majority of students do not meet one objective it may indicate that area needs to be addressed in a different manner. Differentiation could also be addressed with all students aiming to achieve the first objective while more able students are challenged to meet more than one objective.

Peer assessment grid – **Handout 6** can be used to help students assess each other's evaluations, exam answers and essays. Try to anonymise the activity by asking students to write a number between 1 and 999 on their work before giving it in. Give out one piece of work to each student marker with one copy of the peer assessment grid. The student marker should then complete the first box by identifying four key terms that the 'candidate' has used and one key term that they could have used. Then, pass the work and the peer assessment grid to the person on their left. The second marker then, completes the second box, by writing down a good sentence from the work and explaining why it was a good sentence. Then pass to the left … and so on (as shown on the handout). By the end of the activity the peer assessment grid should be completed and handed back to the original 'candidate' by calling out the numbers on each piece of work. Each 'candidate' will get feedback from four student markers and will have reviewed four different pieces of work themselves. The feedback may vary in quality, but the activity of reviewing four different pieces of work should produce plenty of learning gains. Most importantly, the peer assessment was qualitative rather than quantitative … which I think is much more productive than the usual 'look at the mark scheme and give your mate a score' type of peer assessment.

Collaborative learning

Group work can be incredibly productive, but it is also a perilous activity! The danger is this: diligent students in the group do most of the work, the drama students do most of the feeding back to class, and all of the other students are anonymous in the middle!

The trick to making sure group work is successful is by ensuring the tasks you devise are based on the following principles:

- Students are dependent on each other in order to successfully complete the task.
- Students are also individually accountable for the work they have done.
- Students participate equally.

With these aims in mind, here are some simple ideas for structuring your group work:

Random numbers – When setting a discussion question, ask the students to number themselves in their groups. Then make it clear that when you ask the group to feedback their answer, you will randomly choose a number and that person will have to feedback. This ensures that all group members are involved in the discussion and need to pay close attention to what is being said. In addition, it ensures that more gifted students will need to 'teach' their higher-order arguments to the weaker students, so that they are able to feedback that idea.

Group statements – Set your students a discussion question. Individually, students should write their response to that question and elaborate their answers as fully as possible. Following this, students should share their statements with members of their group. Finally, the group should write a group statement which reflects the opinions, arguments and ideas of the group as a whole. This prevents the strongest and most confident students from taking over the activity and writing the statement without input from weaker/less confident students.

Snowballing – Ask students individually to write down 3 ideas in response to a question. For example, "list 3 evaluation points for Asch's study." This works better if you give them a short time limit, say 2 minutes. After those 2 minutes are up, tell students to share their ideas with the person on their left

and write down any new ideas they hadn't thought of – give them another 2 minutes to do this. Then repeat the process with students who sit across from them. Hopefully, by the end of the activity they should have picked up different ideas from the students around them, and shared their own ideas.

Student dimension line – Display some sort of continuum on your PowerPoint or whiteboard. For example, Zimbardo's Prison Experiment was ethical – strongly agree to strongly disagree. Ask your students to stand along that line to indicate their opinion on this matter. As the teacher, you can now use this line to structure group work. For example, you could 'fold' the line so that the person who most 'strongly agrees' ends up facing the person who most 'strongly disagrees'. Students can then discuss their ideas with the students opposite them (e.g. think, pair, share – see below). Alternatively, you could use a 'systematic sample(!)' - go along the line giving students numbers and then asking them to sit in groups, ensuring that your groups are mixed by having people who 'strongly agree', 'agree', 'disagree' and 'strongly disagree' with the original statement. This idea works particularly well when the original question you set is something like: 'To what extent do you understand ethical issues?' Constructing a dimension line like this also means you can sort your students into differentiated, or mixed-ability groups.

Think, pair, share – I am sure many people have heard of this technique already, it is perhaps the most well-known collaborative learning structure. Set your students some kind of discussion question and give them a few moments of thinking time to individually gather their thoughts. Then students should share their ideas with the person next to them. In the feedback phase of this activity, ask students to feedback their partner's ideas as opposed to their own. This encourages active listening and clear communication.

Top 3 starter/plenary – Display around ten key terms/ concepts in the board. Ask the students to select the three terms/concepts they would be most confident explaining to the rest of the class. Then, ask students to compare their list with the list of the person sitting next to them. The students must explain one term/concept on their list which isn't on their partner's lists and vice versa. Crucially, in the whole-class feedback, the students must explain the new term they have learned, rather than the term they taught to their partner.

Developing student's skills

A Level skills are split into three assessment objectives (AOs). AO1 – demonstrating knowledge and understanding, AO2 – applying knowledge and understanding, AO3 – analysis, interpretation and evaluation. Here are just a few ideas for each AO which can then be used to deliver a number of topics from the course.

Activities by skill – AO1 (Demonstrating knowledge and understanding)

Basic to detailed – Often students are not aware that their outlines of theories/studies lack detail. Equally, when our assessment feedback suggests 'needs more detail', the students often do not have a tangible idea of what this might entail. It is only when you talk to the students that this becomes apparent. A very simple activity to help the students understand what is meant by 'detail' is to give them 'basic' outlines for them to improve/annotate. For example, leave out percentages, key terms, definitions… be a bit vague about the procedure etc. After you have taught that study/theory in more detail, set the students the task of improving the 'basic' outline to an 'effective' outline. This should help them to see and understand what is meant by 'detail' and remind them of the type of information they should try and include in future answers. There are a couple of examples of this activity in this book that you can use and copy, see **Handouts 81** and **146**.

Distilling – Ask students to call out key words associated with a certain topic, these words are recorded on the board for all the class to see. Students could be asked to do this from memory as a revision activity or following reading of a passage to identify key features of the information read. As a class the words on the board are then grouped in level of importance: which words should a basic outline include, which additional words would form a reasonable outline and finally, for a well-detailed outline, what words would also be needed? Students are then challenged to write an outline using as many of the words as possible. Once completed students could peer assess colour coding the words included (basic, reasonable and effective) and check the accuracy of the outline produced.

True or false – Students are given a list of statements to determine whether they are true or false. Using their own knowledge or with help from a textbook, students add additional comments to any correct statements and amend any statements which are false. This is a useful way to dispel common misunderstandings as well as encourage students to read a passage in a more meaningful way than simply highlighting sentence after sentence.

Activities by skill – AO2 (Applying knowledge and understanding)

Two-sentence technique – Application questions in research methods often follow the same pattern. They look something like this:

Outline **one strength** and **one limitation** of this research design in the context of this study (2 + 2 marks).

There might be some variation in the wording and marks available, but this is a fairly repetitive question. However, 'research design' (underlined) could be replaced by 'correlation', 'sampling technique', 'measure of central tendency' etc. In these types of questions, students are required to show their *knowledge* and their ability to *apply* their knowledge to the situation. So, I encourage my students to use a two-sentence technique.

Sentence one (show your knowledge): One limitation of the independent groups research design is that group differences may occur.

Sentence two (apply to the context): In this context, the group of participants using the mind map technique may have had better memories than the participants using the repetition technique. This biases the results.

At the start of the psychology course, I actually insist that students also write in two different colours to drive the message home. This technique can be used across the course, not just in research methods. For example, in the approaches topic, students write a knowledge sentence on one of the approaches and then apply that knowledge to the context given. They can keep doing that until they feel they have answered the question. An example is given on **Handout 131**.

Taking the role of… – Students are assigned the role of a professional working in a field related to the topic being studied, (e.g. occupational psychologist, therapist, editor of a psychological journal) and are set a challenge relating to their job role which involves them drawing out key information from a text. If working in groups the challenge set can be split into clear objectives (relating to higher-order thinking levels) and each group member assigned one to action. Alternatively, a more-able group could be asked to identify their own objectives from the overall aim set by the teacher or even have to work out what the actual problem is that needs to be addressed and develop their own aims and objectives.

Bridging the gap – Students are provided with two pieces of information and are asked to bridge the gap between the two texts. For example, a passage relating to the experience of depression, such as an extract from the autobiography *Prozac Nation* by Elizabeth Wurtzel (1994) is shown at the top of a piece of paper. At the bottom of the paper is an extract from a textbook outlining the cognitive explanation of depression. Clues could be added along the bridge to scaffold thinking.

Scaffolded application – This activity relies on sample assessment materials and past exam papers or the creation of your own scenarios. Provide students with an exam question that requires application of knowledge. Students first highlight the key piece of information contained in the question stem and record this in the stem column of **Handout 7**. In the second column they identify a relevant concept. The final column provides space for the student to apply the concept to the stem (application).

Activities by skill – AO3 (Analysis, interpretation and evaluation)

Primark and Savile Row – This analogy can be used to explain the importance of creating evaluations that relate specifically to the research being discussed. Basic evaluations are like Primark jumpers – cheap and cheerful, they fit anyone but are pretty disposable. Basic 'Primark-type' evaluations are those that can be applied to a number of different theories or studies with little direct fit. Comments such as 'this study lacks population validity' would be considered basic. Savile Row suits are expensive and tailored to the individual- they simply wouldn't look right on another individual. Effective evaluations are those which relate explicitly to the research under discussion as they are based on key features of the research and so do not fit anywhere else. When students have written their evaluations ask them to check whether they are Primark (basic) or Savile Row (effective).

Body building – This activity encourages students to add weight to the basic evaluative comment to create an effective evaluative paragraph. Provide students with a range of one sentence evaluations that could apply to a specific research theory or study. Working in small groups students are asked to develop the muscle behind this evaluative point by adding specific details that link the point to the actual research being discussed. For example, 'Point: The Working Memory model is useful as it has had many real world applications'. Students can build up this evaluation by considering how the model has been used in dyslexia research.

Evaluation Ladders – Hands up who has read and been upset by this comment on their students essays: "The ecological validity of the study is low because it is not like real life"?! Aaaaggghhh! Of course, our job as teachers is to help students to elaborate their evaluative comments – something they seem to find really hard, but undoubtedly has a significant impact on their grades if they can develop the skill. Having read the above statement in an Asch essay for the thirtieth time, I (MG) decided to try and devise a memorable teaching technique to help students with this skill. And so, the 'elaboration ladders' were born (see **Handout 8**). The central idea behind the elaboration ladders is that students start with an introductory evaluation comment at the bottom of the ladder and then gradually elaborate this comment further and further until they reach the smiley face at the top! The box on the right-hand side is designed to prompt students into thinking of ways they could elaborate their evaluations, for example, 'have I got evidence?'. To give you an example of how this might work, consider Ainsworth's Strange Situation paradigm:

1. Students could start off by making a generic statement such as: *'It could be argued that Ainsworth's studies lacked ecological validity.'*

2. Students would then need to consider how they could elaborate this. Using the prompts on the right they may decide to include evidence: *'Indeed, Lamb et al. (1995) feels that the Strange Situation is highly artificial (novel and stressful) and therefore might make children more clingy and less likely to look secure.'*

3. Again, students should consider the prompts on the right such as – 'Why does this matter?' For example: *'This is a problem because it means the results of the study may not be generalisable outside of the Strange Situation and that Ainsworth's results may have underestimated the amount of secure attachments.'*

4. Once again, students should consider how they might elaborate this response. This time, it could come in the form of a counterargument: *'On the other hand, it may be relatively common that infants would face novel and stressful situations and Ainsworth's study is able to take that into account. In addition, Ainsworth designed the study deliberately to be artificial and create anxiety in order to judge whether the infants would be able to use their attachment figures as a secure base.'*

By going through this process, the hope is that the student is able to discuss their evaluation and its implications in more depth. This visual technique, used in conjunction with the prompts on the right-hand side of the ladders, seems to have been very successful in developing elaboration skills in the students at our school.

Burger evaluation skills – This technique can be used with your students to develop their ability to evaluate *theories* with studies. I often find that students struggle with the structure of using research evidence to evaluate a theory. What students forget to do is illustrate that they understand how and why the evidence undermines or supports a theory. Instead, they simply describe a relevant study and expect the reader to draw their own conclusions! The burger technique requires students to 'sandwich' their study descriptions with evaluative commentary (AO3). You will see from **Handout 9** that students are first encouraged to outline whether the evidence 'supports' or 'undermines' the theory at the top of the burger. Then, in the middle of the burger they outline that evidence, ensuring that they only outline the relevant information of that study, and not every detail. Lastly, and most importantly, at the bottom of the burger they must explain how that study undermines or supports the theory; usually, this should involve explaining whether or not the data supports what the theory would have predicted and why. Blank burger templates are given on **Handout 10** where students can attempt the technique.

ICT tips and tricks

ICT tricks

Here are just a few ideas you could use to 'jazz up' your lessons!

Rolling shows – These can be created using PowerPoint and essentially consist of a slideshow of images. They are very useful to use when students are coming into lessons. When played with relevant music they create a good atmosphere and let students know that from the moment they walk into your classroom, they are in a learning environment.

Find a series of images related to the content of the lesson. Insert an image onto each slide of your PowerPoint. You could also insert questions for the students to read. When you have finished inserting your images/text, select the <Transitions> or <Animations> tab on the top menu bar. Here you can select which transition you would like to be used to change from one slide to another – I find that 'fade' looks the most professional. Untick the option <On mouse click> and instead select the tick box <Automatically after> and then set the transition to every 5 seconds (or so). Make sure you click the <Apply to all> option beneath this. Lastly, select the <Slide Show> tab from the top menu bar, and then <Set up slide show> from the menu. Clicking the tick box for <Loop continuously until 'ESC'> will ensure that your slideshow will cycle through the images until you want it to stop.

Randomiser – This is another technique that can be used with PowerPoint and enables you to select students randomly, for example to answer a question, or to sort them into groups. Enter your students' names into PowerPoint, with one name on each slide. When you have finished this, follow the procedure outlined above for 'Rolling Shows' exactly, except this time, set the transition between slides to be every 0 seconds – this is important to make the process random as you will see later. To stop the slideshow on one of the names simply press 'S' on your keyboard, this will stop the slideshow. To select another name, simply press 'S' again to start the slideshow.

Although I (MG) have suggested doing this with names, it can also be used to 'randomise' questions, key terms, and even essay titles.

Bluetooth mouse – This idea requires a little investment but is extremely effective if you do not have an interactive whiteboard. Consider purchasing a Bluetooth mouse (search on Amazon, you can get them for around £10 at time of writing). It is essentially a wireless mouse but the signal is much more powerful. This means they can be used at the back of the classroom by your students! You can set up matching games etc. in Publisher, Word, or other software – and your students can play them from their seats! I like to call it the 'Lazy person's interactive whiteboard'. If your laptop or computer is slightly older, you may also need to purchase a 'Bluetooth dongle', perhaps ask your IT technicians about these.

Windows Movie Maker – This is a free programme which is installed on most Windows machines (unless the over zealous IT technicians at your school have removed it!). It is an extremely easy programme to use and allows you to edit videos and insert text on top. This is useful to edit videos you have downloaded (e.g. using the websites above) or videos you have recorded on a digital camera (e.g. a re-enacted student version of Milgram!). There are plenty of tutorials for using this programme on the internet; simply search for 'Windows Movie Maker tutorial' on the internet. Alternatively, I wrote a beginners guide for a staff INSET last year which can be found at www.oxfordschoolblogs.co.uk/psychcompanion/blog/

MonkeyJam – This free software is also relatively easy to use and allows students to make animations, with either drawings, themselves, or plasticine. The process takes a while but is ideal for extended projects or after-school clubs. Searching for monkeyjam in Google should be enough to find this software. Again, there are many tutorials available on the internet. A video camera or good webcam are required.

Making cartoons – There are some fantastic websites that allow students to make professional-looking cartoons with images they want to use. For example, they could recreate a discussion between Milgram and his critics by finding images of the relevant psychologists. Here are some easy-to-use websites you might consider: www.toondoo.com and www.stripcreator.com

Great websites

Here are a list of fantastic psychology-related websites on the internet, invaluable to any teacher! I am sure there are more out there waiting to be found, but these are the ones I have come across:

- www.psychlotron.org.uk *A site packed full of ready-to-use worksheets, information sheets, video clips and interactive whiteboard files. Brilliantly organised and updated every week. A fantastic site!*

- www.resourcd.com *This is a teacher sharing site that contains worksheets, PowerPoints, past-exam papers, video clips, ideas, a forum... everything a psychology teacher would ever need!*

- www.holah.co.uk *Although this site is primarily for teachers of the OCR spec, there is invaluable information on this site relevant to AQA content.*

- www.coolpsychologystuff.co.uk *A great site which specialises in psychology-related products for teachers and students. Includes equipment, gifts, DVDs and posters.*

- www.uniview.co.uk *A similar site to that above with products available for your classroom.*

- www.allpsych.com *A collection of links to further sites, organised by topic.*

- www.theatp.org *A great website and association for psychology teachers. They also run a CPD conference each summer which is cheap and well attended.*

- www.teachpsych.org *Lots of resources and ideas for teaching on this website. It is designed for teachers following the American 'APA' qualification but there are still useful ideas that can be gained from this website.*

Blog sites and twitter accounts

The following sites contain thousands of articles related to AQA topics. They are extremely useful for using as extension tasks. Many of the sites allow you to subscribe to their RSS feeds. This means you do not have to search each of the sites every week or so to find related articles; the articles come to you!

Most of these blogs also have twitter accounts you can 'retweet' to your class if your school allows subject twitter accounts. Alternatively, advertise the twitter accounts to your students and try to convince them to give them a 'follow'!

- www.psychblog.co.uk
- www.psychteacher.co.uk
- www.bps-research-digest.blogspot.com
- www.oxfordschoolblogs.co.uk/psychcompanion/blog/
- www.mindhacks.com
- www.spring.org.uk
- www.thepsychfiles.com
- www.thesituationist.wordpress.com
- www.in-mind.org
- www.psychcentral.com
- www.whatispsychology.biz
- www.badpsychologyblog.org

Introduction to Lesson Notes

Your lesson notes section

This section has been written with some specific objectives in mind…

1. To provide teachers with plenty of ideas for teaching the AQA psychology specification.
2. To provide teachers of psychology with a 'toolkit' that helps to alleviate workload, specifically in the planning and creation of resources.
3. To assist teachers in identifying opportunities for differentiation in their lessons and catering for different 'learning styles'.

Plenty of ideas

Within this section we hope you will find plenty of ideas which you might consider using when delivering the AQA psychology specification.

We have tried to structure this section in a way that mirrors the AQA course so that you can easily identify how the ideas and resources fit in with your delivery of the specification. As a result, those of you who have purchased *The Complete Companion* will find that our structure is borrowed from the chapter breakdown used in the textbook.

The lesson notes include ideas for starters, plenaries, main activities and study replications. We have decided not to include detailed lesson plans as there is rarely a one-size-fits-all approach to teaching – it is often more effective for teachers to adapt ideas to suit their own teaching techniques.

Creation of resources

For many of the ideas and activities included in this section, there are accompanying photocopiable handouts which can be used in lessons.

We hope that these handouts will ease some of your workload and bring you closer to that elusive work-life balance!

These handouts can be found on pages 105–271. They are numbered so that you can find them easily.

Differentiation

Undoubtedly one of the most challenging responsibilities for a teacher is planning opportunities for differentiation in lessons. In our own experience of the classroom, we have taught students predicted A's, alongside other students who are predicted U's (yes I know, hard to believe isn't it?!).

Much of the time we are differentiating without even thinking about it. However, if you are anything like us, you may start to panic when asked to identify 'strategies for differentiation' on lesson plans! To a certain extent, the skill is in identifying what we are already doing, as opposed to reinventing the wheel.

Consequently, we have tried to identify how the lesson ideas in this section may provide opportunities to stretch the gifted and talented, while supporting the weaker students so that you can highlight these on your lesson plans and schemes of work.

Our A Level classes will most probably have a wide range of abilities and if teaching in a sixth form or college with a comprehensive intake you could have a class with target grades ranging from E through to an A grade. As such, differentiation is a vital component of lessons if we wish all our students to progress.

The lesson notes found make reference to methods of adapting activities or social support to help students of different abilities access the lesson based on the principles listed below.

- **P**athways – students of different abilities may benefit from being set different tasks based on their current level of skill or understanding.
- **H**igher order – some activities can be adapted or added to, to encourage higher-order thinking such as evaluating, synthesising or creating as mentioned by Bloom's Taxonomy.
- **S**caffolding – scaffolding provides students with the support needed to access the same activity as others in the class. This may mean providing a list of key words to assist reading of a passage or a writing frame when answering 12 or 16 mark questions.
- **G**rouping – depending on the activity set students may benefit from working in mixed-ability groups, where more-able students can take on the role of lead learners with the responsibility of directing the group and checking understanding, which in turn helps consolidation of their knowledge. For other activities, ability groups may be more suitable with different groups being set different activities.
- **T**argeted intervention – At some points you may wish to work closely with a certain student or small group of students. This could be to support less-able students or challenge the most able to think beyond the obvious. This is challenging when teaching large classes but can be done if the class is provided with tasks that encourage independent learning and the group develops a culture of collaboration with each other rather than relying on their teacher to provide all the answers.

TOPIC: Content Analysis

Considering content analysis

Students are first asked to identify the sampling method, coding and method of representing data in the scenario given on **Handout 11**. This activity reinforces what is involved in conducting a content analysis and gives an example of thematic analysis. The second half of **Handout 11** requires students to apply their evaluative knowledge of the method to the scenario. A stretch question is also included asking students to consider other media that may be analysed, for example, school reports or transcripts of interviews with students.

Less-able students may need a reminder of key terms to support their understanding. Definitions of sampling method, coding, qualitative data, quantitative data and thematic analysis could be provided.

TOPIC: Content Analysis

Creating a content analysis

Students could carry out a mini content analysis of their own. This could be linked to another area of the specification, for example, an analysis of the portrayal of gender roles in magazine adverts or children's story books. Students should consider the media to be analysed and sampling method used, how data is coded and whether data will be represented quantitatively or qualitatively. Students could:

1. Design a study.
2. Write this up as an answer to a 12-mark question.
3. Carry out a content analysis.
4. Rewrite the exam answer.

Additional activities:

The exam may include a question worth as much as 12 marks asking students to design a study. Before students carry out their own content analysis, their write-up of the methodology could be marked using the mark scheme provided here.

A suggested question could be: Design a content analysis into . . . . (insert suitable topic here). . . . In your answer you should provide details of: the media to be analysed and sampling method used, how data will be coded and represented, how reliability of data collection might be established.

Ensure groups comprise students who show good imagination and those who have a secure understanding of content analysis as a method of investigation.

Once students have carried out their content analysis, their initial answer can be revisited and improved based on their new-found knowledge from conducting their own investigation.

Level	Marks	Description
4	10–12	Suggestions are generally well detailed and practical (realistic). Sound understanding of content analysis is demonstrated. All elements requested by the question are presented and reported in sufficient detail for the study to be implemented with success. Only minor details and/or explanation are lacking. Specialist terminology is used effectively and explanations are clear and coherent.
3	7–9	The answer shows some understanding of content analysis with suggestions being mostly sensible and practical. Most of the elements are presented and implementation of some aspects is possible. The answer is mostly clear and well organised with specialist terminology often used effectively.
2	4–6	Although some suggestions are appropriate others may be impractical or insufficiently explained to enable replication. Some elements are presented but the answer lacks clarity, organisation and accuracy making implementation difficult.
1	1–3	Limited understanding of content analysis with only one element requested by the question being considered. Implementation would be very difficult. The answer lacks clarity, has many inaccuracies and is poorly organised.
	0	No relevant content.

TOPIC: Case studies

Case studies match up

Handout 12 requires students to match the individual researched with a description of the case and knowledge gained as a result of the study. Students can assign a different colour for each case study to record the matches identified.

The case studies represented on **Handout 12** relate to topics all students will have studied (Memory: HM, Clive Wearing and Approaches: Little Hans) as well as one optional topic (Gender (the case of David Reimer) - links to nature/nurture debate if gender is not one

of your Paper 3 choices). As such, this activity can provide a useful reminder of other aspects of the A Level.

Additional activities:

A suitable independent research homework would be to ask students to find another example of case study research in psychology. This could involve revisiting class notes from other topics, using textbooks or internet searches. As a starter to the following lesson students could form small

HANDOUT 12

P   H   S   G   **T**

Some students may find it easier to cut out each cell and physically sort them into groups rather than identify matching cells using colour codes.

discussion groups where research found is shared with each other; picking out the key points of each case study and the psychological understanding gained.

TOPIC: Case studies

Explain yourself

Students often need reminders to expand their evaluative points rather than giving a list of strengths and/or limitations. **Handout 13** gives four statements that students are required to explain in their own words.

For example, 'Case studies require consideration of important ethical issues' can be expanded by explaining that the confidentiality of the individual needs to be assured, often using initials rather than full names (such as HM). However, in many cases informed consent has

not been acquired either because the individual was not able to give consent or they were never asked. A further ethical issue might be that repeated testing can risk psychological harm.

Students could complete each expansion individually or work in pairs (one student tackling strengths, the other limitations) then teaching each other.

Additional activities:

Once completed, ask the class, 'What makes a 'good' case study?' This can

HANDOUT 13

P   H   **S**   G   T

Prompts can be given to support expansions. For example, Ethics: confidentiality, protection from harm.

lead to consideration of what we mean by 'good' – ethically sound, rich data, furthered understanding? Students may also debate whether some aspects are sacrificed to achieve others.

TOPIC: Reliability

Applying definitions

By Year 2 of the course, students should have an understanding of reliability and so **Handout 14** can be used to test retention of knowledge for various concepts relating to consistency of measurement. Once each scenario has been read, students identify and define the relevant concept.

Scenario 2: test-retest reliability. Extension - students could consider the problems of using self-report to investigate behaviours such as dieting.

Scenario 3: inter-observer reliability. Extension – students can be introduced to/reminded of correlation coefficients. A result of .80 or more suggests good inter-observer reliability.

Scenario 4: improving inter-observer reliability. Extension – students can be

given an observation scenario (maybe linked to Paper 3 topics) and asked to identify and operationalise suitable behavioural categories.

Scenario 5: improving self-report reliability. Extension – provide students with a questionnaire gathered from the internet or magazine for them to identify any poorly worded questions.

Additional activities:

To encourage revision of previous topics, students identify (or are provided with) research studies to produce a brief summary of reliability in relation to the specifics of each investigation. For example, Bandura et al.'s (1963) use of behavioural categories to identify aggressive behaviour towards a bobo doll, Rutter and Sonuga-Barke's (2010)

HANDOUT 14

P   H   S   G   **T**

Students who found reliability a difficult concept to understand in Year 1 of the course may benefit from referring to a textbook to complete this activity.

measurement of Romanian orphans' development using IQ test scores.

References

Bandura, A., Ross, D. and Ross, S.A. (1963), Imitation of film-mediated aggressive models, *Journal of Abnormal Social Psychology, 63*, 575–82

Rutter, M. and Sonuga-Barke, E.J. (2010), X. Conclusions: Overview of findings from the era study, inferences, and research implications, *Monographs of the Society for Research in Child Development, 75(1)*, 212–29

TOPIC: Reliability

Class research

NO HANDOUT

P H S **G** T

Find a suitable video clip for the class to observe, for example, an extract from a soap opera. Explain that the class is researching gender roles displayed by male and female characters. The class can then identify a list of suitable behavioural categories and devise a recording sheet to be used while viewing the clip. Give students the opportunity to operationalise each category. This is event sampling.

Once data has been collected, students can compare their coding sheet to those of others to determine whether they had good inter-observer reliability.

Additional activities:

Students could create a scattergram comparing the data they collected with one of their peers.

Y axis – observer A, X axis – observer B.

Each point on the scattergram represents a behavioural category and the co-ordinates are number of times observer A and B recorded the category. Separate scattergrams can be created for males and females to determine whether students' observations were more reliable for one gender over another.

Students work in mixed-ability pairs to create a scattergram of data comparing the data collected for male and female characters from two different observers.

TOPIC: Validity

Roll with it

HANDOUT 15

P H **S** **G** T

Working in groups, students take it in turns to roll two dice. Taking either the face of one die or adding the two faces together, the student who rolled the dice answers the question relating to that number. For example, if two dice thrown show 2 and 5, students can choose from question 2, 5 or (2 + 5) 7. Students can record the answers their group gives to each question in their notes.

Additional activities:

If groups did not have access to a textbook during the activity then once all questions have been answered, students check each response is correct using their notes and/or the textbook (*Complete Companion*, pages 18 and 19), making any corrections or adding any missed details. Students could even score their group's performance. Two

Mixed-ability groups supported with access to a textbook ensures students are able to consolidate and check understanding when answering each question.

marks are available for each question; 1 mark for vague but accurate response, 2 marks if the answer is detailed and accurate.

TOPIC: Validity

Unjumble the jumble

HANDOUT 16

P H S G **T**

In my (RG) experience those students who sailed through GCSE with little revision really struggle with the vast content and level of detail needed to succeed at A Level. As they have not tested different ways of revising in their GCSEs they often try to write notes out again or simply highlight comments; neither being effective methods of revising. Other students struggle with organising material to be revised into succinct blocks as shown on **Handout 16**. For this activity, students

improve the revision notes shown on the handout by imposing order and utilising a more effective method of revision such as mind map or flash cards.

Additional activities:

Once revision notes have been created, students can take a quick spotcheck (10 multiple choice questions) to check how successful their revision has been. This is another important revision skill students need to be constantly

Students can be provided with a choice of revision techniques to suit their abilities/preferences, e.g. mind map, flash cards, information table, PowerPoint.

reminded of – revision isn't making the mind map; it's using the mind map to test retention of information by recalling items unaided then using the mind map to check missed details.

TOPIC: Features of science

Features of science

Handout 17 can be used in conjunction with a textbook (*Complete Companion*, page 20) if introducing the features of science or used as a revision technique to test retention of knowledge.

Once completed, split the class into two groups for a game of Pictionary. One student from each group is given a mini white board and told one feature of science. They then return to their group and begin drawing. The first group to guess the feature wins a point. Note that induction and deduction

are not in the specification, but have been included in the handout to help develop students' wider understanding of scientific method.

Additional activities:

Students could revisit previous topics and select one or two studies to create a features of science revision poster identifying any empirical methods, attempts to maintain objectivity, the hypothesis and related theory as well as giving a detailed account of the procedure.

HANDOUT 17

P **H** S G T

Before this activity, hold a class vote requiring students to give a YES or NO response to the question, 'Is psychology a science?' Students should support their decision with examples.

TOPIC: Features of science

Examining answers

Students often find it difficult to effectively apply their knowledge to a scenario. The candidate response provided on **Handout 18** models how to embed aspects of the question into an explanation of various features of science. On reading the answer, students are asked to comment on the following aspects of the answer before using the mark scheme to award a score. Some possible answers for the examiner's report:

Knowledge – the candidate shows an understanding of objectivity, the need for operationalisation and replication and empirical measurements.

Application – features of science content makes explicit reference to aspects of the question, concepts of 'blonde, fun'.

Specialist terms – student refers to features by name and inclusion of subjectivity (students could propose that the candidate could suggest her mother may be basing her claims on 'anecdotal' evidence).

Clarity and organisation – paragraphs are used to create a logical response that is easy to follow.

Additional activities:

Before sharing the answer on **Handout 18** students could attempt the question in pairs. Their response can then be compared to the model response.

HANDOUT 18

P H S **G** T

Students work in mixed-ability pairs when commenting on the answer.

TOPIC: Probability

Research reminder

Before considering inferential statistics in more depth, **Handout 19** gives students the opportunity to refresh their basic understanding of the research process by identifying:

Population – A Level psychology students, Sample – selected students from each class (n = 10).

IV – coloured or traditional (black/white) resources and slides.

DV – score on a multiple choice quiz (max. 20).

H1 – There may be a difference in scores on a multiple choice quiz between students taught using coloured resources/slides and those taught with traditional black/white materials.

H0 – There may be no difference in scores on a multiple choice quiz between students taught using coloured resources/slides and those taught with traditional black/white materials.

p ≤ 0.05 – 5% likelihood results are due to chance.

For arithmetic skills practice students could also be asked to calculate the mean score for each condition. You could even set percentage calculation practice, e.g. what % of students scored over half marks in each condition?

Once completed students could be asked to explain the likelihood of a Type 1 error being made at p ≤ 0.05 in the study shown on **Handout 19**. Students could also consider strengths and limitations of the study presented, for example, why did the teacher randomly select ten students from each class?

Additional activities:

Give students the following two situations and ask them to identify which type of error has occurred.

- Tom is tackled badly while playing football. The pain is intense and his ankle immediately starts to swell. He is certain he has broken his ankle however; a hospital x-ray shows no broken bones. (Type I error: Tom thinks something has happened (broken bones) but no breaks have occurred.)

HANDOUT 19

P H S G **T**

A 'cheat sheet' showing key terms with generic definitions may help students who need a recap of Year 1 research methods.

- Jenny is tired all the time, very thirsty and needs to use the toilet frequently. She is sure she is fine, just a little rundown at the moment. However, she is later diagnosed with diabetes. (Type II error – Jenny thinks nothing is wrong but her symptoms are actually due to a serious medical condition.)

Students could try to create their own example and test each other's ability to identify type I and II errors. Creating a memory tool to help remember the difference is also useful. I (RG) tend to use: 'Type I: the hypo SHOULD be gone' meaning it should have been rejected not accepted.

'Type II: the null is POO' meaning the null was accepted in error and is indeed incorrect.

TOPIC: Probability

Cookie challenge

I (RG) have used this practical example to bring to life concepts of probability and statistical testing. Explain to students that you are interested in which cookies are best if you love chocolate chips: a top range brand that costs a little more or a cheaper supermarket value brand. Whilst you can ask one or two students to manually calculate the test, either quickly calculate it yourself or run it through the computer. This allows you to quickly check the results are correct, freeing up time to work with the less-able students.

1. Divide the class into two groups and provide each student with either one top brand cookie (group A) or one value brand cookie (Group B).

2. As a class set the alternative and null hypotheses and probability level (p ≤ 0.05).

3. Before counting the number of chocolate chips in their cookies the class needs to standardise the procedure, e.g. do we count both top and bottom? Do we break the cookie in half and count any in the middle? Are 'half' chips counted? This may seem silly but it is a good opportunity to remind students of the importance of standardisation and operationalisation.

4. Students record the class data in their notes. Mean chocolate chip count for each brand can also be calculated.

5. Introduce the Mann-Whitney test as a suitable statistical measure (looking for a difference, unrelated data, interval data). Explain that the test helps to determine whether the difference between the two groups is large enough to be deemed significant.

6. Either quickly calculate the test yourself or ask selected students to conduct the test while the rest of the

NO HANDOUT

P H S G T

Students can carry out the Mann-Whitney calculation themselves (they will not be asked to do this in the exam) to practice numeracy skills.

class write up the procedure so far. The *Complete Companion*, page 27 provides a step-by-step guide to conducting a Mann-Whitney test and tables of critical values.

7. Once the U value has been found students identify whether data is significant.

Additional activities:

To further reinforce Type I and II errors ask students to rephrase Type I and II errors in terms of this study, e.g. if it is accepted that top brand cookies contain more chocolate chips than value brands but actually there is no difference, then a Type I error has been made.

TOPIC: Statistical tests

Statistical testing terms

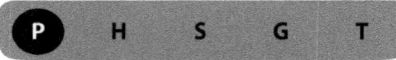

Handout 20 provides a simple task that produces a glossary of specialist terms to help students understand subsequent statistical topics, improve exam responses and is a useful revision tool. Students can colour code or draw lines to match each specialist term to the relevant definition. Alternatively, students may wish to cut out each definition to stick into their class notes alongside the relevant term.

Additional activities:

The specialist terms shown on **Handout 20** can be used to create a crossword (there are lots of free crossword creators on the internet) or be used in a game of bingo where students select nine terms to be crossed off when they think the definition has been read aloud.

> Think-pair-share encourages students to test their own recall of Year 1 topics before collaborating to support each other.

TOPIC: Statistical tests

Try-Talk-Target-Text

P	H	S	G	T

Students are given sets of questions to answer (*Complete Companion*, page 25 contains questions in the 'Can you' section of the spread).

Try – students work alone without notes to answer as many questions as possible, in as much detail as possible.

Talk – students then discuss their answers with a peer, making any additions or amendments to their responses following peer feedback.

Target – Working in pairs, students colour code each question: red – we did not know how to answer the question, amber – we think we have a correct answer but it lacks detail, green – we are confident we have given an accurate and detailed response.

Text – Students then use their textbook or class notes to mark any green

answers, improve any amber ones and develop their understanding of red questions (asking for teacher support when needed).

Additional activities:

Students will need to be able to identify a suitable statistical test from memory and as such need to create their own revision tool for the different tests. This could take the form of flow chart, table, visual image or set of flash cards. Students should use this to regularly test their ability to select an appropriate test. For example, use the start of lessons to present a scenario and ask students to select the appropriate test. The AQA website has legacy material for PSYA 4 which can be used to identify suitable scenarios from past research methods questions.

> Students can be given different sets of questions to answer, e.g. basic 'What is meant by the term . . .?' to more complex, 'Explain the relationship between the calculated value and the critical value'.

TOPIC: Non-parametric tests of difference

Non-parametric testing 1 and non-parametric testing 2

Handout 21 presents three studies that use non-parametric tests to analyse the data collected. Students identify the correct test, use the critical value tables on **Handout 22** to select a suitable value then determine whether data were significant or not.

Study 1– Smokers/Non Smokers and ban: Chi-Squared test as looking for a difference, nominal level of measurement, unrelated data (independent groups). One-tailed test (directional hypothesis stated). Critical value = 2.71. Data are significant.

Study 2 – Cigarettes and attitudes: Spearman's Rho as looking for a correlation, ordinal level of measurement, related data. One-tailed test. Critical value = 0.634. 0.886 Data are significant. This is a non-parametric test of correlation.

Study 3 – Hungry/full participants: Mann-Whitney as looking for a difference, unrelated data, interval level

of data. Two-tailed test non-directional hypothesis stated). Critical value = 23. Data are significant.

Additional activities:

After completing **Handout 21**, students reflect on their own level of understanding by rating the following statements on a scale of 1 (I am still confused) to 7 (I have a clear understanding):

- I know when to use a one-tailed test and when to use a two-tailed test.
- I know which tests require the observed value to be greater than the critical value to be significant.
- I know which tests require the observed value to be less than the critical value to be significant.
- I am able to find the appropriate critical value in a table of values.
- I can explain what $p \leq 0.05$ refers to.
- I can explain what $p \leq 0.01$ refers to.
- I understand the difference between a Type I and Type II error.

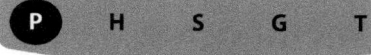
Once completed, more-able students could create further scenarios including ones for the Sign test and Wilcoxon test. These can be presented to the class for other students to solve.

References

Fisher, R. A. and Yates, F. (1974). *Statistical tables for Biological, Agricultural and Medical Research 6e.* Longman Group UK Ltd.

Gross, R., McIlveen, R., Coolican, H., Clamp, A. & Russell J. (2004). *Psychology: A new introduction for A-level 2e.* Hodder & Stoughton.

Runyon, R. and Haber, A. (1979). *Fundamentals of Behavioral Statistics 3e.* Addison-Wesley.

Zar, J. H. (1972). Significance Testing of the Spearman Rank Correlation Coefficient, *Journal of American Statistical Association, 67*, 578-80.

TOPIC: Parametric tests of difference

Parametric tests of difference

The first section of **Handout 23** shows two candidates' answers to possible exam questions. Students read each response to determine which candidate gave a better response.

a. Identify the test – Both answers are correct but Candidate 2 saves time as they state just what is needed to earn the mark.

b. Justify the choice of test – Candidate 2 shows clearer links to the scenario but both 1 and 2 can receive credit for stating 'looking for a difference' and 'related data'. Candidate 1, however, needs to be more specific when stating the level of measurement.

c. State the non-directional hypothesis – Candidate 1 mistakenly gives a directional hypothesis.

The second section of the handout requires students to apply the strengths

and errors of the two candidates to answer questions in response to a second scenario.

a. Unrelated t-test.

b. Independent measures (newspaper or TV), interval level of measurement (score on test), looking for a difference in retention of information between the two medias.

c. (Either direction is acceptable.) Participants who read newspapers score higher on a test of current affairs than participants who watched televised news programmes.

Additional activities:

When studying the use of statistical tests, students have to comprehend a lot of specialist terminology, concepts and procedures. This can become confusing at times and sometimes

You may wish to work through the first section of **Handout 23** as a class. Students then use points raised to attempt the second section individually.

students may leave a lesson feeling they understand only to become muddled in the next lesson. Allow time in lessons for students to check their understanding. One way to do this is to ask students to write a list of questions they need to ask to improve their understanding. Students then move around the class helping each other answer the questions. Any unanswered questions at the end of this activity need to be addressed as a whole class.

TOPIC: Tests of correlation

Venn diagram

As a starter activity, provide students with a simple template of a Venn diagram: one circle for Spearman's rho, the other for Pearson's r. Students then assign the following terms to relevant areas of the Venn (give terms out in a random order):

- Spearman's rho: ordinal level data, non-parametric, normal distribution not required.
- Pearson's r: interval level data, parametric, normal distribution required.
- Both: looking for a relationship, related data, repeated measures, calculates a correlation co-efficient.

Additional activities:

Students often become experts at talking about methods that allow psychologists to look for a difference. This can mean that mistakes creep in when talking about looking for a relationship using correlations. Provide students with a range of scenarios to identify whether they are looking for a difference or correlation, identify the IV/DV or variables and state directional/non-directional hypotheses (students frequently make the mistake of stating, 'there is a difference between . . .' for correlations).

NO HANDOUT

| P | H | S | G | T |

Students who are confident in their maths knowledge can identify the similarities and differences themselves rather than being given terms.

Handouts 21 and 22, 'Non-parametric testing 1 and 2' also contain a Spearman's rho example.

TOPIC: Tests of correlation

Testing correlations

Handout 24 outlines a study into the effect of institutionalisation on children's development for students to explain using their understanding of correlational analysis.

a. Spearman's rho.

b. Looking for a relationship/correlation, related data (time in months/score on 11+ test), interval level data that can be assumed to have a normal distribution.

c. There is a negative correlation between time spent in institutional care and score on the 11+ test (the longer spent in care the poorer the educational performance).

d. 1 mark each for correctly labelling x and y axis, 1 mark for correct direction of correlation.

e. At $p \leq 0.05$ the critical value for N = 27−2, one-tailed test is .323. Therefore, data are not significant and the directional hypothesis is rejected.

Additional activities:

As a revision homework, students can look through class notes from previously learned topics to identify correlational studies. They can create a revision sheet for correlations using the past examples from their notes. This reinforces the reasons for choosing

HANDOUT 24

| P | H | S | G | T |

Once it has been established that data were not significant, students can consider why this might be the case, i.e. what helped infants overcome their negative start in life? They could also consider the strengths and limitations of correlations as a method of investigation.

correlational analysis, the strengths and limitations of the method as well as refreshing memories for other topics.

TOPIC: Chi-Squared

Chi-Squared test

Students apply their knowledge of Chi-Squared test to the three scenarios presented on **Handout 25**.

Scenario 1 – bedtimes. Chi-Squared test was chosen because researchers were looking for a difference/association, data are independent (parent or child) and level of data is nominal as each person belongs to one category.

Scenario 2 – pets and gender. Missing data: 3 females found pets to be stressful. 19 females were surveyed in

total. 7 males found pets reduced stress. In total 37 people were surveyed. A suitable directional hypothesis would be, 'More females will report pets reduce stress than males'. Percentage of males who found pets reduced stress = males/all males × 100 = 7/18 × 100 = 39%.

Scenario 3 – luck and gambling. Critical value for a two–tailed test where df = 2 (R − 1) × (C − 1) is 5.99. As the observed value is greater data are significant.

HANDOUT 25

| P | H | S | G | T |

Students work in ability pairs enabling teacher to target students who struggle with the statistical component of the course.

Additional activities:

Students who complete **Handout 25** quickly can devise their own Chi-Squared investigation. If deemed ethical this can be carried out and data analysed using the Chi-Squared formula (*Complete Companion*, page 32 provides instructions of how to do this.)

TOPIC: Reporting investigations

Reporting investigations

As an introduction to the topic of reporting investigations, students use different colours to highlight the six sections of a report shown at the top of **Handout 26**. They then match the different items to be reported to the six sections by highlighting each speech bubble in the relevant colour.

Once completed, students can use the information to answer the following questions:

What is the purpose of writing an introduction? (2 marks)

Explain the difference between descriptive and inferential statistics. (2 marks)

Why do researchers present an abstract at the start of the report? (2 marks)

What influences a researcher's choice of (non)directional hypothesis? (2 marks)

Additional activities:

As a stretch activity, students can be provided with one or two abstracts from journal articles and challenged to identify what was done and what

> Once completed, ask students why it is important these conventions are followed. Students should consider the importance of replicability and the use of peer review to ensure the quality of research entering the public domain.

was found. Although it can be difficult to gain (free) access to whole articles, abstracts can be obtained from internet searches using Google Scholar.

TOPIC: Reporting investigations

Creating a report

To practise report writing skills, the following templates (suitable topics added in bold italics) can be used to create questions for students to answer either alone or working in pairs.

a. Design a study to investigate **the presence of cues when recalling information**. Include sufficient details to permit replication, for example, hypothesis, IV/DV, detail of design, procedure and sampling. (12 marks)

b. Design a study to investigate **the correlation between score on locus of control questionnaire and self-reported likeliness to conform in a range of hypothetical situations**. Include sufficient details to permit replication, for example, hypothesis, variables (correlation), detail of design, procedure and sampling. (12 marks)

c. The psychologist noticed that mothers and fathers offered different types of care for their children: she observed mothers tended to deal with emotional needs while fathers offered more opportunities for play and exploration. She decided to test the following hypothesis: Mothers tend to children's emotional needs more than fathers.

She observed mothers and fathers interacting with their child over a period of a month. Every time the child showed distress she recorded who the child turned to for comfort.

Imagine you are the psychologist and are writing up the report of the study. Write an appropriate methods section which includes reasonable detail of design, participants, materials

> When constructing a method, students should be encouraged to justify all decisions in terms of improving reliability and validity.

and procedure. Make sure that there is enough detail to allow another researcher to carry out this study in the future. (12 marks)

NB - methodology sections of reports should be written in past tense.

Additional activities:

Once completed student responses can be marked using the mark scheme presented below.

Level	Marks	Description
4	10–12 marks	Suggestions are generally well detailed and practical (realistic). Sound understanding of the chosen research method is demonstrated. All elements of the question are presented in sufficient detail for the study to be implemented successfully. The outline is clear and coherent with only minor details/ explanation missing. Specialist terms are used effectively.
3	7–9 marks	Suggestions are mostly sensible and practical. At least three of the named elements are addressed with responses showing some understanding of the chosen method. Ideas are mostly clear and well organised with specialist terminology mostly applied effectively.
2	4–6 marks	At least two elements requested by the question are addressed but ideas may be impractical, under developed or even inaccurate. Based on the information given it would be difficult to implement the methodology proposed. The answer lacks clarity and organisation in places.
1	1–3 marks	At least one element is addressed but knowledge of the chosen method is very limited. Due to a lack of clarity and inaccuracies it would be very difficult to implement the suggested methodology. The answer is poorly organised.
	0	No relevant content.

TOPIC: Gender in psychology: gender bias

Gender and alpha bias

Handout 27 contains a revision passage created by a student revising alpha bias. Students read the three questions shown below the passage and assign one colour to each question which can be recorded in the key provided. Students then use each colour to highlight sections of the passage that can be used to address each question.

Additional activities:

On completing this activity students can discuss the following questions to deepen their understanding of alpha bias:

- How might Freud have been influenced by the dominant culture during the period in which he developed his theories?
- How can the feminist perspective counter androcentrism and reverse alpha bias?
- Is it possible for researchers to investigate human phenomenon without being influenced by pre-existing notions of gender?

These questions can lead to lengthy debates using a Socratic seminar. Students work in pairs to discuss ideas with each other before one member of the pair joins the debate circle. Students in the circle discuss each question while students outside the circle make notes on interesting points

HANDOUT 27

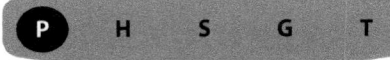

Students could be challenged to answer the questions shown on **Handout 27**. This could be either using the revision passage shown for support or attempting questions from memory then reading the revision passage to identify other relevant comments that could be added to their responses.

and additional questions raised. When the conversation starts to be repeated or flag, the teacher invites those in the outer circle to recap, reinforce or refine ideas for the inner circle with the option of adding new ideas or posing questions.

TOPIC: Gender in psychology: gender bias

Gender and beta bias

Handout 28 summarises the main ways in which beta bias can occur. Once students have recorded their own examples of beta bias, the handout can be used to form a discussion about gender in psychology.

Students could consider the following questions:

- Have issues in the lives of women been neglected by psychology? If so why?

  Students may consider wider patriarchal society, dominance of male psychologists, access to funding (are topics of male interest more likely to be funded?), peer review and journal editors.

- What are the strengths of minimising the differences between men and women?

  E.g. access to education, voting due to acceptance of equal intellectual ability between the genders. Defence secretary Michael Fallon argued in 2014 roles in the armed forces should be, 'determined by ability not gender'.

- What are the limitations of presuming men and women as the same?

  Arguing for equality may draw attention away from the special needs of each gender, e.g. male suicide rate is higher than females means differences may

be overlooked in diagnosis, support and treatment. Biological demands of pregnancy, childbirth and breastfeeding ignored in equal parental leave.

- Which is more damaging to psychology and/or wider society; alpha or beta bias?

  Students need to revisit work on alpha bias such as the long held view of sexual selection where women are portrayed as choosey and men as focused on reproduction.

Before debating their ideas, students would benefit from time to formulate their responses using class notes or wider reading (*Complete Companion*, pages 42–3). This could be done individually or in pairs with students recording their initial opinions and evidence. Following the discussion, students can return to their original thoughts and make any amendments or additions based on what they have heard.

Additional activities:

Cross curricular links may be made here with students studying sociology providing the class with a summary of the feminism perspective. This will help students place the issue of gender in psychology in a wider social context.

HANDOUT 28

P	H	S	G	T

Less-able students may require a little guidance as to where to look in the specification for a suitable example of beta bias in which differences between the genders are minimised. More-able students may be able to identify this area for themselves. You could modify the handout and remove the examples of Mednick and Payton so setting students a research challenge to find their own examples of psychology ignoring women's issues.

References

Mednick, M. T. S. (1978). Psychology of women. Research issues and trends. *New York Academy of Science Annuals, 309*, 77–92. Reprinted in S. Cox (Ed.). *Female Psychology: The Emerging Self* 2e (page 91–107). New York: St Martin's. Cited in Biaggio, M., Hessen, M (Eds). (2000). *Issues in the Psychology of Women* (p22) Springer.

Payton, C. R. (1984). Who must do the hard things? *American Psychologist, 39*, 391–7. Cited in Biaggio, M., Hessen, M (Eds). (2000). *Issues in the Psychology of Women* (p22) Springer.

TOPIC: Culture in psychology: cultural bias

Cultural bias crossword

The crossword on **Handout 29** can be completed as an individual using class notes to consolidate their understanding of key terms or as a revision activity to test retention of knowledge. It could also be set as a group activity in the form of a competition: first group to enter answer all clues correctly are the winners.

Across:

2 – etic
5 – beta
6 – two
7 – Afrocentrism
8 – collectivism
9 – indigenous
11 – emic
12 – morals.

Down:

1 – ethnocentrism
3 – imposed

4 – relativism
10 – alpha.

Additional activities:

Once the crossword is completed, students can highlight which clues referred to alpha bias (10 down, 8 across) and which referred to beta bias (5 across, 3 down) to help them answer the question: Explain what is meant by the terms alpha bias and beta bias (2 + 2 marks). Students could then consider how alpha bias and beta bias may occur in ethnocentrism and cultural relativism.

Should you not wish to use the crossword, the clues can also be used in the form of a class quiz to test recall of key terms.

References

Sears, D.O. (1986). College sophomores in the laboratory: Influences of a narrow

> Less-able students may find a list of the answers helpful allowing them to match the key word to the clue before entering them into the grid. Alternatively, you could provide them with the answer to 1 down and 4 down to provide them with letters for a number of other clues.

data base on psychology's view of human nature. *Journal of Personality and Social Psychology, 51*, 515–30.

Smith, P. and Bond, M.H. (1998). *Social Psychology Across Cultures: Analysis and perspectives (2nd edition)*. New York: Harvester Wheatsheaf.

Takano, Y. and Osaka, E. (1999), An unsupported common view: Comparing Japan and the U.S. on individualism/collectivism. *Asian Journal of Social Psychology, 2(3)*, 311–41

TOPIC: Culture in psychology: cultural bias

Cultural bias commentary

Handout 30 gives three extracts containing common errors students make when writing evaluations. Students are requested to record their feelings towards the extract, e.g. 'Would you use the comments exactly as they are in your essay or do they need to be improved?' Should students feel the extracts need improvement they should give detailed comments as to how this could be done.

Candidate 1 – marker's commentary:

The opening sentence suffers from, what I (RG) like to call, 'The mysterious this'. Students frequently use 'this' presuming the reader knows what they are referring to. A clearer opening would be, 'One example of the consequences of cultural (beta) bias . . .'. Although the candidate has chosen a relevant example, it lacks detail. For example, they could have included data from European immigrants and explained why ethnic groups performed worse than White Americans.

Candidate 2 – marker's commentary:

This response is more detailed than Candidate 1 and has made use of key

terms associated with indigenous psychologies. They could finish their commentary by considering that any theories arising from indigenous psychologies like Afrocentrism may only be helpful to our understanding of behaviour within the culture in which it was developed.

Candidate 3 – marker's commentary:

The candidate has structured their response using PEEL (**P**oint – sample choice can lead to bias, **E**vidence – Sears' data, **L**ink – commented on unrepresentativeness) but they have forgotten to **E**xpand on the evidence – explaining why samples of undergraduates may not be generalised to other groups within, and beyond, society. As a considerable amount of university students will be middle-class, academic, young adults we cannot assume they will be representative of other cultural groups.

Additional activities:

Using these three responses for guidance, students could create their own evaluations. They could either rewrite

> Students may benefit from a recap of evaluation writing tips before analysing the three extracts shown. For example:
> - signpost evaluations
> - PEEL structure helps construct a coherent commentary
> - detail needed to ensure effective use of evidence.

the three extracts shown on **Handout 30** adding a fourth paragraph of their own creation, or using their class notes and/or text books (*Complete Companion*, page 44) produce their own paragraphs.

A 16-mark 'discuss' question would allocate 6 marks for AO1 with the remaining 10 marks for AO2 and AO3 depending on question requirements. For example, if asked to 'discuss with reference to . . .' students would need to evaluate (AO3) and apply (AO2) their knowledge to a question stem. If simply asked to 'discuss' then marks are awarded for AO1 and AO3.

TOPIC: Free will and determinism

NO HANDOUT

An introduction to the debate

| P | H | S | **G** | T |

This activity can be used to introduce the concepts of determinism, soft determinism and free will. Display a continuum spanning from determinism to free will on the white board. Once students have been allocated to groups, provide each group with a specific coloured pen or Post-it® notes to record their ideas – this helps identify ideas from each group during the feedback session.

Ask students to decide where they would place the following behaviours on the continuum:

- acting aggressively when frustrated
- falling in love
- career choice
- sleeping.

Once decided, students record where they placed each idea along the continuum with teacher questions prompting further discussion. Possible questions could include:

- if groups felt aggression is often determined, e.g. genes, childhood

experiences or due to the situation, then should criminals be punished if they were driven to behaviour in this way? This is a good question in which to play devil's advocate to really get students engaging with the concepts. It is also a useful cross curricular link with law and the notion of moral responsibility.

- a useful link to research methods would be to ask the class to consider the advantages of taking a determinist approach when carrying out scientific research.

Through their discussions, students may unknowingly refer to the concept of soft determinism which can be developed by asking the class to consider examples of where they feel soft determinism is evident in human behaviour.

Additional activities:

Provide students with a simple summary of different types of determinism: biological, environmental, psychic and scientific. Challenge students to find at least one example for each type from

Organise students into mixed-ability groups. In each group you may wish to nominate the more-able student as spokesperson to feed back the ideas discussed to the class. Assign the role of group leader to a less-able student. The group leader needs to ensure all group members have a say and record the key points arising from the discussions, asking questions where needed to clarify their (and others') understanding of the views expressed.

previously studied topics. This task provides a valuable opportunity to reflect on prior learning and reinforces the concept of determinism. Students can also find evidence to support or criticise the theories identified. For example, concordance rates in monozygotic twin studies are never 100%, suggesting that behaviour is not the sole product of biology.

TOPIC: Free will and determinism

HANDOUT 31

Free will and determinism sound bites

| P | H | S | **G** | T |

The activity briefly summarises key considerations when discussing free will and determinism. Students need to develop the points beyond a basic sound bite to create an effective commentary of each concept. This can be a useful handout to help model the detail needed when creating evaluations, especially for those students who continue to think a list of evaluative points will enable them to access level 3 or 4 mark bands.

The first two sound bites (the importance of . . .) encourage students to focus on the benefits of determinism or free will. For example, science believes all events have a cause, and so independent variables are manipulated to identify the causal effect on dependent variables. The implication that behaviour has a cause means it can be predicted and even controlled. Free will is important if an individual is to take responsibility for their actions, a

central aspect of humanistic psychology and the legal system.

Handout 31 then gives four sound bites relating to issues with taking a determinist or free will stance. Depending on your class, students may be able to discuss their initial ideas without the use of class notes or textbook, drawing their opinions from prior learning. However, should students need support, page 46 of the *Complete Companion* can be used to develop a commentary for each sound bite.

Additional activities:

Students could be provided with a set of cards showing a range of opinions, evidence and examples relating to free will and determinism. Initially students sort the cards into four categories: support for concept of free will, support for concept of determinism, issues with concept of free will, issues with concept of determinism. They then order

Less-able students may find a cheat sheet helpful when completing **Handout 31**. This sheet provides comments that can be added to each sound bite with the students' task being to identify which comment relates to which sound bite then explaining them in their own terms on the handout.

each set from strongest to weakest argument/evidence. Once decisions have been made, split the group in half and hold a mini debate. Debate topics may include:

'There is no role for free will in the scientific study of human behaviour.'

'Modern psychology needs to accept the concept of free will.'

TOPIC: The nature-nurture debate

Study in a bag

A good starter to this topic might be to prepare a bag/tub with cut up pieces of cards each with a study on from Year 1 (e.g. Asch, Milgram, Loftus and Palmer, Little Albert, twin studies, interactional synchrony research etc.). Try to include a variety of different studies.

Give a brief outline of the nature-nurture debate and then asks students to pick a study from the bag/tub . . . Ask students to state how that study contributes to the nature-nurture debate. Students might like to consider the following questions:

- What behaviour was being studied?
- What environmental variables/factors (if any) were researched that influenced that behaviour?
- What biological/nature variables/factors (if any) were researched that influenced that behaviour?
- What environmental or biological variables were not researched in this study that you feel may affect the behaviour?

An alternative method to using a bag/tub is to use a PowerPoint randomiser template (see page 8).

NO HANDOUT

The nature of this activity lends itself to higher-order thinking, particularly the analysis and application of the research to the nature-nurture debate.

Using collaborate learning structures (see page 5) can also ensure that your higher-ability students are stretched and that your lower-ability students are supported.

You could also include two bags/tubs. One bag could have relatively straightforward studies which clearly indicate nature or nurture roles. The other bag could have more complex studies which indicate an interaction between nature and nurture. Students could choose the bag that they select the study from.

TOPIC: The nature-nurture debate

Table mat - nature versus nurture

This activity can either be used as a starter activity or consolidation activity.

If you have a lovely technician in your department, ask them to laminate enough copies of **Handout 32** for the class. Then, they should cut out the statements on **Handout 33** and place them into envelopes; there should be enough envelope 'sets' for each member of the class. If you don't have a lovely technician . . . consider doing it yourself or setting it as a detention activity!

In essence, this is a very simple matching exercise. It is more difficult as a topic starter exercise because the students will need to draw on their Year 1 knowledge in order to place the cards correctly; this may be difficult because you haven't taught the content, but it is by no means impossible.

Alternatively, you could use these table mats as a simple progress check tool at the end of the topic and as a consolidation activity.

Laminating the table mats and statement sets will save you cutting out

HANDOUTS 32 and 33

You could use this activity to provide structure and scaffolding for a 'nature-nurture debate' AO1 examination question.

If this activity is used as a topic starter activity before you have actually taught the content, then students will need to use higher-order thinking skills.

the statements again the following year (and I'm sure you'll agree, we spend far too much time cutting up paper!).

TOPIC: The nature-nurture debate

Interactionist approach (Nature vs Nurture revisited)

It is very easy for students to slip into the nature versus nurture mindset as opposed to developing a more nuanced understanding of the interaction between the two. **Handout 34** is an attempt to help students understand this more nuanced interaction in the context of examples.

Students need to choose one characteristic/skill and then try to apply this to the nature affecting nurture and nurture affecting nature relationship types.

For example: Good at playing football.

- Reactive: Parents notice talent for kicking ball so take you to football coaching.
- Passive: You inherit ability to play football from parents. As such, your environment involves playing football a lot with your parents and watching football matches.
- Active: You notice you're good at football so you choose friends at school who you can play football with.

HANDOUT 34

The inclusion of examples will help support the less-able students to create their own examples.

However, you may need to identify and support less-able students who may struggle to apply these ideas to new examples.

- Neural plasticity: Playing football a lot at school and at home strengthens the neural connections and pathways involved in the motor activity required to kick and control a ball accurately.

TOPIC: The nature-nurture debate

Understanding twin studies

Handouts 77, 78 and 79 could be easily adapted for any topic/behaviour area. These particular handouts were designed to help students understand the contribution of twin studies for understanding the role of genetics in the development of schizophrenia. However, they also work very well for helping students to understand how twin studies help us to resolve the relative contributions of nature and nurture in the development of lots of behaviours. A possible question is related to twin studies and mathematical reasoning (see AQA website; the handouts mentioned could be used to help support an answer to this question).

These handouts provide excellent scaffolding for students' responses to tricky examination questions. Less-able students are likely to need targeted support in order to articulate their understanding in a written form.

TOPIC: Holism and reductionism

Exploring experimental reductionism

During this topic, there is a good opportunity to try to consolidate research methods understanding and link a few concepts together: reductionism, operationalisation, ecological validity, independent and dependent variables and causal relationships.

Handout 35 could be used as an introduction to this topic. The material in the grey box could be used with material from Year 1 in order for students to explore reductionism with research they are already familiar with.

Students should write out the material in the grey box but insert material as instructed by the numbers on the handout. They should try this first with A: Loftus and Palmer. They could then try B: Peterson and Peterson . . . and so on.

Again, this handout provides excellent scaffolding for students' extended writing on a conceptually-difficult topic. Less-able students are likely to need targeted support in order to articulate their understanding in a written form. Teachers might also consider asking more-able students to attempt a second or third example without the aid of the writing frame.

TOPIC: Holism and reductionism

Levels of explanation

The *Complete Companion* (page 50) states that '*the reductionist approach in psychology suggests that explanations begin at the highest level and progressively look at component elements:*

- *Highest level: cultural and social explanations of how our social groups affect our behaviour.*
- *Middle level: psychological explanations of behaviour.*
- *Lower level: biological explanations of how hormones and genes etc. affect our behaviour.*

We can consider any behaviour in terms of all three levels.'

A simple table on the board could help structure students' understanding of this with the use of examples they are familiar with. The table below also includes some examples from Year 1 that might be useful to explore with your students:

For less-able students it might be best to create a matching exercise with 3–4 examples pre-prepared. More-able students could either be asked to fill in the explanations from memory/educated guesses, or be given the Year 1 textbook in order to identify the relevant information.

Example	Highest level (cultural and social explanations)	Middle level (psychological explanations)	Lower level (biological explanations)
Episodic memories	Remember more if they have significance.	Time-stamped, require conscious thought.	Hippocampus and temporal lobe.
Conformity	We feel pressure to act in a similar way to the group.	Normative social influence (wanting to be liked).	Evolutionary origins for survival.
Stress			
Phobias			
Depression			
Attachment			

Dead Poets Society

There is an excellent clip I (MG) have used for years when introducing the positivism versus interpretivism debate in sociology. Although I suspect the clip is more suited to that debate, I think it has good links to this one too so I've included the idea here for you to consider!

There is a scene in Dead Poets Society where Robin Williams' character (Mr Keating) asks students to rip out the forward of a poetry textbook. At the time of writing a short version was available here (ideally, you'd watch a couple of minutes beyond this clip): https://www.youtube.com/watch?v=tpeLSMKNFO4. Keating takes exception to the idea that you can quantify poetry in order to evaluate it. He goes on to talk about how the students' thoughts, interpretations and words matter. He references Shakespeare to explain that the whole world is a stage and that they are actors on that stage and that THEY can contribute a verse.

Start by asking students a simple question in a collaborative learning structure (see page 5): Why could you argue that poetry should not be evaluated quantitatively?

Most groups will explain the idea that it is because people react to poetry differently, they interpret the meaning differently and therefore measuring it with numbers does not reflect the variety of opinion on the poem . . . I think there is a great opportunity to discuss whether there are links to psychology and research methods here. Can behaviour be measured quantitatively? Do individuals interpret situations differently? Does psychology need to reflect how individuals explain their own behaviour? Should we use more qualitative methods?

If you want to take this further I often offer the following dichotomy by using the 'all the world's a stage' reference.

The play is improvised (the interpretivist/idiographic approach): We all play different characters but we interpret those characters in different ways. I might be a teacher, but my opinion on what that means might differ to someone else playing that character. So, in order to study the play, we need to ask the actors the way in which they have interpreted their character and improvised the behaviour of that character – we'll need qualitative

The nature of this activity lends itself to higher-order thinking, particularly the analysis and application of the clip to the debate.

Using collaborate learning structures (see page 5) can also ensure that your higher-ability students are stretched and that your lower-ability students are supported.

research methods in order to ask them and gain a proper insight.

The play is scripted (the positivist/ nomothetic approach): We all play different characters but the behaviour is scripted. As a result, we act on the stage in a predictable way because our behaviour is determined by that script. So in order to understand behaviour we need to study the script. In terms of psychology, studying the script refers to studying the laws/theories which govern behaviour. This requires quantitative research in order to find patterns and causal laws.

I'm aware this might seem odd . . . but take a risk and see if it helps your students' understanding of the philosophical debates and the links to research methods choices . . . I've always found it does.

Connect 3

It is important that students develop a good understanding of the idiographic and nomothetic approaches with a deep understanding of the implications these approaches have for research methods choices.

Rather than dive straight into the text, **Handout 36** is designed to help students concentrate on their understanding of individual elements and then bring them together to develop a deeper and more holistic understanding.

In the grey shaded areas, students should articulate their understanding of the principles, i.e. the approaches,

qualitative methods etc. Students should be told to ONLY define the terms in the boxes. They could do this using their textbooks (in the *Complete Companion* see page 52).

In between the grey shaded areas, students should try and explain how the elements link together. For example, the nomothetic approach uses quantitative methods in order to generate laws about behaviour, large groups of people need to be studied and their data then needs to be averaged/ analysed statistically in order to make generalisations about behaviour.

The instruction to define key terms is a lower-order thinking skill which requires knowledge and understanding.

The instruction to 'link' elements of the approaches together constitutes a higher-order thinking skill which some of the students may find more difficult.

As such, you could group students in mixed-ability pairs and give the students different roles to complete the activity, i.e. less-able students complete the definitions, more-able students complete the links. Crucially, however, in the whole-class feedback session, reverse the roles so that you ask less-able students about the links and more-able students about the definitions. This will ensure that all students are accountable for all aspects of the work and the students work collaboratively to understand all aspects.

TOPIC: Ethical implications of research studies and theory

Ranking ethical issues

NO HANDOUT

| P | H | S | **G** | T |

Ask the class to divide into small groups and instruct each group to list the ethical issues they know and then rank them in order of importance. Discuss the results.

Alternatively, students could be asked to rank the issues in the context of particular studies.

Either way, the purpose is to try to get students to identify their previous knowledge so that you can build on this knowledge in Year 2.

There is plenty of scope to use collaborative learning structures in this activity (see page 5) to ensure that more-able students are stretched and less-able students are supported by their peers.

TOPIC: Ethical implications of research studies and theory

A trauma I'd forgotten

HANDOUTS 37 and 38

| P | H | S | G | T |

The suggested activity relates to the newspaper article 'A trauma I'd forgotten' on **Handouts 37 and 38**. It permits students to think about the impact of research, and especially socially sensitive research, from a participant's point of view. In this case the researchers found the 'participant' after going through some hospital records. The participant, Peter Moss, was unaware he was a disturbed child until he took part in this research 35 years later. They started the research, thus triggering old memories etc., but when the funding ran out, they had to stop and lost interest, leaving him in the lurch without any answers to his questions.

The exercise illustrates the dilemma between doing the research and possibly finding out something important, or not doing anything but risking learning nothing at all. The article also introduces the concept of funding.

There is plenty of scope to use collaborative learning structures in this activity (see page 5) to ensure that more-able students are stretched and less-able students are supported by their peers.

Teacher-class Q&A should also involve targeted questions; that is, asking higher-order questions to more-able students and less intimidating questions to the less-able.

TOPIC: Ethical implications of research studies and theory

Role play an ethics committee

NO HANDOUT

| P | H | S | **G** | T |

Arrange for small groups of students to identify a set of studies that you have covered, trying to select them from different topic areas. Each study should then be considered by an 'ethics committee' to determine whether they feel it is acceptable. The ethics committee will need a set of guidelines (can be downloaded from http://www.bps.org.uk/documents/Code.pdf or use the framework outlined on page 54 of the *Complete Companion*).

Students could then make notes on the ethical issues raised by each study. When answering exam questions on this topic the emphasis should always be on the issues raised in named studies – but not on the studies themselves. Students might fill in a table listing the studies considered, the issues raised, suggestions for dealing with the issues and the effectiveness of any solutions (the AO3 component) Students can use the headings from page 54 as the headings for their table.

The groups could be arranged with ability in mind.

This could be in mixed-ability groups and utilising collaborative learning structures (see page 5).

Alternatively, the groups could be arranged by ability. More-able groups could be given studies with lots of factors to consider which are less clear-cut. In contrast, less-able groups might be given more straight-forward studies where the outcome of the committee should be more obvious.

TOPIC: Evolutionary explanations for partner preferences

Evolutionary monsters

This is a really effective student activity designed to help them understand concepts such as the EEA (environment of evolutionary adaptiveness), genome lag, natural selection etc. Although the evolutionary approach seems quite straightforward, many students do struggle to get their heads around the different terms and how they relate to modern-day behaviour. I (MG) often find that students are disbelieving of evolutionary explanations because they do not make sense in a modern context. As such, I think it is vital that you spend time teaching them about **genome lag**: the idea that the environments that species (including us) have adapted to have since changed, and continue to change. Evolution is a relatively slow process, environments can change overnight. This can result in behaviours that seemingly do not look adaptive in a modern-day context.

The activity will require you to print off some pictures of 'monsters', I usually use Google images from a 'flanimal' search.

Ask the students to explain how one of the 'monsters' evolved to fit in with the current environment, and why some of its features might be maladaptive to the current environment. When using this activity you should emphasise how environments can change overnight, but how evolution is an extremely slow process. The activity can be used as a building block to understanding specific explanations of human behaviour.

I use these instructions on my whiteboard:

Feel free to be imaginative during this exercise, particularly when thinking about the EEA! Include all the bold words in your explanations.

- Choose one of these monsters.
- Explain how it's unique features are **adaptive** to the environment.
- To do this, it will be necessary for you to describe the **environment of evolutionary adaptiveness (EEA)**.

NO HANDOUT

This activity lends itself to group activity and collaborative learning structures (see page 5) which ensure equal participation, stretch of the more-able and support for the less-able.

The more able could also be set the task of explaining the features by sexual selection as well as natural selection.

- Explain the process of how/why their features evolved via **natural selection**.
- Describe their **current environment** (i.e. how the environment has changed).
- Explain how their features are now **maladaptive**.
- Explain the role of **genome lag**.

TOPIC: Evolutionary explanations for partner preferences

Register questions

One way to introduce this topic is via a simple 'register questions starter technique'.

Rather than asking your students to say 'Yes Sir' or 'Yes Miss' (or grunting) in response to your register, ask the males to say what they think is deemed to be attractive in males, and the females what they think is deemed attractive in females!

Ask one of the students to write a list on the board and introduce the rule that there can be no repeats.

After the register is completed, ask students to try and explain the results. Why are there gender differences. Students are likely to point out more immediate social differences, so after while, try and provoke more evolutionary explanations by asking questions such as 'What might this have to do with humans one million years ago?'

NO HANDOUT

The activity itself is difficult to differentiate but the follow-up discussion may lead to an opportunity to ask higher-order questions which can be particularly targeted at high-ability students.

TOPIC: Evolutionary explanations for partner preferences

NO HANDOUT

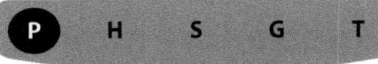

Lonely hearts ads

This is an activity that has been included in the previous two versions of this book and still works in this specification. If you have the previous editions, you'll know that we have included four pages of lonely hearts adverts with which to conduct a content analysis. For the sake of space, we haven't included those in this edition but I'm (MG) happy to be contacted about them via email. If not, any local newspaper should provide useful material.

A number of studies have investigated evolutionary explanations of mate preference using 'lonely hearts' ads in newspapers. The idea could be done on a small scale as a classroom activity to enable a deeper discussion of sexual selection.

Waynforth and Dunbar (1995) found that 42% of men sought a youthful mate compared to 25% of females; 44% of males sought a physically attractive partner compared with 22% of women.

In another variation the focus has been on caring – as times have changed and women are more financially independent, they may seek a partner who is willing to offer support in terms of being caring rather than in terms of resources.

For example, Bereczkei et al. (1997) found that females advertised for men who were family-orientated as well as financially sound.

In a slightly different type of study, Buss (1989) explored what males and females looked for in a marriage partner. Among the results were that women more than men desired mates who had 'good financial prospects', e.g. ambition, and qualities linked to resource acquisition.

There are a number of hypotheses that can be tested:

Wealth/status

- Females will ask for financial resources and economic security more than males.
- Males will offer financial resources more than females.

Physical attractiveness

- Males will ask for traits indicating physical attractiveness more than females.
- Females will offer traits indicating physical attractiveness more than males.

Age

- Females will ask for males who are older than they are (females will prefer to mate with older males).
- Males will ask for females who are younger than they are (males will prefer to mate with younger females).

Family commitment

- Females will ask for family commitment more than males.
- Males will offer family commitment more than females.

Some thought will need to be given to how these variables will be operationalised and recorded.

One issue that may arise as a result of this activity is that not all lonely-hearts adverts will fit the criteria of the study. For example, people may be seeking same-sex relationships. In terms of the hypotheses stated, it is clear that these types of adverts would need to be excluded from the sample. But, of course, this leads to an interesting discussion about some of the

> Less-able students could perhaps be assigned easier variables to operationalise such as physical characteristics. More-able students might be encouraged to consider how to operationalise concepts such as 'advertising resources'.

assumptions that evolutionary theories make and the extent to which they ignore non-heterosexual relationships and attraction.

You could perhaps have different members of the class researching different hypotheses and then feeding back their results to the class at the end.

Try and encourage your students to relate their findings back to previous research (such as those discussed here), the concepts and logic of sexual selection, and whether their findings support or undermine the hypotheses.

References

Berezckei T. et al. (1997) Resources, attractiveness, family commitment; reproductive decisions in human mate choice. *Ethology*. ALQ, *103*, 681–99.

Buss (1989) Sex differences in human mate preferences: Evolutionary hypotheses tested in 37 cultures. *Behavioral and Brain Sciences, 12*, 1–49.

Dunbar, R. (1995) Are you lonesome tonight? *New Scientist, 145* (February), 26–31.

Waynforth, D. and Dunbar, R. I. M. (1995) Conditional mate choice strategies in humans: Evidence from lonely hearts advertisements. *Behaviour, 132*, 755–9.

TOPIC: Evolutionary explanations for partner preferences

6 key points – 25 words

On the righthand side of the double-page spread in the *Complete Companion* (page 65), some very useful exam advice is included which is the basis of this **Handout 39** activity.

A summary of the advice is included at the top of the handout. Students need to explain the 'six key things' included on the handout but aim to use the 25 word count mentioned. Of course, they can go over that word count, but they should try to keep to the 150 word count in total.

This is a good activity for those students who feel the need to copy verbatim what is included in text books and/or PowerPoints but make no attempt to précis the information or engage with it in any meaningful way.

Handout 39 provides students with scaffolding for an 'outline' question on this topic.

You could set up this activity so that more-able students are paired with less-able students. The more-able student could have access to the full text on page 65 of the *Complete Companion*. It is their job to summarise that information and explain it to the less-able student. Then, without the help from the more-able student, the less-able student must write their 25 word version of the key point.

TOPIC: Attraction: Physical attractiveness and self-disclosure

Research activity: the matching hypothesis

Find pictures of around eight couples on the internet/magazines and separate the photos so that the males are on one sheet and the females are on the other. Ensure that each photo is labelled A–H and randomise the photos so that both the 'A' photos are two halves of an actual couple etc. You now have the materials to run a classic research study on the matching hypothesis.

Students should rate each of the photographs on a scale of 1–10 for attractiveness (where 10 is very attractive).

The simplest method is to ask half the class to rate the males and half to rate the females. You could divide the class by sex and ask each to rate faces of the opposite sex if you feel that your students will be reluctant to rate members of the same sex.

Afterwards you have to pair the couples and then examine their scores.

- First calculate an average score for each photograph.
- Next fill this score in the appropriate place in the table like the one shown below (changed to match the photo order you used) – the score for female photo G goes in the first box. The score for male photo D (her partner) goes at the top of the male column and so on.
- Use the data to draw a scattergraph or calculate the correlation coefficient using Excel.

Female photo	Mean score	Male photo	Mean score
G		D	
D		A	
C		H	
F		C	
B		E	
H		B	
A		G	
E		F	

The matching hypothesis would predict a positive correlation between the male and female photos because it suggests that we are attracted to, and form relationships with, individuals who closely match out perceptions of our own level of attractiveness.

As this is a class research activity, there are less opportunities for differentiation in the collection of data.

However, the ensuing class discussion and/or write up gives the teacher the opportunity to target individual students with comprehension and higher-order questions depending on ability.

e.g. How do these results support the matching hypothesis?

e.g. Is there any threat to the internal validity of this study?

e.g. What ethical issues need to be considered in this study?

TOPIC: Attraction: Physical attractiveness and self-disclosure

Application skills – Two-sentence technique

Application (AO2) skills need to be developed. It is the element of the examination where revision of content can only help to an extent . . . the ability to use that content in a new scenario is a skill that requires practice.

For the past few years, I have taught students the 'two-sentence technique' (see page 6). This technique is outlined on **Handout 40** and students can read through a worked example.

Essentially, the 'two sentence technique' is a writing structure to help students illustrate both the appropriate selection

of material, and then the appropriate application of that knowledge to a new scenario – both required by the AQA mark schemes to secure top level scores.

So, go through an example if you can with the students, and then ask them to complete **Handout 40** which requires them to select appropriate knowledge from the attraction topic (physical attraction and self-disclosure in particular).

The 'two-sentence technique' is a little rigid in its structure and does not always lend itself easily to some application

HANDOUT 40

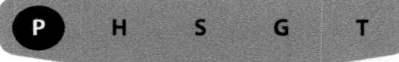

P   H   **S**   G   T

Handout 40 provides scaffolding to students attempting application questions towards the start of the A Level course.

questions. However, it is an excellent teaching tool and scaffolded support for the students. More-able students may learn to use the technique in a more flexible way whilst the technique remains a good crutch for less-able students.

TOPIC: Attraction: Filter theory

Filtering filter theory

Handout 41 is a very simple activity designed to either help students organise their understanding of the topic as they are reading the notes from the textbook (page 70) and/or as a consolidation activity at the end of the topic.

The handout forms a visual representation with the large 'potential partners' pool at the top, being slowly being filtered

down to just a few possible partners at the bottom of the page. More and more potential partners are filtered at the various stages pinpointed in the theory: early stages, as the relationship develops and final relationship assessment.

All the students need to do is to sort the various key words and phrases at the bottom into those various stages.

HANDOUT 41

P   H   S   G   T

This is a reasonably simple activity. If using as a consolidation task, you could perhaps instruct the more-able to cover the key terms and phrases at the bottom to make the task more difficult.

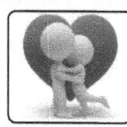
TOPIC: Social exchange theory

Feedforward marking

The concept of A B C and feedforward marking is outlined on page 2. I've (MG) found it to be a really effective marking and feedback technique that genuinely has an impact on student progress.

As a result, I've now started to use the concept to design handouts.

Handout 42 shows a fictitious student answer to the following exam question: Outline the social exchange theory of romantic relationships. (6 marks)

In addition, in the grey boxes are some fictitious teacher comments and A B C . . . tasks. The students are therefore required on **Handout 42** to complete those tasks in order to improve the answer. It is always worth mentioning to the students during/after this task how small additions/sentences can have a huge impact on the quality of a piece of work.

Possible task improvements:

A: Rewards that we may receive from a relationship include companionship,

being cared for, and sex. Costs may include effort, financial investment and time wasted (i.e. missed opportunities with others because of being in that particular relationship).

B: It should be 'their' because 'their' is possessive and 'there' usually refers to a place.

C: This is developed through our experience in other relationships together with our general views of what to expect from a relationship.

D: Someone with a low CL may be perfectly happy in a poor relationship. Someone with a high CL may struggle to maintain relationships due to very high expectations.

E: individual's

F: The comparison level for alternatives is where the person weighs up the potential increase in rewards from a different partner, minus the costs associated with ending the current relationship.

HANDOUTS 42 and 43

P   H   S   G   **T**

It is inevitable that some students will find the improvements harder to make than others – some students will need individual support during the activity in order to prompt the correct responses.

You could ask the students to help each other in pairs/threes using a collaborative learning structure (see page 5) as long as it is set up in a way where all students are responsible and have to engage in the task.

References

Thibaut, J.W. and Kelley, H.H. (1959), *The Social Psychology of Groups*, New York: Wiley.

TOPIC: Social exchange theory

Q&A: Equity theory dominoes

Handouts 44 and **45** provide question and answer dominoes so the activity is relatively straightforward to explain; the students have to match the concepts in bold with the answers on the left of the dominoes! All being well, they should end up in a big circle.

You could either use this as a plenary/consolidation activity or as a way to

make students engage in reading the text on page 74 of the *Complete Companion*.

References

Schafer, R.B. and Keith, P.M. (1980). Equity and depression among married couples. *Social Psychology Quarterly*, 430–5.

HANDOUT 44 and 45

P   H   S   **G**   T

More-able students are likely to finish faster than less-able students so could be used to support other students when they have finished. However, this should be in an instructive way rather than simply telling them the answers!

TOPIC: The investment model of relationships

Investment model: Annotation

I (MG) often think that it is best to start teaching new ideas/theories/concepts in a very simple way and then to build on that foundation; often, students are intimidated when presented with lots of information because they are not used to doing that at GCSE level (rightly or wrongly).

So on **Handout 46** there is the simplest possible outline of the investment

model in diagram form. I would go through this simple concept with the students. Then, the students can start to annotate the diagram with the extra information included in the box on the right hand side of the page. They can do this by reading page 76 of the *Complete Companion* or similar.

Alternatively, this could be used as a plenary/consolidation activity.

HANDOUT 46

P   H   S   G   T

To increase the pressure and difficulty for more-able students, you could instruct that they only read the relevant page of the textbook once. This encourages the more-able students to read and engage with the text with more concentration than they might if they know they can keep going backwards and forwards from the text to the handout.

TOPIC: The investment model of relationships

Investment model scale

Showing students the tools used by researchers to measure variables helps to make the research they are studying a bit more tangible. It can also provide a useful opportunity to consider research methods.

Handouts 47 and **48** provide a short version of the investment model scale mentioned on page 77 of the *Complete Companion*.

Here are some questions you could ask the students:

- Which of the questions are designed to operationalise relationship satisfaction?
- Which of the questions are designed to operationalise relationship alternatives?
- Which of the questions are designed to operationalise relationship investment?
- Which of the questions are designed to operationalise relationship commitment?
- What is the danger of measuring these variables using self-report?

- Why might anonymity help the validity of this study?
- How is the scoring of Q11 different to all of the other questions? What could the researchers do when analysing the data to keep the scoring consistent?
- Why might it be useful to include more questions like Q11?
- Why might filler questions have been useful?
- How could the internal reliability of this questionnaire be assessed?
- How could the external reliability of this questionnaire be assessed?
- This is a shortened version of the investment model scale. How could the validity of this shortened version be assessed against the original scale?

Scoring the scale:

'Relationship satisfaction' (Q1–3). High score indicates good satisfaction.

'Relationship alternatives' (Q4–6). High score represents a potential increase in rewards from a different partner.

HANDOUTS 47 and 48

| P | H | S | **G** | **T** |

The questions below could be asked in collaborative learning structures (see page 5) and/or targeted at particular students based on their ability and confidence.

'Relationship investment' (Q7–9). High score indicates that the individual invests heavily in the relationship.

'Relationship commitment' (Q10–12). However, the score for Q11 must be reversed; for example, a score of 5 becomes a score of 1 and vice versa. High score indicates that the individual is highly committed to the relationship.

References

Rusbult, C.E., Martz, J.M. and Agnew, C.R. (1998). The investment model scale: Measuring commitment level, satisfaction level, quality of alternatives, and investment size. *Personal relationships, 5(4)*, 357–87.

TOPIC: Relationship breakdown

Report: Relationship breakdown

Encouraging students to apply their knowledge and understanding in order to analyse different situations and case studies is an excellent way to develop psychology students' understanding and steer them away from simple rote learning.

Handout 49 asks students to produce a psychological report into a relationship breakdown – from a film, soap, celebrity etc. It will obviously be important here that students analyse a fictional relationship or high profile relationship as opposed to a private and personal relationship. Inevitably students may start to apply some of the theories to situations close to their

own lives but this subject matter would obviously not be suitable for an explicit classroom activity.

Ensure that the students include all the factors listed on the report brief and encourage them to maintain a psychological focus rather than drifting into more anecdotal speculation.

References

Rollie, S.S. and Duck, S.W. (2006). Stage theories of marital breakdown. In J.H. Harvey and M.A. Fine (eds) *Handbook of Divorce and Dissolution of Romantic Relationships*, Hillsdale, N.J: Lawrence Erlbaum, 176–93.

HANDOUT 49

| P | **H** | **S** | G | **T** |

The application of the research to a chosen scenario is a higher-order skill but the students are supported with scaffolding in the form of the required elements for the report.

For less-able students, you could allocate them a well-known relationship breakdown in the media that you know will be reasonably easy for them to apply to research to.

TOPIC: Virtual relationships in social media

HANDOUT 50

Reasons why virtual relationships are better

P   H   S   G   **T**

I suspect our adolescent A Level students are repeatedly told about the dangers of social media and the fact that 'we actually talked to each other face-to-face in our day'!

So I am sure the students will enjoy an activity that requires them to think through why virtual relationships are better and to justify those reasons with psychology/evidence. This is what **Handout 50** requires the students to do.

They should be able to complete the table using page 80 of the *Complete Companion* or similar.

For example . . .

Reason: It is easier for the less attractive, shy and less socially skilled.

Psychology: In online relationships there is an absence of the barriers or 'gates' that normally limit their opportunities. Online interactions reduce personal factors such as physical appearance, age, ethnicity and mannerisms determining who is initially approached.

For less-able students who find it difficult to organise texts, you could give them a list of pre-prepared reasons that they then have to find the psychology/research to justify. For example:

- Potential relationships are more likely to get off the ground.
- Individuals can make themselves more socially desirable on the internet.
- People can copy other daters' ideas in order to make themselves more popular.
- People are more likely to self-disclose which helps relationships develop.
- Individuals with the internet are more likely to be partnered.
- The quality of online relationships can match offline relationships.
- Shy people can improve the quality of their friendships.

TOPIC: Parasocial relationships

HANDOUT 51

Celebrity attitude scale

P   H   S   G   T

The 'Celebrity Attitude Scale' is often used to research the absorption addiction model and so it is a useful activity for students to attempt the scale themselves first. A version of this scale is included on **Handout 51** for you to use and discuss with your students as an introduction to this topic.

The 'Celebrity Attitude Scale' is a 17-item scale with lower scores indicating more individualist behaviour, (e.g. watching or reading about celebrities) and higher scores indicating over-identification and obsession with celebrities.

It uses a Likert scale where strongly agree is equivalent to a score of 5, and strongly disagree equivalent to a score of 1.

Therefore final scores will be between 34 and 170.

It might be useful to ask students afterwards to identify which of the items would fit each of the categories described by Giles and Maltby (2006):

- Entertainment-social
- Intense-personal
- Borderline-pathological

This activity is not differentiated.

References

Giles, D. and Maltby, J. (2006). Praying at the altar of the stars, *The Psychologist*, *19*, 82–5.

TOPIC: Parasocial relationships

Connect 4

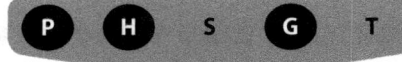

Handout 52 encourages students to deconstruct the attachment theory explanation of parasocial relationships into its basic parts, and then to help them link it together. This should help the students to be more analytical in their commentary.

In the grey shaded areas, students should articulate their understanding

of the key terms/ideas, i.e. parasocial relationships, anxious ambivalent attachment, secure base etc.

In between the grey shaded areas, students should try and explain how the elements of the theory link together.

The instruction to define key terms is a lower-order thinking skill which requires knowledge and understanding.

The instruction to 'link' elements of the theory together constitutes a high-order thinking skill which some of the students may find more difficult.

As such, you could group students in mixed-ability pairs and give the students different roles to complete the activity, i.e. less-able students complete the definitions, more-able students complete the links. Crucially however, in the whole-class feedback session, reverse the roles so that you ask less-able students about the links and more-able students about the definitions. This will ensure that all students are accountable for all aspects of the work and the students work collaboratively to understand all aspects. See page 5 for detail on collaborative learning structures.

TOPIC: Parasocial relationships

Eysenck Personality Questionnaire (EPQ)

P	H	S	G	T

This activity is not differentiated.

The following is included as evaluation/commentary on page 83 of the *Complete Companion*:

Maltby et al. (2003) used the Eysenck Personality Questionnaire (EPQ) to assess the relationship between parasocial relationship level and personality. They found that whereas the entertainment-social level was associated with extraversion (i.e. sociable, lively, active), the intense-personal level was associated with neuroticism (i.e. tense, emotional, moody). As neuroticism is related to anxiety and depression, this provides a clear explanation of why higher levels of

parasocial relationship are associated with poorer mental health. Maltby et al. suggest that future research might explore the implications of a reported connection between the borderline-pathological level and psychoticism (i.e. impulsive, antisocial, egocentric), as measured by the EPQ.

Versions of this questionnaire can be found all over the internet which might be interesting for the students to complete in order to understand the paragraph above in a little more depth. There is a short version on page 255 of the *Complete Companion*.

One internet version of the questionnaire is here: http://similarminds.com/eysenck.html

References

Maltby, J., Houran, M.A. and McCutcheon, L.E. (2003). A clinical interpretation of attitudes and behaviors associated with celebrity worship. *Journal of Nervous and Mental Disease, 191*, 25–9.

TOPIC: Sex-role stereotypes and androgyny

Men are from Mars, Women are from Venus . . .

A good way to introduce the topic of gender might be to play a class game of 'Men are from Mars, Women are from Venus'. The board game contains some excellent questions which tease out gender stereotypes. Just search for the board game online. Or perhaps consider buying the CD-Rom version to show on the digital projector. At the time of writing these were available on Amazon for less than £5.

TOPIC: Sex-role stereotypes and androgyny

Completing the Bem Sex-Role Inventory (BSRI)

NO HANDOUT

P H S **G** T

The discussion element of this activity could utilise a collaborative learning structure (see page 5) to ensure the less-able are supported and the more-able are stretched.

Students like completing questionnaires/scales etc.

It might be worth asking students to complete the BSRI as a homework task before you start this topic. There are plenty of places online where students can do this (and it is on page 91 of the *Complete Companion*):

http://personality-testing.info/tests/OSRI/

http://garote.bdmonkeys.net/bsri.html

Remember that it is important to prepare students for the possible results first in case any issues arise from the outcomes. In addition, you might want to consider the students in your group and whether it is appropriate at all.

If you feel it is appropriate, it can be a useful discussion starting point:

- What did you think of the questions?
- What did you think about the results?
- Do you think that gender can be measured using this technique?
- Can you spot any potential problems with the validity of the study?
- How could the reliability of the research be assessed?

TOPIC: Sex-role stereotypes and androgyny

Bem Sex-Role Inventory (BSRI)

HANDOUT 53

P **H** S G **T**

For less-able students, you could provide them with definitions of the keys terms, (i.e. independent variable, dependent variable, research design etc).

In the feedback and progress-checking session, ensure that you target the highest-order questions at the most able (i.e. potential problems).

Research methods is embedded throughout the examination papers; in fact, research methods questions are worth at least 25% of all marks. As such, research methods teaching and learning should be embedded throughout the course.

One way to encourage this is to ask your students to deconstruct psychological studies, or in this case, the Bem Sex-Role Inventory, into their constituent parts and to consider the reliability/validity/ethics of the research. **Handout 53** provides students with a framework to do this.

If there is time, encourage students to contextualise the criticisms on the back on the handout because it is easier to just write generic evaluation statements.

References

Bem, S.I. (1981). *Bem Sex-Role Inventory: Professional Manual*. Palo Alto, CA: Consulting Psychologists Press.

Spence, J.T., Helmreich, R.I. and Stapp, J. (1975). Ratings of self and peers on sex-role attributes and their relation to self-esteem and conceptions of masculinity and femininity. *Journal of Personality and Social Psychology, 32*, 29–39.

NO HANDOUT

TOPIC: Sex-role stereotypes and androgyny

The Story of X

A summarised version of the story by Lois Gould 'X', from Ms. magazine, May 1980 can be found here: http://www3.delta.edu/cmurbano/bio199/AIDS_Sexuality/BabyX.pdf

It links in nicely to some of the issues surrounding psychological androgyny and gender dysphoria.

You could read the story to the students, they could take it in turns to read it out loud, or they could read it on their own.

Another real-life story is mentioned on page 93 of the *Complete Companion*; that of a British couple who raised their son in a gender-neutral manner (Time magazine, 2012).

Possible discussion points:

- Could it happen today?
- Why not?
- What might the consequences be – to the individual child, and its peers?
- How would society have to change (e.g. shops, media, marketing etc)?
- How does this study relate to theories of gender?
- How might this study relate to psychological androgyny and gender dysphoria?

| P | H | S | **G** | T |

The discussion element of this activity could utilise a collaborative learning structure (see page 5) to ensure the less-able are supported and the more-able are stretched.

TOPIC: The role of chromosomes and hormones in sex and gender

HANDOUT 54

Spot the deliberate mistakes

Once you have taught your students the role of chromosomes and hormones in sex and gender, you could test your student's knowledge and understanding by asking them to spot the 11 deliberate mistakes on **Handout 54**. This can be a good activity to consolidate key terms of key principles, as well as build their confidence about biological mechanisms.

The correct version of the text is shown below, with the words in bold replacing wrong ones on the handout.

Each person has **23** pairs of chromosomes (in each cell of the body). Each of these chromosomes carries hundreds of genes containing instructions about physical and behavioural characteristics such as eye colour and predisposition to certain mental illnesses.

One pair of chromosomes is called the sex chromosomes because they determine an individual's **sex**. In the case of a **female** this pair is called XX because both chromosomes are shaped like X's. The **male** chromosome pair is described as XY. The Y chromosome carries very little genetic material although it does determine the sex of a child.

There is usually a direct link between an individual's chromosomal sex (XX and XY) and their **external** genitalia (vagina or penis) and **internal** genitalia (ovaries or testes). During prenatal development all individuals start out the same – a few weeks after conception both male and female embryos have external genitalia that look essentially **feminine**. When the foetus is about three months old, if it is to develop as a male, the testes normally produce the male hormone **testosterone** which causes male external genitalia to develop.

Genetic transmission explains how individuals acquire their sex. It may also explain some aspects of gender (a person's sense of whether they are male or female) because of the link between genes, genitalia and hormones.

| **P** | H | S | G | T |

It might be necessary, for your less-able students, to give them more instruction as to where the mistakes might be. You could do this by highlighting the sentences where the mistakes are located.

Genes/chromosomes initially determine a person's sex and they also determine which hormones are produced. Most gender development is actually governed by **hormones**. The hormone testosterone is produced in greater quantities in males, and the hormones **oestrogen** and **oxytocin** are mainly female hormones.

TOPIC: The role of chromosomes and hormones in sex and gender

Hormone quadruplets

Handout 55 would be a good activity to use once you have gone through the various ways hormones are involved in sex and gender. Alternatively, you could give students the information on the hormones (e.g. page 94 of the *Complete Companion*) and ask them to complete the activity by reading the information.

The students must sort the twelve numbered statements into three groups using the handout, (i.e. group A, B and C). Then, once they have done this, they should name the three groups. The group names should be 'testosterone', 'oestrogen' and 'oxytocin'.

Once the students have grouped the statements, they should then write a brief summary of each hormone and its role in sex/gender by using the statements as part of the summary.

Answers

Group name: Testosterone

Numbers: 2, 3, 6, 10

Group name: Oestrogen

Numbers: 5, 7, 9, 11

Group name: Oxytocin

Numbers: 1, 4, 8, 12

References

Berenbaum, S.A. and Bailey, J.M. (2003). Effects on gender identity of prenatal androgens and genital appearance:

For less-able students it would be advisable to give them the group names before starting the activity as they may need this support to sort the statements into groups.

Evidence from girls with congenital adrenal hyperplasia. *The Journal of Clinical Endocrinology and Metabolism, 88(3)*, 1102–6.

Shi, L., Lin, Q. and Su, B. (2015). Estrogen regulation of microcephaly genes and evolution of brain sexual dimorphism in primates. *BMC Evolutionary Biology*, 15, 127.

TOPIC: The role of chromosomes and hormones in sex and gender

Flipped learning: The girl who was raised a boy

We included the idea of flipped learning in our Year 1 book and there are plenty of opportunities for flipped learning in Year 2 as well. We all know that students like to watch videos. Mainly, I (MG) might uncharitably suggest, because it means they can relax and not do any writing. Well, not in my classroom!

I have a very simple rule for my lesson planning and that rule states that if a video is over ten minutes long, there must be a handout that goes with it.

However, a really interesting new concept that has been gathering pace is that of 'flipped learning'. A really useful summary is here: http://www.edudemic.com/guides/flipped-classrooms-guide/. Essentially, the idea is that the lecture (or in this case, watching a video) occurs outside the classroom and before the lesson; the lesson in the classroom is used to explore the themes and ideas.

I would advocate using this idea with the case study of David Reimer. This classic piece of gender research concerned twin boys involved in an accidental castration, providing Dr John Money with the perfect opportunity to test the nature versus nurture explanations of gender identity. In recent years the true facts of this case became known (see John Colapinto's

book, *As Nature Made Him*, Quartet Books (2006)). In November 2004 the BBC's *Horizon* programme provided a further update of this case after the tragic suicide of 'David Reimer' (see http://www.bbc.co.uk/sn/tvradio/programmes/horizon/dr_money_prog_summary.shtml). Students never fail to be fascinated by this extreme case study and it is definitely worth reviewing the story in more detail.

At the time of writing, an online version of this documentary could be found here:

https://vimeo.com/55409956

The alternative is to set this as an independent study activity, with students seeking information from a variety of sources: the internet, textbooks, the library etc.

During the homework task and 'flipped learning', students should write comments on what they see, which they can discuss in the next lesson. To give this homework some structure, provide the students with themes they should comment on. For example:

- What accident occurred to David Reimer in his first year of life?
- Outline some of Reimer's experiences and case details from when he was a young child.

Structure can be provided in this activity by giving themes/categories that students must comment on when watching/reading about the case of David Reimer.

During class feedback and discussion, higher-order questioning should be targeted at more-able students. In contrast, retention and comprehension questions can be targeted at lower-ability students.

- Outline some of Reimer's experiences and case details from when he was an older child.
- Outline some of Reimer's experiences and case details from when he was an adolescent.
- Dr Money suggested that Reimer's sex should be 'reassigned' and he be raised as a girl ('Brenda'). What psychological justification did he give for this?
- In what way did the experiment work?
- In what way did it not work?
- What theory was Dr Money's ideas about gender development based on?
- What does the case of David Reimer suggest about that theory?
- What would you conclude about gender development from this case study? What are the problems with generalising those conclusions?
- What ethical issues arise as a result of this research?

TOPIC: Cognitive explanations of gender development: Kohlberg's theory

Gender constancy theory cartoons

HANDOUT 56

| P | H | S | G | **T** |

On **Handout 56** students must illustrate the limitations children have in their gender thinking at each stage according to Kohlberg's theory. They should use their textbooks to help.

You can encourage them to draw silly images with stick-people, thought bubbles and speech bubbles.

I (MG) personally could not stand drawing when I was at school so do

reassure your students that the end results will not be entered into any competitions and that you are more concerned with the process of the activity as opposed to the end result!

Simple activities like these help students process the information in their textbooks, make the theory relevant in terms of concrete examples, and help the students revise the topics with visual aids.

This might be an activity you target particularly at students who are struggling to understand the abstract concepts involved in order to make the theory more tangible.

TOPIC: Cognitive explanations of gender development: Gender scheme theory

Gender schema theory: AO3 signposts

HANDOUT 57

| P | H | S | G | **T** |

The rationale for **Handout 57** is included at the top of the page.

In summary, over the years of teaching and marking for AQA I (MG) have come to the conclusion that AO3/ evaluation signposts are actually crucial to successful evaluation for several reasons. As such, I work hard to develop students' skills in writing their own.

Here are some rough suggestions for **Handout 57** for your guidance (and based largely on page 98 of the *Complete Companion*).

- Evidence supports the GST prediction that children begin acquiring information about gender schemas before they reach gender stability.
- A potential challenge to GST is evidence that children can label their gender group even earlier than indicated in previous studies.
- Evidence supports the idea that gender schemas organise memory; we would expect children to pay greater attention to information consistent with gender schemas if gender schemas are important in acquiring information.
- Further evidence to confirm GST can be found in the way children distort

information inconsistent with their gender schemas.
- An application of GST is that it can explain why children are frequently highly sexist despite parental attempts to be gender-neutral.

References

Bandura, A. and Bussey, K. (2004). On broadening the cognitive, motivational, and sociostructural scope of theorizing about gender development and functioning: Comment on Martin, Ruble, and Szkrybalo (2002). *Psychological Bulletin, 130*, 690–701.

Bradbard, M.R., Martin, C.L., Endsley, R.C. and Halvesron, C.F. (1986). Influence of sex stereotypes on children's exploration and memory: A competence versus performance distinction. *Developmental Psychology, 22*, 481–6.

Hoffman, L. (1998). The effects of mother's employment on the family and the child. See http://parenthood.library. wisc.edu/Hoffman/Hoffman. (accessed June 2012).

Martin, C.L. and Halverson, C.F. (1983). The effects of sex-typing schemas

This may prove to be a very difficult activity for some students.

It might be best to work through some of the predictions of GST first in order to ensure students are confident in how the studies relate to the theory.

To reduce the difficulty of the activity, the suggestions in the bulleted list could be given to students who then have to choose which is the most appropriate for each paragraph.

on young children's memory. *Child Development, 54*, 563–74.

Martin, C.L. and Little, J.K. (1990). The relation of gender understanding to children's sex-typed preferences and gender stereotypes. *Child Development, 61*, 1427–39.

Zosuls, K.M., Ruble, D.N., Tamis-LeMonda, C.S., Shrout, P.E., Bornstein, M.H. and Greulich, F.K. (2009). The acquisition of gender labels in infancy: Implications for sex-typed play. *Developmental Psychology, 45(3)*, 688–701.

TOPIC: Psychodynamic explanation of gender development

Choose the right word

HANDOUT 58

| P | H | S | G | **T** |

Handout 58 includes a very simple activity to consolidate students' learning on the psychodynamic explanation of gender development.

The text on the handout is taken from page 100 of the *Complete Companion*. When they are given the choice, the

students must choose the correct words from the ones given in bold. Students can easily get themselves in a tangle with all the various key terms in this topic so this is designed to help them think that through and increase their confidence in the understanding of this explanation.

This activity is difficult to differentiate other than by outcome. Less-able students may struggle in some areas so you should be on hand to support.

TOPIC: Psychodynamic explanation of gender development

NO HANDOUT

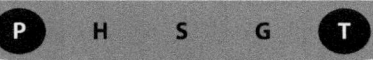

What is science?

Teaching about Freudian theory is always a good opportunity to explore the concept of science and what it means.

Using a collaborative learning structure (see page 5), ask simple questions: What is science? What is scientific research?

To help prompt and shape their answers, you could insist that certain words are

included in their answers; for example, evidence, objective, replicable etc.

On the board, note down the key features of the students' definitions and discuss why it could be argued that Freud's theory and his chosen research methods could be considered unscientific.

> The use of a collaborative learning structure (see page 5) ensures the less-able are supported and the more-able are stretched.

TOPIC: Social learning theory as applied to gender development

HANDOUT 59

P H S G T

Social learning: Make it relevant

There are a few topics in psychology that pop up quite a lot, which students appear to remember well; social learning theory is one of them and they would have met this theory once or twice in Year 1.

The danger with this is that students remember the theory and its key concepts well but fail to apply them to the topic at hand – in this case gender. I've (MG) seen my own students make this mistake and I have seen students across the country make this mistake in their examination papers.

Handout 53 is based on these experiences and was designed to show my own students how a very detailed and accurate description of social learning theory could actually only attract 2–3 marks if it lacks focus.

The student activity on **Handout 59** is to improve the description with brief examples, words and sentences to

ensure that the description is focused on gender and achieves closer to a 'level 4' mark band. You may need to tell your students that sometimes all it will need is the addition of one word, sometimes a sentence will be more appropriate.

For example:

1. Gender-role.
2. Children witness many gender behaviours at home, at school and in the media.
3. For example, they may witness a male being popular on television because he is strong and good at sport.
4. This means that girls are more likely to perform behaviours they see performed by other girls/women.
5. Gender-appropriate.
6. Gender.
7. For example, a boy might see another boy dressing as a girl and getting a lot of attention. But if the boy tries

> The suggestions for improvements below could be given to less-able students. Although they should attempt the handout on their own first, they could be given the suggestions to select from as options for the parts they are finding difficult.

it himself he may be 'punished' by disparaging remarks which means he does not repeat it.

8. Gender-appropriate.

Once students have completed this activity, the powerful point to make is that with a few small tweaks, you could argue that this description has moved from a level 1/2 answer to a level 4 answer. *Focus and relevance in an answer is very important.*

TOPIC: Cultural and media influences on gender roles

Feedforward marking

The concept of A B C and feedforward marking is outlined on page 2. I've (MG) found it to be a really effective marking and feedback technique that genuinely has an impact on student progress.

As a result, I've now started to use the concept to design handouts.

Handout 60 shows a fictitious student answer to the following exam question: Evaluate the influence of culture and media on gender roles. (10 marks)

In addition, in the grey boxes are some fictitious teacher comments and A B C . . . tasks. The students are therefore required on **Handout 61** to complete those tasks in order to improve the answer. It is always worth mentioning to the students during/after this task how small additions/sentences can have a huge impact on the quality of a piece of work.

Possible task improvements:

A: For example, childbearing and nursing of infants mean that women are well placed to care for children but are less able to take on roles which require extended absence from home, such as commuting to work. Men's greater speed and strength makes them more able to perform other tasks.

B: Evidence about cultural differences may be flawed, which challenges the conclusions of the research.

C: That is, there are very few children who have NOT watched television to compare them to.

D: Williams (1985) studied children in a valley in Canada which had received television for the first time. He found that their views on gender had become significantly more sex-typed after the introduction of the TV.

E: One might expect males to act more aggressively after the introduction media-driven male stereotypes. In addition, although the study is not directly about gender, it does indicate that simply exposing children to stereotypes is not enough for them to change their attitudes.

F: It is possible that this 'backlash' occurs because boys of this age want to take a view that is opposed to the view held by adults.

References

Appell, G.N. (1984). Freeman's refutation of Mead's coming of age in Samoa: The implications for anthropological inquiry. *The Eastern Anthropologist, 37*, 183–214.

Charlton, T., Gunter, B. and Hannan, A. (eds) (2000). *Broadcast Television Effects in a Remote Community*. Hillsdale, NJ: Lawrence Erlbaum.

Eagly, A.H. and Wood, W. (1999). The origins of sex differences in human behavior: Evolved dispositions versus social roles. *American Psychologist, 54*, 408–23.

Freeman, D. (1984). *Margaret Mead and Samoa: The Making and Unmaking of an Anthropological Myth*. Cambridge, MA: Harvard University Press.

It is inevitable that some students will find the improvements harder to make than others – some students will need individual support during the activity in order to prompt the correct responses.

You could ask the students to help each other in pairs/threes using a collaborative learning structure (see page 5) as long as it is set up in a way where all students are responsible and have to engage in the task.

Pingree, S. (1978). The effects of nonsexist television commercials and perceptions of reality on children's attitudes about women. *Psychology of Women Quarterly, 2*, 262–77.

Signorelli, N. and Bacue, A. (1999). Recognition and respect: A content analysis of prime-time television characters across three decades. *Sex Roles, 40*, 527–44.

Williams, T.M. (1985). Implications of a natural experiment in the developed world for research on television in the developing world. Special issue: Television in the developing world. *Journal of Cross-cultural Psychology, 16(3)*, 263–87.

TOPIC: Cultural and media influences on gender roles

Content analysis of advertisements

This is an excellent idea that was included in the previous version of the *Teacher's Companion*. In the days when students had to do a non-experimental piece of coursework, a popular choice was to conduct a content analysis of advertisements on TV related to gender stereotypes. The importance of ads is that they affirm existing gender stereotypes which lead us to have different expectations for female and male behaviour, which then has a profound influence on how we behave. Research has not just focussed on TV ads but also looked at ads in magazines.

There is a variety of research on this topic.

- **Women are underrepresented.**

Sommers-Flanagan et al. (1993) found that music videos feature roughly twice as many males as females. Women are not seen much, but they are heard even less. You can simply count the gender of the person doing voiceovers on ads or gender representation in music videos.

- **Women's and men's bodies are represented differently.**

In magazine advertisements women are much more likely than men to serve a decorative function. Women recline in seductive clothing, caressing a liquor bottle, or they drape themselves coyly on the nearest male. They bend their bodies at a ludicrous angle, or they look as helpless as six-year-olds. They also may be painfully thin. In contrast, men stand up, they look competent, and they look purposeful (Jones, 1991).

- **Women and men are shown doing different activities.**

In magazine advertisements, men are rarely portrayed doing housework. Instead, men are more likely than women to be shown working outside the home. The world of paid employment is not emphasised for women. For example, an analysis of the articles in *Seventeen* magazine demonstrated that only 7% of the contents concerned career planning, independence, and other self-development topics. In contrast, 46% of the contents concerned appearance (Peirce, 1990). Basically, the media world often represents men and women as living in separate spheres.

- **Women are cast in a dependent role.**

One of the classic studies of TV advertising was conducted by Manstead and McCulloch (1981). They analysed 170 ads (they started with about 300 observed over a one-week period on British TV but ignored those that contained only children and animals). The adult central figure in each ad was identified and classified on a number of criteria. Women were found to be more likely to be portrayed as product users, to be cast in a dependent role, to produce no arguments in favour of the product and to be shown at home.

Similar results were produced in a later study by Harris and Stobart (1986) which also compared daytime versus evening ads. Harris and Stobart analysed eight aspects of the central figures' behaviour: credibility basis, role, argument, product type, location of central character, type of reward provided by the product for central character, gender of the background figures and humour. These categories could form the basis of a detailed content analysis.

Copyright [1981] by Psi Chi, the National Honor Society in Psychology [www.psichi.org]. Reprinted with permission. All rights reserved.

Possible activities:

- Ask students to bring in teen magazines and analyse the gender stereotyping in the ads in terms of central character, how male/female bodies are represented, what men and women are portrayed doing.

- Ask students to watch music videos and compare male and female vocalists in terms of what they are portrayed doing.

- Ask each student to observe TV ads. For each ad they should record the product being advertised, and the programme that was being shown either side of it, (e.g. children's programme, male-interest, female-interest, family-interest). For each central character they should record gender and what that person is doing in the ad (were they the user or the authority or other role?). You could compare daytime and evening advertising, or compare advertising during 'male' type programmes and 'female' type programmes.

NO HANDOUT

P	H	S	G	T

The suggested activities are not differentiated. However, depending on the activity chosen, it would be wise to provide some scaffolding/structure to support students' data collection.

- If you discuss these results with the students, consider if/how the results may now be different. Do they think these results lack temporal validity?

References

Harris, P. R. and Stobart, J. (1986) Sex-role stereotyping in television advertisements. *British Journal of Social Psychology, 25*, 155–64.

Jones, M. (1991) Gender stereotyping in advertisements. *Teaching of Psychology, 18*, 231–3.

Manstead, A. and McCulloch, C. (1981) Sex-role stereotyping in British television advertisements. *British Journal of Social Psychology, 20*, 171–80.

Peirce, K. (1990). A feminist theoretical perspective on the socialization of teenage girls through Seventeen magazine. *Sex Roles, 23*, 491–500.

Sommers-Flanagan, R., Sommers-Flanagan, J. & Davis, B. (1993). What's happening on music television? A gender role content analysis. *Sex Roles, 28*, 745–53.

TOPIC: Atypical gender development

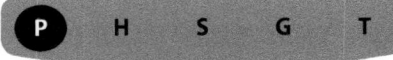

Atypical gender development crossword

A crossword may seem a little too juvenile for A Level students but, as an activity, it certainly has its merits (and in my (MG) experience, there is no such thing as *too* juvenile for A Level students!). This activity can be used to force students to engage with textbook material in more depth and to read for meaning; the clues on this crossword are designed to encourage this. The crossword would work well with page 106 of the *Complete Companion*.

The answers are as follows:

Across

2. thalamus
5. rejection
6. illness
8. genderidentity
9. preferred

Down

1. innately
3. sensitive
4. testosterone
7. longer
10. DDT

References

Hare, L., Bernard, P., Sanchez, F., Baird, P., Vilain, E., Kennedy, T. and Harley, V. (2009). Androgen receptor repeat length polymorphism associated with male-to-female transsexualism. *Biological Psychiatry, 65(1),* 93–6.

Ramachandran, V.S. (2008). Phantom penises in transsexuals. *Journal of Consciousness Studies, 15(1),* 5–16.

It is likely that some students will finish earlier than others. This is because some students will be able to work out the answers more easily and may read more quickly than others. As such, you may wish to have an extension activity up your sleeve. You could ask students to add two to three questions/answers to the crossword using the text provided.

Zucker, K.J. (2004). Gender identity development and issues. *Child and Adolescent Psychiatric Clinics of North America, 13(3),* 551–68.

TOPIC: Piaget's theory of cognitive development

HANDOUT 63

P H **S** G T

Applying Piaget's theory

Students often struggle with applying theories to novel situations (AO2) and so regular opportunities to model and practice this skill are vital. The question set on **Handout 63** requires students to use their understanding of Piaget's theory of cognitive development to explain how Grace's understanding of birds develops through experience.

Possible answer:

Grace has developed a schema for birds through her interactions with the family pet. She knows they have a beak, eat seeds, and have feathers and wings. She uses this schema to identify the wildlife in her garden. Through assimilation she has fitted the new experience of seeing different birds using the bird feeder into her existing bird schema. When she visits the zoo, the penguins she sees do not fit into her schema which causes a state of imbalance. She is told they are birds but their features and actions do not fit her current schema. Her granddad's explanation of why penguins are birds helps her adjust her schema to accommodate this new experience.

If students are struggling to answer the questions then the following key terms and prompts could be provided to help students structure their ideas:

1. **Schema** for birds
2. **Assimilation** of birds seen in the garden
3. **Accommodation** due to seeing penguins
4. **Equilibration** drives the development of the bird schema.

References

Piaget, J. (1926). *The Language and Thought of the Child*. New York: Harcourt Brace Jovanovich.

Piaget, J. (1954). *The Construction of Reality in the Child*. New York: Basic Books

Mark scheme:

Level	Marks	Description
2	3–4	Knowledge of components of Piaget's theory of cognitive development is clear and mostly accurate. The material is used appropriately to explain how Grace's thinking develops. The answer is generally coherent with effective use of terminology
1	1–2	Some knowledge of the theory is evident. Links to the development of Grace's thinking are not always effective. The answer lacks accuracy and detail. Use of terminology is either absent or inappropriate

Additional activities:

When introducing Piaget's theory (AO1), provide students with an explanation of the four concepts stated in the AQA specification: schemas, assimilation, accommodation and equilibrium. After discussing each term and giving examples to aid understanding, challenge students to produce a concise summary of each concept. This could be achieved by imposing a word limit (25 words) or a format, e.g. text message. Once completed, students share their summaries with each other adding to / amending their own summaries if needed.

TOPIC: Piaget's theory of cognitive development

P   H   S   G   **T**

Support or refute?

Handout 64 introduces research studies that can be used to evaluate (AO3) Piaget's theory of cognitive development. Students consider whether the findings of each study can be seen to support or refute Piaget's explanation, recording their judgement on the continuums provided and explaining how they arrived at their decision.

Possible commentary:

Fantz (1961): Supports Piaget's suggestion of infants being born with a few schemas, in this case a mental representation of a human face. The inclusion of a jumbled face and one with equivalent light and dark shading suggest it was the arrangement of the features on the schematic face that held the infant's attention rather than interest or shading. However, it is unclear whether infants were simply drawn to the symmetry. Although, a preference for human faces would have adaptive significance.

Bennett (1976): This study casts doubt on Piaget's emphasis of the importance of 'discovery learning'. However, the differences may be explained by the amount of time teachers in formal classrooms spend teaching these

specific skills and that discovery learning requires teachers to be more sensitive and knowledgeable in how to guide students.

Sinclair-de-Zwart (1969): Findings support Piaget's claim that cognitive maturity is needed for linguistic development, rather than language and social factors driving forward cognitive understanding (as proposed by Vygotsky).

Additional activities:

Themes relating to issues and debates (Paper 3) can be identified when evaluating Piaget's theory. Piaget combines biological maturation with experience to explain cognitive development. As well as keeping a glossary of key terms, students may find it helpful to note down examples of issues and debates as they arise in other topics.

References

Bennett, N. (1976). *Teacher Styles and Pupil Progress*. London: Open Books.

Fantz, R.L. (1961). The origin of form perception. *Scientific American, 204(5)*, 66–72.

Less-able students may find this task difficult and so splitting the class into working groups may be necessary.

Group 1: working with the teacher to complete the handout. This involves discussing what the findings of each study suggest then prompting students to make links to Piaget's theory.

Group 2: Provide students with an AO1 clue for each study linking research to relevant concepts. Fantz clue – Piaget proposes infants are born with a few schemas. Bennett clue – Piaget states, 'Each time one prematurely teaches a child something he could have discovered for himself, that child is kept from inventing it and consequently from understanding it completely' (Piaget, 1970). Sinclair-de-Zwart clue – Piaget believed linguistic development was dependent on cognitive maturity.

Sinclair-de-Zwart, H. (1969). Developmental psycholinguistics. In D. Elkind and J. Flavell (eds) *Studies in Cognitive Development*. Oxford: Oxford University Press

TOPIC: Piaget's stages of intellectual development

Sort it out

This activity is designed to help students consolidate their understanding of Piaget's four stages. Before attempting the task, students would benefit from experiencing examples of Piaget's logic tasks (conservation of volume using counters or liquid, the three mountains task and class inclusion tasks). This could be achieved by asking students to attempt the tasks themselves or watching video clips of children being tested. For example, watching the clip found at https://www.youtube.com/watch?v=TRF27F2bn-A prepares students for the sort it out activity.

Answers:

Stage 1: 0 to 2 years. Sensorimotor stage.

Children learn to co-ordinate sensory input with motor actions.

Children come to realise that objects out of sight still exist (object permanence).

'Circular reactions' describes the repetition of actions to test sensorimotor relationships.

Stage 2: 2 to 7 years. Pre-operational stage.

Due to a lack of logical thinking children rely on appearance rather than reality.

Egocentric thinking prevents children taking the doll's perspective in the three mountains task.

Children cannot identify smaller groups contained in a larger category (class inclusion).

Stage 3: 7 to 11 years. Concrete operational stage.

Conservation is the most important achievement at this stage.

Children acquire the basics of logical reasoning.

Children are able to use logical thinking to solve conservation tasks.

Stage 4: 11 years +. Formal operational stage.

Children can now solve abstract problems.

Children can think like a scientist – developing hypotheses and testing them.

Children can engage in idealistic thinking – they can imagine an ideal world.

Additional activities:

When studying this topic, students are introduced to a range of new vocabulary. Give students time in class, or set a homework activity, to create a glossary for cognitive terms. This can later be added to when studying Vygotsky.

HANDOUT 65

P   H   **S**   **G**   T

This activity could be set as a group task with students of mixed abilities working together. Once strips for each stage have been arranged correctly, students can then record a concise description of each stage in their notes.

Alternatively, students can work individually using, if needed, a textbook for support (*Complete Companion*, page 118).

Key terms for Piaget should include: object permanence, conservation, egocentric and class inclusion. Words can also be added from previous lessons on Piaget's theory of cognitive development: schemas, assimilation, accommodation and equilibrium.

An extension activity could be set for more-able students asking them to design a task to test a child's intellectual ability at one of the four stages. Links could be made here from Piaget's tasks to criticisms of their methodology – could students design a more realistic task?

References

Piaget, J. (1926). The Language and Thought of the Child. New York: Harcourt Brace Jovanovich.

TOPIC: Piaget's stages of intellectual development

Testing intellectual development

Handout 66 can be used to introduce issues with Piaget's tests of intellectual development (AO3 skill). Students outline the procedure and findings of Piaget's conservation task and three mountains task. After reading the issue stated they explain how later research has shown children of a younger age, than that predicted by Piaget, are able to conserve or take another's perspective.

Additional activities:

McGarrigle and Donaldson's (1974) naught teddy task involves conservation of counters. As an extension activity students could be set the challenge of improving Piaget's conservation of liquids task.

When revising research, students may find it helpful to draw an image to represent each study. This can be labelled to record findings and conclusions. Students should test their recall by redrawing the image and applying labels without using their textbook or referring to the original image. Following this memory test students can add any missed information from their class notes, using a different coloured ink to highlight details that need further revision.

References

Hughes, M. (1975). *Egocentrism in Preschool Children*. Unpublished PhD thesis, University of Edinburgh.

HANDOUT 66

P   H   **S**   G   T

Role modelling the conservation task and three mountains task as designed by Piaget and later modifications by McGarrigle and Donaldson (naughty teddy) and Hughes (naughty doll) will help students visualise the procedure and distinguish between the two methodologies. If you do not want to create mountains or cannot source the toys needed then a quick YouTube search will access a range of relevant video clips.

McGarrigle, J. and Donaldson, M. (1974). Conservation accidents. *Cognition, 3*, 341–50.

Piaget, J. (1954). The Construction of Reality in the Child. New York: Basic Books.

TOPIC: Vygotsky's theory of cognitive development

Explain the image

The activity on **Handout 67** can either be used to develop students' understanding of the theory allowing them to create a record of Vygotsky's explanation or be used as a revision activity testing students' recall of key concepts.

Students can use this handout to help them prepare the AO1 section of the following exam question: Describe and evaluate Vygotsky's theory of cognitive development. (16 marks). In 16-mark questions AO1 is worth 6 marks. Comments relating to AO1 can be picked out from each level of the mark scheme and used as a marking guide for the handout.

Most students should be able to use a textbook (*Complete Companion* page 120) to explain each concept in their own words. Less-able students can be supported by providing descriptions of each concept (without naming that concept) for students to place into each textbox on **Handout 67**.

Alternatively, each student could be assigned one or two concepts to explain. Students then move around the classroom working with students teaching each other the concepts they have completed until each student has a completed handout.

Level 4	Knowledge of the theory is accurate and detailed. The answer is clear coherent and focused with specialist terminology used effectively.
Level 3	Knowledge of the theory is evident, though occasional inaccuracies may be seen. The answer is clear, organised and specialist terminology mostly used effectively.
Level 2	Some knowledge of the theory is evident but the answer lacks clarity, accuracy and organisation in places. Specialist terminology may be used inappropriately.
Level 1	Knowledge of the theory is limited. The description lacks clarity, has many inaccuracies and is poorly organised. Specialist terminology is absent or inappropriate.

Additional activities:

In helping students prepare for the 16-mark question stated above encourage the class to use PEEL format for each evaluative paragraph. Providing students with a PEEL template for each paragraph supports the formation of detailed evaluative comments. For example:

Point: Cross-cultural research has supported Vygotsky's emphasis on the role of culture in cognitive development.

Evidence: Gredler (1992) suggested the primitive counting system used in Papua New Guinea makes subtraction and addition of large numbers difficult which is a limiting factor for cognitive development.

Expansion: Furthermore, some psychologists believe immersing non-human animals in human culture can transform elementary functions into higher mental functions. Savage-Rumbaugh (1991) showed how Bonobo apes were able to communicate using a lexicon.

Link: These studies suggest that culture does play a role in limiting or promoting cognitive development.

References

Gredler, M. (1992). *Learning and Instruction: Theory into Practice*. New York: Macmillan Publishing.

Savage-Rumbaugh, E.S. (1991). Language learning in the bonobo: How and why they learn. In N.A. Krasnegor, D.M. Rumbaugh, R.L. Schiefelbusch and M. Studdert-Kennedy (eds), *Biological and Behavioural Determinants of Language Development*. Hillsdale, NJ: Lawrence Erlbaum Associates.

Vygotsky, L.S. (orig. 1934, reprinted 1962). *Thought and Language*. Cambridge, MA: MIT Press.

TOPIC: Baillargeon's explanation of early infant abilities

Baillargeon reading record

Students complete the reading record (**Handout 68**) to make their own notes on Baillargeon's research into the cognitive abilities of very young children. The reading record encourages students to consider Baillargeon's claims in relation to Piaget's theory of cognitive development.

Students use their textbook (*Complete Companion*, page 122) to summarise the procedure and findings of Baillargeon's studies and make links to Piaget's theory. It should be remembered that for 16-mark questions AO1 is worth 6 marks so it is important that students' note making is concise.

Additional activities:

Students can be set the following exam question: Baillargeon studied early infant abilities by conducting violation of expectation studies. What is meant by the term 'violation of expectation'? (1 mark)

Possible answers:

General answer – What is expected to happen does not occur, leading to surprise (increased looking) in infants.

Specific answer – The image of a row of tall carrots passes behind a screen with a window. The tall carrots should be seen in the window but when they do not appear the infant shows surprise in response to this unexpected event.

References

Song, H. and Baillargeon, R. (2008). Infants' reasoning about others' false perceptions. *Developmental Psychology, 44*, 1789–95.

Students who quickly complete their reading record can be challenged to consider wider issues relating to Baillargeon's research.

For example:

Internal validity: Does the violation of expectation methodology measure what it intends to measure?

Nature/nurture debate: Baillargeon emphasises the role of innate mechanisms but she has not specifically researched the effect of different cultural experiences of infant's development.

These students can feed back their wider research to a small group of students before the whole class moves on to evaluating Baillargeon's research.

TOPIC: Baillargeon's explanation of early infant abilities

Violation of expectation

Handout 69 outlines Baillargeon and DeVos' (1991) violation of expectation experiment (suitable for an AO1 question such as: Outline an example of violation of expectation research. (4 marks). Beneath this students are asked to consider why the researchers implemented certain controls. These comments can form an evaluation (AO3) of Baillargeon's research of early cognitive abilities.

Possible commentary:

Use of birth announcements – reduce bias in sample selection, improved population validity. Piaget's research has received criticism for the use of middle-class children.

Parents did not interact with their child – reduce any effect parental behaviour may have on child's interest in the event: either increasing their interest or distracting the child from the scene.

Two observers in a double blind study – reduces observer bias as the type of event is unknown. Having two researchers allows inter-rater reliability to be assessed.

Additional activities:

On completing **Handout 69**, students should consider critics' claims that violation of expectation studies may lack internal validity and questions as to whether showing surprise is enough to imply an understanding of object permanence. (*Complete Companion*, page122). After considering both the strengths and limitations of Baillargeon and DeVos' study, the class can indicate where they fall on the continuum:

Strong evidence for OP ←--------------------→ Weak evidence for OP

HANDOUT 69

P H S **G** T

Mixed-ability groups would work well for this activity. Students who have previously shown themselves to have a secure understanding of research methods should be distributed amongst the groups to support other students.

Provide each student with a Post-it® note to justify their decision then ask them to stick the note at a suitable point along the continuum displayed on the board/wall.

References

Baillargeon, R. and DeVos, J. (1991). Object permanence in infants: Further evidence. *Child Development, 62*, 1227–46.

TOPIC: The development of social cognition: Selman's theory

Who said what and why?

The activity on **Handout 70** can be used to consolidate Selman's five-stage model of perspective taking. Before sharing the model with students, ask the class to complete the handout matching the child's response (shown in speech bubbles) to the stage and abilities at that age (shown in dashed text boxes). Once students have come to understand the theory, they revisit their handout to determine how accurate their predictions were. Alternatively, the activity can be used as a revision tool to consolidate understanding of the model and Selman's dilemmas.

Additional activities:

Set the assessment: Evaluate Selman's levels of perspective taking. (10 marks). Provide students with a list of evaluative points they need to investigate to answer the question. Remind students that quality is better than quantity so they need to focus on three, maybe four, detailed PEEL paragraphs rather than a list of underdeveloped statements.

Evaluate points you may wish to provide for students include:

- Selman's original research has been supported by later studies.
- The development of perspective-taking is both biological and environmental.
- Research suggests perspective-taking skills are important in social behaviour.
- Research cannot claim perspective-taking skills cause higher levels of social competence.
- Research has a number of important implications for schools, therapy and treatment of criminals.

Students could work in small groups to make notes on one of the points shown above in the form of a poster to be displayed. This forms a 'learning library' for the class – as students write their evaluation they are able to visit the displays to gather ideas for their evaluation. Reading the poster and then returning to their desk to write (hopefully) encourages students to understand what they have read rather than simply copying information word for word without considering the meaning of what they have read.

HANDOUT 70

P H S **G** T

Students can work in mixed-ability groups to complete the activity, maybe giving one student in the group the role of 'expert'. This student has access to the textbook (*Complete Companion*, page 124) and while they cannot tell their group the answers, they can tell the group how many accurate matches they have made and how many errors are still present allowing the group to re-work their matches. If setting this activity as a group task, cutting out each statement makes it easier for students to continually re-work their ideas.

References

Selman, R. (1976). Social cognitive understanding. In T. Lickona (ed.), *Moral Development and Behavior*. New York: Holt, Rinehart and Winston.

Selman, R.L. (1977). A structural-developmental model of social cognition: Implications for intervention research. *The Counseling Psychologist, 6(4)*, 3–6.

TOPIC: The development of social cognition: Theory of mind

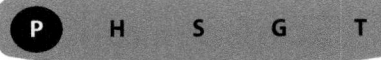
Theory of mind exam answers

Think-pair-share (described on page 5) can be used with **Handout 71**. Initially students work alone to mark Selina and Alan's answers to the two exam questions (think). They then join a friend to moderate their marking (pair). Finally, they ask for whole class feedback and decide on marks as a group (share).

Briefly outline theory of mind as an explanation for autism. (2 marks)

Selina provides a stronger answer to this question. She has identified 'mindblindness' and shown understanding of how this relates to the difficulties faced by autistic individuals.

Alan's answer is less detailed. His first sentence is a re-wording of the question and subsequent comments do not focus on theory of mind as an explanation.

Explain two limitations of theory of mind as an explanation for autism. (6 marks)

Selina only focuses on one limitation and so would be unable to score full marks. She identifies that research supporting lack of theory of mind as an explanation for autism may be low in internal validity. However, she loses her way in the middle of her answer and describes procedure and findings of Baron-Cohen's Eyes-Task.

Alan's answer is more successful as he clearly identifies two limitations (students should be encouraged to following this example, 'one limitation is . . . . ., a second limitation is . . .'). He has identified an evaluative point and explained why this is a limitation. Annotating answers using ID (identify) and EX (explain) may help students visualise the structure of Alan's answer and is a helpful way of encouraging students to develop their own responses to this kind of question.

Once students have discussed the mark they would award Selina and Alan for each question, they may then choose one of the following extension activities:

- Improve any answers that did not score full marks.
- Use the answers to create a 16-mark response to the question, 'Describe and evaluate theory of mind as an explanation for autism'.
- Write an examiner's report commenting on what students did well and what needed to improve for both questions.
- Create your own answers for the two questions.

References

Baren-Cohen, S., Jolliffe, T., Mortimore, C. and Robertson, M. (1997). Another advanced test of theory of mind: Evidence from very high functioning adults with autism or Asperger Syndrome. *Journal of Child Psychology and Psychiatry, 38,* 813–22.

Mark scheme for 6 mark question in Handout 71:

Level	Marks	Description
3	5–6	Two limitations are explained in a clear and effective manner. The answer is coherent and well organised. Specialist terminology is used effectively.
2	3–4	Two limitations are given, but one or both may lack explanation. The majority of the answer is clear and organised with appropriate use of specialist terminology. **OR**, one limitation is given at top of level 3.
1	1–2	At least one limitation is given but explanation lacks detail, is vague or muddled. Specialist terminology is used inappropriately or is absent. **OR**, one limitation is explained at the top of level 2.

TOPIC: The mirror neuron system

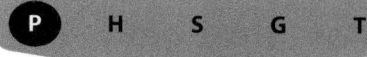

If this is the answer . . . what is the question?

Handout 72 shows a set of answers to various AO1 questions relating to mirror neurons. Students read each answer carefully to determine what is being explained and use this understanding to hypothesise what question could have triggered each response.

Possible questions students could create:

(moving clockwise from top left hand of **Handout 72***).*

- What are mirror neurons?
- How were mirror neurons discovered?
- In relation to behavioural regulation, explain the terms 'on-line' and 'off-line'.
- How have mirror neurons been linked to the concept of theory of mind (ToM)?
- Are mirror neurons the same in non-human and human animals?
- What other aspects of social development seem reliant on mirror neurons?

- In what area of the brain are mirror neurons most active when trying to understand the intentions of others?
- Why is it important that humans and other animals are able to imitate others?

Additional activities:

When recapping the role of mirror neurons either at the start of a lesson, to check progress or as a revision activity, instruct students to form small groups and on a piece of paper write the term 'mirror neurons' vertically down the left-hand side of their paper. For each letter, students have to write word, phrase or sentence relating to mirror neurons.

For example.

M – macaque monkeys were the first species in which mirror neurons were identified

If students find it too challenging to create their own questions in response to the answers shown on **Handout 72**, a series of possible questions (you may even wish to include a few irrelevant ones) could be shared with the class/given to targeted students to help them consider what the answer is explaining.

Alternatively, more-able students could be set the questions to answer with **Handout 72** being used as a feedback sheet allowing students to check their responses independently.

I – imitation is possible due to mirror neurons

R – research has shown . . .

Setting a time limit or making it a race to finish first adds a competitive element to the task.

TOPIC: The mirror neuron system

Develop the detail

The level 4 mark scheme for 16-mark questions states that evaluations should be, 'thorough and effective' with, 'minor detail and/or expansion of argument sometimes lacking'. The essay extract on **Handout 73** is underdeveloped but text boxes to the right of the extract can be used to add detail to the candidate's answer. Students need to identify which commentary applies to each paragraph to produce a 10-mark evaluation (the remaining 6 marks are allocated for AO1, 'describing the role of mirror neurons in social cognition').

Additional activities:

Handout 73 can also be used as a peer assessment activity. Students could use the mark scheme shown below to decide what level the undeveloped extract would reach. They could then suggest ways to improve the evaluation (just cover the textbox comments when photocopying the handout!).

References

Heyes, C. (2009). Where do mirror neurons come from? *Neuroscience and Biobehavioral Review, 34(4)*, 575–83.

Students can be challenged to add a final, developed evaluation to consider the use of mirror neurons in explaining autism.

Hickok, G. (2009). Eight problems for the mirror neuron theory of action understanding in monkeys and humans. *Journal of Cognitive Neuroscience, 7*, 1229–43.

Mukamel, R., Ekstrom, A.D., Kaplan, J., Iacoboni, M. and Fried, I. (2010). Single-neuron responses in humans during execution and observation of actions. *Current Biology, 20*, 750–6.

Ramachandran, V.S. (2000). Mirror neurons and imitation learning as the driving force behind 'the great leap forward' in human evolution. See www.edge.org/3rd_culture/ ramachandran/ramachandran_p1.html (accessed November 2008).

Tranel, D., Kemmerer, D., Adolphs, R., Damasio, H. and Damasio, A.R. (2003). Neural correlates of conceptual knowledge for actions. *Cognitive Neuropsychology, 20(3)*, 409–32.

Level 4	Evaluations are thorough and effective. Ideas are expressed clearly in a coherent manner. Commentary is focused with only minor details lacking and/or underdeveloped arguments.
Level 3	Evaluations can be identified and comments are mostly effective. The majority of the answer is clear and organised but may lack focus in places.
Level 2	Any evaluation present is only partially effective and may lack clarity in places. Some commentary may contain inaccuracies and be poorly organised.
Level 1	Evaluation is absent or limited and poorly focused. Many inaccuracies can be identified with commentary being poorly explained and organised.

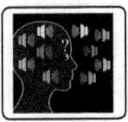

TOPIC: Classification of schizophrenia

What I thought . . . and what it actually is

| P | H | S | G | T |

This activity is not differentiated.

Students often have misconceptions about what schizophrenia is, usually due to sensationalised stories in the media.

Start by asking students to write down what they think schizophrenia is.

At the end of the topic, ask them to complete the following Venn diagram to visually represent how their understanding of the disorder has (hopefully!) developed:

TOPIC: Classification of schizophrenia

HANDOUT 74

Matching clinical key terms

| **P** | H | S | G | T |

The clinical diagnosis of schizophrenia in particular does seem to intimidate some students because it involves numerous unfamiliar terms.

A simple way to help students learn these or to recap their learning is a matching exercise (**Handout 74**).

Students can either cut out the boxes and rearrange, or, they could simply draw lines from the term to the definition (although this can get messy).

An extension activity could be that students highlight the symptoms of schizophrenia in terms of positive symptoms (those that appear to exaggerate or distort normal functions) and negative symptoms (those that reflect a loss of normal functions).

Not, as some students think, positive and negative symptoms in terms of which are nice and which are bad.

TOPIC: Classification of schizophrenia

A beautiful mind

| P | H | S | G | T |

This activity is not differentiated.

As previously mentioned, schizophrenia can and has been extremely poorly portrayed in the media, with teenage soaps in particular being guilty. In fact, many students think that schizophrenia is more like split-personality disorder as a result of their viewing experiences.

One film which I (MG) believe portrays schizophrenia in an excellent way is 'A Beautiful Mind', which stars Russell Crowe as John Nash, a famous economics academic who suffered from the disorder.

From what I am led to believe there are some fairly large inaccuracies in the film when compared to the experiences of

John Nash (for example, he only ever suffered from auditory hallucinations whereas in the film his hallucinations are visual which I guess makes it a more watchable film!). However, the film gives a much better sense of how a person can actually live a relatively normal life whilst suffering from the disorder when it is under control.

In addition, he does not kill or bomb anyone, and the camera does not zoom in and out incessantly nor the focus blur when it is from his perspective in order to 'illustrate' his madness. Unfortunately all too many TV shows do depict schizophrenia in this way.

As such, to cut a long rant short, I would advise showing some clips from the film to your students so they get a more rounded perspective! Perhaps even show the whole thing after school. Copies can be purchased on Amazon for as little as £3.

There probably isn't time to watch this film in class but it could be set as a homework task.

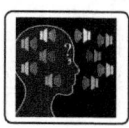

TOPIC: Reliability and validity in diagnosis and classification

It's not as clear cut as you think...

Until now, many students will have probably considered schizophrenia an objective and absolute mental illness. They've heard about it on the TV and doctors talk about it.

However, as psychologists, we know that to some extent schizophrenia is actually a social construction and merely a collective of symptoms bundled together and called 'schizophrenia' (I suppose this depends on your opinion).

In many ways it is difficult to open students' minds to the possibility that 'schizophrenia' as an objective and definitive illness doesn't actually exist (despite the fact that the symptoms do ...!).

A good starting point might be Rosenhan's (1973) 'On being sane in insane places' study which opens the possibility that psychiatrists and their diagnoses might be fallible. There are a number of good short video clips about this on YouTube.

Then consider using **Handouts 75** and **76** with your students.

They should use the list of symptoms in the box on **Handout 76** and place them in the Venn diagram on **Handout 75**. Then check their answers using their textbook or the internet.

Hopefully, this activity will illustrate to students that diagnosis of schizophrenia is not 'clear cut' and that many of the symptoms used to

diagnose schizophrenia are also used to diagnose depression and bipolar disorder. This would hopefully lead to a good discussion about the validity of the current clinical characteristics of diagnosis of this mental disorder.

For answers (according to my research!) see below:

Schizophrenia only:

- disorganised speech
- affective flattening
- alogia (poverty of speech).

Schizophrenia and bipolar disorder:

- delusions
- hallucinations
- psychomotor disturbances
- subjective experience that thoughts are racing
- inflated self-esteem and feelings/beliefs of grandiosity.

Bipolar disorder only:

- periods of mania (elevated mood)
- alternating moods between depression and mania
- excessive involvement in pleasurable activities.

Bipolar disorder and depression:

- depressed mood most of the day, nearly everyday
- significant weight loss or weight gain
- insomnia or hypersomnia
- feelings of worthlessness
- recurrent thoughts of suicide.

This activity could be followed with a discussion question using a collaborative learning structure (see page 5): What does this activity suggest about the reliability and validity of schizophrenia classification and diagnosis?

This is a very open-ended and higher-order question that should stretch the higher-ability students who will then need to share and articulate their ideas with the rest of the group.

Depression only:

- depressed mood most of the day, nearly every day without any periods of elevated mood (mania).

Depression, schizophrenia and bipolar disorder:

- inability to do everyday tasks
- difficulty concentrating
- anhedonia (inability to feel pleasure in normally pleasurable activities).

References

Rosenhan, D.L. (1973) On being sane in insane places. *Science, 179*, 250–8.

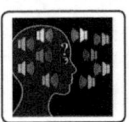
TOPIC: Biological explanations for schizophrenia

Understanding twin studies

Investigating the genetic basis of any behaviour usually involves the use of twin studies – schizophrenia is no different.

Students sometimes find the logic of twin studies and the interpretation of the results very difficult and therefore it is good to give them an opportunity to try and work through the design of the study in order to understand how and why twin studies support or challenge the concept of a genetic basis for behaviour.

Suggested answers to **Handout 77**.

Two types of Twin –

Identical twins share 100% of their genes and are also known as monozygotic twins (MZ). Non-identical twins are likely to share about 50% of their genes and are also known as dizygotic twins (DZ).

Assuming schizophrenia is completely genetic, what are the chances of Dave's identical twin Arnold developing the disorder?

If you assume that schizophrenia is completely genetic, the chances of

Arnold developing the disorder is 100%. This is because Dave and Arnold are genetically identical so the gene(s) determining Dave's disorder will also be present in Arnold.

Arnold does NOT suffer from schizophrenia. Are Dave and Arnold concordant?

No they are not concordant. Concordant would mean they BOTH have the disorder.

What is a concordance rate?

This is measured by researchers when they wish to find out the influence that genetics have on behaviour. It refers to the percentage of twins that share a particular trait. If a behaviour is completely genetic, the percentage in MZ twins should be 100%, and in DZ twins it should be somewhere around 50%.

It is assumed that MZ and DZ twins share 'equally similar environments'. What does this mean?

MZ twins usually grow up in the same household, with the same parents, in the same area and culture, go to the

This handout provides all students with scaffolding in order to deconstruct and understand twin studies; this should then help with their interpretation of twin studies.

I (MG) often find that some students need hand-holding during this topic so be ready to offer one-to-one support for students who are struggling.

same school, share friends etc. They have very similar environments.

In addition, DZ twins usually grow up in the same household, with the same parents, in the same area and culture, go to the same school, share friends etc.

Therefore, it is said that MZ and DZ twins share equally similar environments.

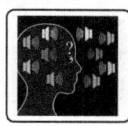

TOPIC: Biological explanations for schizophrenia

Writing about twin studies

Several A Level topics require students to understand (see previous handout) and write about twin studies in a successful way. **Handouts 78** and **79** can be easily adapted for use in any of those topics, it is just the research findings that will need amending (i.e. remove Joseph (2004) for a different twin study).

Handout 78 is focused on AO1; outlining the twin study and explaining what the findings suggest about the genetic role in schizophrenia and why.

Handout 79 is focused on AO3; evaluating the twin study methodology and explaining how this impacts the evidence supporting the genetic explanation of schizophrenia.

Suggested answers AO1:

- **Joseph (2004) reported a mean concordance rate of 40.4% for MZ twins and only a 7.4% rate for DZ twins. This suggests** that schizophrenia is at least in part genetically influenced.

- **This is because** MZ twins shared 100% of their DNA and DZ twins share only 50% of their DNA which may explain the higher concordance rates for schizophrenia in MZ twins.

- **In addition, the difference in concordance rates cannot be explained by the environment because** twin studies assume that MZ and DZ twins share equally similar environments; for example, both MZ and DZ twins share the same parents, homes, locations, schools, teachers, similar friendship groups etc.

- **Therefore** only the difference in genes shared can explain the difference in MZ and DZ concordance rates which suggests a genetic role in the development of schizophrenia.

Suggested answers AO3:

- **There could be a flaw in the argument that MZ and DZ twins share equally similar environments because** MZ twins are often treated more similarly than DZ twins due to their identical nature. In addition, MZ twins are always same-sex whereas DZ twins can be a male/female combination so it could be argued that MZ twins share a more similar environment with each than DZ twins do.

- **This is a problem for the conclusions drawn from the study** because the difference in MZ and DZ concordance rates for schizophrenia can now also

HANDOUTS 78 and 79

P **H** **S** G **T**

These handouts provide all students with scaffolding in order to interpret and write about twin studies in the context of schizophrenia.

I (MG) often find that students need hand-holding during this topic so be ready to offer one-to-one support for students who are struggling.

be explained by the difference in environments between MZ and DZ twins which confuses the conclusion.

- **Therefore** it is no longer clear that genes can explain the difference in schizophrenia concordance rates which undermines the evidence used to support the idea of a genetic role in the development in schizophrenia.

References

Joseph, J. (2004). Schizophrenia and heredity: Why the emperor has no genes. In J. Read, L. Mosher and R. Bentall (eds), *Models of Madness: Psychological, Social and Biological Approaches to Schizophrenia*. Andover: Taylor & Francis.

TOPIC: Psychological explanations for schizophrenia

Explaining double-binds

Bateson et al. (1956) suggest that children who frequently receive contradictory messages from their parents are more likely to develop schizophrenia. For example, if a mother tells her son that she loves him, yet at the same time turns her head away in disgust, the child receives two conflicting messages about their relationship on different communicative levels, one of affection on the verbal level and one of animosity on the non-verbal level.

According to the theory, these interactions prevent the development of an internally coherent construction of reality, and in the long run, this manifests itself as schizophrenic symptoms.

Bateson et al. (1956) called these contradictory messages 'double binds'. Below are some examples of double binds to help your students put this in context.

- 'You need to be more independent!'

- 'Do not read this sign!'

- When Josh arrived home from school his mum asked him to give him a hug. When Josh gave her a hug she seemed to stiffen up and look away. She then broke away, turned round and said 'I love you'.

Share these with your students, (e.g. on PowerPoint) and ask them to explain how and why these examples are double binds.

NO HANDOUT

P H S **G** T

Using collaborative learning structures (see page 5) can help to ensure that your higher-ability students are stretched and that your lower-ability students are supported. More-able students can be asked to find further examples of double binds.

References

Bateson, G., Jackson, D.D., Haley, J., and Weakland, J.H. (1956) Towards a theory of schizophrenia. *Behavioural Science, 1*(4).

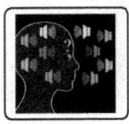

TOPIC: Psychological explanations for schizophrenia

Feedforward marking

The concept of A B C and Feedforward marking is outlined on page 2. I've (MG) found it to be a really effective marking and feedback technique that genuinely has an impact on student progress.

As a result, I've now started to use the concept to design handouts.

Handout 80 shows a fictitious student answer to the following exam question: Evaluate the family dysfunction explanation of schizophrenia. (10 marks)

In addition, in the grey boxes are some fictitious teacher comments and A B C . . . tasks. The students are therefore required on **Handout 81** to complete those tasks in order to improve the answer. It is always worth mentioning to the students during/after this task how small additions/sentences can have a huge impact on the quality of a piece of work.

Possible task improvements/responses:

A: The question asked for evaluation, these two paragraphs are a description of the explanation and therefore not worth any marks.

B: They found that the difference was only found when the adopted family was rated as 'disturbed'. This means, whilst genetic vulnerability is clearly involved, environmental conditions and family relationships are needed to trigger the illness.

C: There is research evidence to support the idea that particular types of family relationships may lead to schizophrenia.

D: However, not all research supports the explanation and the evidence is contradictory.

E: Expressed emotion (a family communication style in which family members of the patient talk about the patient in a critical and hostile manner).

F: This suggests that people with schizophrenia have a lower tolerance for intense emotional stimuli, especially involving family members. Ultimately, this supports the idea that family relationships explanation of schizophrenia.

References

Altorfer, A., Kasermann, M.L. and Hirsbrunner, H. (1998). Arousal and communication: I. The relationship between nonverbal, behavioral, and physiological indices of the stress response. *Journal of Psychophysiology, 12*, 40–59.

Bateson, G., Jackson, D., Haley, J. and Weakland, J. (1956). Toward a theory of schizophrenia. *Behavioural Science, 1*, 251–64.

Berger, A. (1965). A test of the doublebind hypothesis of schizophrenia. *Family Process, 4*, 198–205.

P	H	S	G	T

It is inevitable that some students will find the improvements harder to make than others – some students will need individual support during the activity in order to prompt the correct responses.

You could ask the students to help each other in pairs/threes using a collaborative learning structure (see page 5) as long as it is set up in a way where all students are responsible and have to engage in the task.

Lebell, M.B., Marder, S.R., Mintz, J., Mintz, L.I., Tompson, M., Wirshing, W., Johnston-Cronk, K. and McKenzie, J. (1993). Patients' perceptions of family emotional climate and outcome in schizophrenia. *The British Journal of Psychiatry, 162(6)*, 751–4.

Liem, J.H. (1974). Effects of verbal communications of parents and children: A comparison of normal and schizophrenic families. *Journal of Consulting and Clinical Psychology, 42(3)*, 438.

Tienari, P., Wynne, L.C. and Moring, J. (1994). The Finnish adoptive family study of schizophrenia: implications for family research. *British Journal of Psychiatry, 163(23)*, 20–6.

TOPIC: Drug therapy

Choose the right word

Handout 82 includes a very simple activity to consolidate students' learning on drug therapies used to treat schizophrenia.

The text on the handout is taken from page 146 of the *Complete Companion*. When they are given the choice, the students must choose the correct words from the ones given in bold. Students can easily get themselves in a tangle with all the various key terms in this topic so this is designed to help them think that through and increase their confidence in the understanding of this explanation.

References

Kapur, S., Zipursky, R., Jones, C., Remington, G. and Houle, S. (2000). Relationship between dopamine D2

P	H	S	G	T

This activity is difficult to differentiate other than by outcome. Less-able students may struggle in some areas so you should be on hand to support.

occupancy, clinical response, and side effects: A double-blind PET study of first-episode schizophrenia. *The American Journal of Psychiatry, 157(4)*, 514–52.

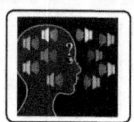

TOPIC: Drug therapy

Psychology story time – Magic dancing shoes

P H S **G** T

Using collaborative learning structures (see page 5) can help to ensure that your higher-ability students are stretched and that your lower-ability students are supported.

Below is the story of Dave, his poor dancing and the (fake) 'magic shoes' which he buys from a con man.

The story tells the tale of a man who hates dancing and has no confidence in his ability. That is, until a man sells him 'magic shoes' which transform his dancing moves and coordination.

The twist in the tale is that the 'magic shoes' are actually fake, yet Dave's dancing improved anyway.

This sounds to me like the perfect tale to explain the **placebo effect** which students need to understand in order to interpret the findings of studies which investigate the effectiveness of drug therapies for schizophrenia. It may seem juvenile, but that's often the way students like it!

Twenty past six every Thursday was the time Dave dreaded the most. "Are you ready?" his wife Sue would call up from the hallway while he tried to desperately think of an excuse to get out of their weekly salsa dancing class. "Yes," he'd inevitably gloomily reply.

On the drive to his local community centre Dave would imagine he was off down to the pub with his mates instead, before predictions of the insults dance instructor Julio would have in store for him invaded his thoughts. "Spaghetti arms" and "Billy bow legs" had been last week's favourites.

As they entered the hall, Dave's stomach twisted into a knot at the sound of the

salsa music blaring from Julio's CD player. With a sigh he grabbed Sue's hand and walked towards his fate.

As the previous four weeks' classes had shown, try as he might Dave was just a horrible dancer. He just couldn't seem to pick up the steps like everyone else, and even when he did manage a few he was always a second behind. As he told himself for the millionth time that night 'you're doing this for Sue', he heard a loud "Psssst!" behind him.

Turning around, Dave saw an unfamiliar face looking at him. "I'm Clive," the man said. "I've been watching your moves." Dave shifted from one foot to the other, embarrassed, not knowing where to look.

"No, don't worry – I want to tell you I think I might have something that will work for you," Clive said, nodding down at his feet. "See these shoes? They're magic. I was just like you before I found them, but once I put them on I never looked back." As he spoke, Clive broke into a spin before giving a perfect performance of the choreography Dave had tried – and failed – to pick up over the last month.

Dave's mouth fell open. "I know, pretty magic, eh?" said Clive. "But do you know what the best part is? I'll let you buy them – £50."

"Deal," said Dave, looking behind him to check Sue was still chatting to her friend Anne. As Clive took Dave's money and handed over the shoes he broke out into

a huge grin, thinking 'I can't believe he bought those fake shoes! That was the easiest money I've ever made' smugly to himself.

Dave couldn't wait to get home and try out his new shoes. As soon as he was sure Sue had fallen asleep that night, he got up and went down to the living room. To his utter amazement he could remember the routine and not only that, he thought he was pretty good.

For the first time ever, Dave looked forward to twenty past six the next Thursday and couldn't wait to see Julio's face when he started dancing.

The moment was just as good as Dave had hoped – gradually everyone around him stopped and stared as he swung Sue around with perfect timing and movement. "I don't believe it," said Julio, open mouthed.

Turning around to see the amazed faces around him, Dave caught sight of Clive at the back of the room. He wondered for a moment why Clive looked more surprised than everyone else but as the class all burst into applause suddenly it was only dancing – and how good he was – on Dave's mind.

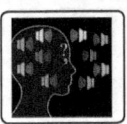
TOPIC: Cognitive Behavioural Therapy

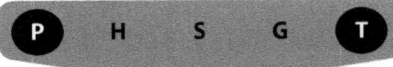
Better in 10: Make CBTp relevant to schizophrenia

Students will have met CBT in Year 1 so should have some basic knowledge. However, I (MG) have found in the past that when writing about CBT, they tend to write about it generally and forget to make it relevant to the particular mental disorder they are supposed to be outlining.

I've seen my own students make this mistake many times and I have seen students across the country make this mistake in their examination papers.

Handout 83 is based on these experiences and was designed to shock my students; I would show them an accurate and detailed answer but reveal that it would only count as level 1 or 2 because it is a generic description of CBT rather than a description of a therapy for schizophrenia.

The student activity on **Handout 83** is to improve the description with brief examples, words and sentences to ensure that the description is focused on schizophrenia and achieves closer to a 'level 4' mark band. Students should try to find 10 improvements that they can make and indicate where those improvements can go into the text.

Sometimes those improvements can be as simple as including the word 'schizophrenia'. In other places it might involve including an example relevant to schizophrenia. The text is based on page 148 of the *Complete Companion* but most of the specific references/examples to schizophrenia have been removed.

Once students have completed this activity, the powerful point to make is that with a few small tweaks, you could argue that this description has moved from a level 1/2 answer to a level 4 answer. Focus and relevance in an answer are very important.

A list of suggestions for improvements below could be given to less-able students. Although they should attempt the handout on their own first, they could be given the suggestions to select from as options for the parts they are finding difficult.

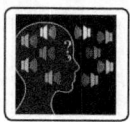

TOPIC: Family Therapy

Family therapy: Evaluation elaboration

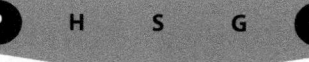

Handout 84 is designed to illustrate to students the level of depth required to achieve top AO3 marks.

Students should start by reading the boxes on the far left-hand side of the page, which outline simple evaluation points. Ask them to highlight (or shade in) each of the boxes in that column with a different colour.

The students should then read the boxes in the next column. Each represents further explanation/ elaboration of one of the evaluation points, but they are not in the same order. Students should highlight (or shade in) those boxes with the correct, corresponding colour.

They should repeat this until all boxes in all columns are shaded in. This will require some thought from the students.

Purpose:

Explain to students that the more they can elaborate their original evaluation points, (e.g. 'A strength of the cognitive approach is that it has many applications'), the more AO3 marks they are likely to get. This is denoted at the top of the handout. The evaluation comments start at 'Level 1', and then increase in marks the further they are elaborated, through 'Level 2', 'Level 3' and 'Level 4'. These are loosely based on the AQA essay mark schemes.

Answers:

The correct answers are as follows:

"Research evidence suggests that family therapy can be effective in improving clinical outcomes."

- For example, Pharoah et al. (2010) reviewed 53 studies published and found that patients showed some improvement in social functioning and mental state. Patients were also less likely to relapse.
- However, the authors suggest that the main reason for its effectiveness may have less to do with the interventions themselves and more to do with that fact that it increases medication compliance.
- As such, this undermines the evidence. It suggests that the beneficial effects are NOT the result of family therapy itself, but because family therapy

means patients are more likely to take their drugs (which are effective).

"There are a number of methodological issues in research into family therapy."

- Pharoah et al.'s meta-analysis identified the problem of random allocation. A large number of studies were from China. Evidence has emerged that in many Chinese studies, random allocation had been stated as having been used, yet was not (Wu, 2006).
- In some studies, the observers were not 'blinded' to the condition (family therapy or standard care) which increases the possibility of observer bias.
- The issues with the evidence mean that conclusions on the effectiveness of family therapy are difficult to determine.

"An advantage of this therapy is the considerable economic benefits."

- The NICE review of family therapy studies demonstrated that it was associated with significant costs savings when offered to patients *alongside* the standard care.
- The extra cost of family therapy is offset by a reduction in costs of hospitalisation because of the lower relapse rates.
- There is also evidence that relapse rates are lower after the completion of the intervention – which suggests that the savings could be even higher.

"Family therapy has an additional advantage in having a positive impact on family members."

- Lobban et al. (2013) analysed the results of 50 family therapy studies that had included an intervention to help relatives.
- 60% of these studies reported a significant positive impact on at least one outcome category for relatives, e.g. coping, relationship quality, problem-solving skills.
- However, the researchers also concluded that the methodological quality of the studies was poor, making it difficult to distinguish effective from ineffective interventions in terms of family members.

"Some of the evidence questions the worthiness and value of family therapy."

- Garety et al. (2008) failed to show any better outcomes for patients given

> To challenge your more-able students, you could decide to cut out the twenty boxes and instruct the students to match them up to make five evaluation points. Once they have cut out the boxes, they should mess the boxes up so it is no longer clear which boxes belonged to which columns. This is a more difficult activity because the students must decide on the order of the elaboration as well.

family therapy compared to those that simply had carers.

- Individuals in both groups were found to have low relapse rates compared to the no therapy/carer control group. The researchers also found that the carers displayed low rates of expressed emotion.
- This suggests that family intervention may not improve outcomes further than a good standard (carers with low expressed emotion) of treatment as usual.

References

Garety, P., Fowler, D., Freeman, D., Bebbington, P., Dunn, G. and Kuipers, E. (2008). A randomised controlled trial of cognitive behavioural therapy and family intervention for the prevention of relapse and reduction of symptoms in psychosis. *The British Journal of Psychiatry, 192*, 412–23.

Lobban, F., Glentworth, D., Chapman, L., Wainwright, L., Postlethwaite, A., Dunn, G., Pinfold, V., Larkin, W. and Haddock, G. (2013). Feasibility of a supported self-management intervention for relatives of people with recent-onset psychosis: REACT study. *The British Journal of Psychiatry, 203(5)*, 366–72.

Pharoah, F., Mari, J., Rathbone, J. and Wong, W. (2010). Family intervention for schizophrenia. *Cochrane Database of Systematic Reviews, 12*.

Wu, T., Li, Y., Liu, G., Bian, Z., Li, J., Zhang, J., Xie, L. and Ni, J. (2006). Investigation of authenticity of 'claimed' randomized controlled trials (RCTs) and quality assessment of RCT reports published in China. *Proceedings of the 14th Cochrane Colloquium*; Dublin. 2006.

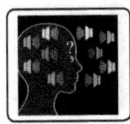

TOPIC: Token economy and the management of schizophrenia

Design your own token economy

As an introduction to this topic, you could ask the students to quickly design their own token economy.

This activity could work by roughly working through the following steps (which could be displayed on the board):

- Choose a context where you want behaviour to change, (e.g. behaviour in school, scouts, lunchtime, little brothers/sisters at home etc.).

- Pinpoint the behaviours that need to be changed – these should be specific, observable and measurable.

- Choose the types of tokens to be used, (e.g. plastic chips, gold stars, play money etc.).

- Choose the reinforcers that the tokens can be exchanged for, (e.g. TV time, chocolate).

- Set the reinforcer cost, i.e. determine how many tokens are required for each reinforcer.

Although the examples the students might use are quite different to schizophrenia, it might help them understand the concept of a token economy in a more tangible context first.

| P | H | S | **G** | T |

Using collaborative learning structures (see page 5) can help to ensure that your higher-ability students are stretched and that your lower-ability students are supported.

TOPIC: Token economy and the management of schizophrenia

Brief summaries: Token economy

This is a fantastic idea stolen (with permission!) from Jo Gotts at www.psychexchange.co.uk (now part of www.resourcd.com).

Essentially the activity involves students summarising information and as such, choosing the most important to retain in the synopsis. The information they need to summarise is on page 152 of the *Complete Companion*. Each 'brief' will be a summary of a key aspect of the token economy as a method used to manage schizophrenia behaviour. One rule that should be maintained is that the students write full sentences. The idea here is that students have to read

an evaluation, process it, understand it and then write it back down in summarised form; this stops students simply copying text into their notes without actually thinking about what they are writing or understanding it.

Handout 85 therefore provides four briefs in which to write 'brief summaries' (do you see what Jo did?!) of evaluation of token economies for schizophrenia.

Beneath each 'brief' are some key words/studies which students should aim to include in their summary. You could change/adapt this sheet to suit your needs.

| P | **H** | S | **G** | T |

You could set up this activity so that more-able students are paired with less-able students. The more-able student could have access to the full evaluations on page 153 of the *Complete Companion*. It is their job to articulate that evaluation and explain it to the less-able student. Then, without help from the more-able student, the less-able student must write their 'brief summary'.

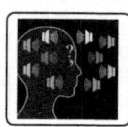

TOPIC: An interactionist approach

Moving up the levels

I (MG) have found myself in the last few years writing 'needs more detail' in some of my essay marking feedback. Of course, this is pretty useless feedback for students who genuinely do not understand what is meant by 'detail'. It is much easier to show them and *illustrate* to them what is meant by 'detail' and how this translates into examination marking.

It is feasible that within this topic the following question might be asked in an A Level examination: Outline the interactionist model for explaining schizophrenia. (6 marks)

Suppose that you have taught your students this explanation and that they need to outline this information in good detail. This activity should help them to know what 'good detail' means. Try using **Handout 86** with your students after you have outlined the explanation to them in detail.

Handout 86 outlines the explanation accurately, but with some vague details in places or key examples/ideas missing. The students should add details to the description by using the table at the bottom of the handout.

Suggested additions:

1. (diathesis)
2. (stress)
3. The fact that identical twin concordance is not 100% also suggests that environmental factors must also play a role in schizophrenia.
4. There was a relationship between the level of trauma and the likelihood of developing schizophrenia; those severely traumatised as children were at greater risk.
5. Vassos et al. (2012) found in their meta-analysis that the risk was 2.37 times higher in urban areas compared to rural areas.
6. It is possible that adverse living conditions and densely populated areas may contribute.
7. Which suggests the relationship between urban stress and schizophrenia requires some other factor, e.g. genetic vulnerability.
8. For example, minor stressors may lead to schizophrenia in a vulnerable individual. Or a major stressful event may cause schizophrenia in a person with low vulnerability.

This provides less-able students with a tangible example of what examiners mean by 'detail'. It could be given to less-able students in order to increase their examination skills and to structure their answers.

References

Varese, F., Smeets, F., Drukker, M., Lieverse, R., Lataster, T., Viechtbauer, W. and Bentall, R.P. (2012). Childhood adversities increase the risk of psychosis: A meta-analysis of patient-control, prospective and cross-sectional cohort studies. *Schizophrenia Bulletin, 38(4)*, 661–71.

Vassos, E., Pedersen, C.B., Murray, R.M., Collier, D.A. and Lewis, C.M. (2012). Meta-analysis of the association of urbanicity with schizophrenia. *Schizophrenia Bulletin, 38(6)*, 1118–23.

TOPIC: The evolutionary explanation for food preferences

Eating past and present

Using their knowledge of the evolutionary explanations of food preferences, students either discuss or record their responses to the questions shown on **Handout 87**. Questions in speech bubbles refer to demands of the EEA and can be addressed using a textbook (*Complete Companion*, page 164). The thought bubbles contain questions that require students to hypothesise based on their own experiences. For example, the rise in globalisation, multi-culturalism and travel means people have access to more and more foods which may reduce fear of new foods as we see examples of people eating unfamiliar foods.

Additional activities:

Prior to this activity, students could compile their top food likes and dislikes to determine whether a pattern exists, e.g. are 'liked' foods high in calories/ sweet? Are 'disliked' foods bitter to taste

HANDOUT 87

| P | H | S | **G** | T |

> Working in pairs allows one student to tackle the past questions, referring to the EEA (information available in textbooks), while the other student addresses present questions referring to modern society, requiring deeper thinking.

or less common to their culture? Students could also be shown more unusual foods and asked if they would be willing to taste them, such as offal and a century egg.

TOPIC: The evolutionary explanation for food preferences

Data--------Analysis

On the left-hand side of **Handout 88**, four studies into food preference are listed. Students have to match the findings from these studies to comments on the right-hand side of the handout. These comments model how to analyse the findings by relating data collected to the various concepts proposed by the evolutionary explanation.

Once completed, students could be asked to conduct their own research into 'the scapegoat technique' which is mentioned on the handout in relation to Bernstein and Webster's (1980) research with chemotherapy patients.

Additional activities:

Once they have completed **Handouts 87** and **88**, students can attempt the following question:

Sammi is a fussy eater. He dislikes bitter tasting food and often refuses to eat food claiming it 'smells funny'. He will only eat foods he is familiar with, many of which are sweet tasting. Recently he was sick after eating cheese on toast and now he refuses to eat anything with melted cheese.

Use your knowledge of evolutionary explanations for food preferences to explain Sammi's eating behaviour.

References

Bernstein, I. L. and Webster, M. M. (1980). Learned taste aversions in humans. *Physiology & Behavior, 25(3)*, 363–6.

Birch, L. L., McPhee, L., Shoba, B. C., Pirok, E. and Steinberg, L. (1987). What kind of exposure reduces children's food neophobia? Looking vs. tasting. *Appetite, 9(3)*, 171–8.

HANDOUT 88

| **P** | H | S | G | T |

> More-able students could be given the data only to develop their own analytical comments relating the findings to evolutionary explanations.

Grill, H. J. and Norgren, R. (1978). The taste reactivity test. I. Mimetic responses to gustatory stimuli in neurologically normal rats. *Brain Research, 143(2)*, 263–79.

Knaapila, A., Tuorila, H., Silventoinen, K., Keskitalo, K., Kallela, M., Wessman, M. and Perola, M. (2007). Food neophobia shows heritable variation in humans. *Physiology & Behavior, 91(5)*, 573–78.

TOPIC: The role of learning in food preferences

Reading between the (head)lines

For each headline, students rate the validity of each story, 1 = invalid, 10 = valid. To encourage informed decision making, students need to include at least one piece of evidence to support their judgement. Judgements could be informed by methodological issues, associated research and wider issues.

Additional activities:

Controversial statements: students work in groups, give each group a controversial statement for them to discuss for 5 minutes. The whole group must agree on a final sound bite in response to the statement which is then shared with the group. This can be made more difficult by insisting the group either agrees with or disagrees with the statement as it is presented: no sitting on the fence!

Statements used could include:

- Parents are to blame if their child eats unhealthily.
- TV Adverts for high fat/high sugar foods should be banned (as is the case for tobacco).
- The rise of TV has led to the death of the family meal.

HANDOUT 89

| **P** | H | S | G | T |

> More-able students may wish to take one headline and develop it into a complete news article through their own research.

TOPIC: The role of learning in food preferences

On the one hand or the other

NO HANDOUT

P H S **G** T

This is a simple activity that could be used for almost any topic really. Ask your students to draw around both their hands on an A3 sheet of paper. They should include the title, 'On the one hand social and cultural influences have shaped our food preferences, on the other hand . . .'. Using a textbook (*Complete Companion*, pages 166–7) students write an argument or explain evidence to support the argument that food preferences are learned, on the fingers of the left hand. Once completed, students can either record criticisms of parental/cultural influences or evidence for evolutionary explanations on the fingers of the right hand. In the palm of both hands students record their own opinion about the origin of food preferences.

Additional activities:

For homework, students could carry out a content analysis of adverts for unhealthy food shown on television at different times over a two-day period. They could consider the message promoted and the extent to which nutritional content is discussed. Once data is compiled the class can, for example, discuss the extent to which media plays a role in food preference.

> Students initially work alone before sharing ideas with another. They then snowball into groups of four where they are able to check the accuracy and detail of points recorded.

TOPIC: Neural and hormonal mechanisms in the control of eating

Neural and hormonal mechanisms

HANDOUT 90

P H S G **T**

Handout 90 provides a diagram showing the interaction between the lateral hypothalamus (LH – switches 'on' eating) and the ventromedial hypothalamus (VMH – switches 'off' eating). Students need to add detail of these two structures in the boxes provided. Along the dotted lines, students should record the effect of eating on blood glucose levels. Finally, details need to be recorded for the role of ghrelin (stimulates appetite) and leptin (reduces urge to eat). When explaining hormonal influences students should be encouraged to make reference to the hypothalamus.

Additional activities:

Once completed, students can use **Handout 90** to revise for the following exam question: Outline the role of the hypothalamus, ghrelin and leptin in the control of eating behaviour. (6 marks). Students could answer this question using their handout which would be a good test of the usefulness of their completed diagram.

The diagram can also be used to prepare for a game of *Guess Who*. Prepare three clues for each technical term. Students who guess correctly after the first clue score three points, a correct guess after two clues scores two points and so on. For example, damage leads to aphagia = 3 points, stimulation causes feeding = 2 points, an area of the hypothalamus considered to be the 'on switch' for eating = 1 point.

> This is often a tricky section for students who struggle with science so the interaction between LH and VMH may need to be modelled first.

TOPIC: Neural and hormonal mechanisms in the control of eating

Construct a critique

Handout 91 presents a brief summary of four studies into neural and hormonal control of eating. Once each have been read and understood, students consider wider issues relating to this area of investigation.

Answers:

Free will / determinism: research implies feelings of hunger and satiety drive our eating behaviour but we do exercise some personal choice; for example, those on a diet may try to ignore feelings of hunger, sometimes we do eat beyond satiety and feel uncomfortably full (though this unpleasant feeling does prevent further eating), we sometimes eat when we are not hungry out of boredom. Neural explanations don't comment on what we choose to eat to satisfy hunger.

Non-human animals: Studies often use rodents who, like humans, have a hypothalamus so some generalisations can be made. However, should we consider the reasons for eating, e.g. for survival as opposed to affirming social bonds, altering mood etc? Furthermore, if animals are provided with a constant supply of food this may not be the case for wild animals who need to seek out food.

Real-life application: Students could consider obesity treatments derived from research such as leptin injections. This could lead to developed discussion of biological verses psychological treatments (CBT).

Additional activities:

Before considering evidence to evaluate neural and hormonal control of eating, a suitable starter activity is needed to remind students of the role of the hypothalamus, ghrelin and leptin. Assign one component to each group and ask them to create a 10-word summary of the role the component plays in controlling eating. These summaries can be displayed on the board while the class reads the four evaluation studies on **Handout 91** to help students make sense of the evidence.

| P | H | S | G | **T** |

Providing students with 'think-hints' – a brief sentence to get them thinking may be helpful. For example, 'what brain structures do rats and humans have in common?'

References

Gold, R.M. (1973). *Hypothalamic Obesity: The myth of the ventromedial nucleus. Science, 182*: 488–90.

Heymsfield, S.B., Greenberg, A.S., Fujioka, K., Dixon, R.M., Kushner, R., Hunt, T., Lubina, J.A., Patane, J., Self, B., Hunt, P. and McCamish, M. (1999). Recombinant leptin for weight loss in obese and lean adults: A randomized, controlled, dose-escalation trial. *Jama, 282(16)*, 1568–75.

Wren, A.M., Seal, L.J., Cohen, M.A., Brynes, A.E., Frost, G.S., Murphy, K.G., Dhillo, W.S., Ghatei, M.A. and Bloom, S.R. (2001). Ghrelin enhances appetite and increases food intake in humans. *Journal of Human Endocrinology and Metabolism, 86(12)*, 5992.

TOPIC: Biological explanations for anorexia nervosa

Magic numbers

The top section of **Handout 92** displays nine numbers (three per type of study) which students link to each type of study.

Answers:

Family studies (Strober et al., 2000): 1st degree relatives, share 50% DNA, 10x greater risk if family member has anorexia nervosa (AN).

Twin studies (Wade, 2000): 28–74% heritability found in one specific study. In one study, in over 2000 interviews heritability rate found to be 58%.

Adoption studies (Klump et al., 2009): 123 adopted females and their adopted sisters compared to 56 adopted females and their biological sibling. Heritability rate of 59–82% for different aspects of disordered eating.

Once students have matched the numbers they use these to create a summary of findings for each type of study.

Additional activities:

When considering neural explanations, provide students with a series of claims which they need to expand with evidence (*Complete Companion*, page 170).

Claims:

- High levels of serotonin lead to increased anxiety which may trigger AN.

- Increased dopamine activity alters the way people interpret rewards which may affect attitudes to food dysfunction of the limbic system. This may lead to difficulty regulating and processing emotions which may lead to pathological thoughts seen in AN.

References

Klump, K.L., Suisman, J.L., Burt, S.A., McGue, M. and Iacono, W.G. (2009). Genetic and environmental influences on disordered eating: An adoption study. *Journal of Abnormal Psychology, 118(4)*, 797–805.

| P | **H** | S | G | T |

Once completed, set the following extension question: 'Can we isolate the effect of genetics from environmental variables?' Information for environmental variables refers to students making links to other AN explanations such as family systems theory and Social Learning Theory.

Strober, M., Freeman, R., Lampert, C., Diamond, J. and Kaye W. (2000). Controlled family study of anorexia and bulimia nervosa: evidence of shared liability and transmission of partial syndromes. *American Journal of Psychiatry, 157*, 393–401.

Wade, T.D., Bulik, C.M., Neale, M. and Kendler, K.S. (2000). Anorexia nervosa and major depression: shared genetic and environmental risk factors. *American Journal of Psychiatry, 157*, 469–71.

TOPIC: Biological explanations for anorexia nervosa

Create a learning library

The aim of this activity is to produce a learning library that can be used in later lessons to support students answering a 16-mark question: Discuss biological explanations for anorexia nervosa.

Provide each group with an A3 sheet showing evidence for one of the biological explanations of AN: genetic (you could assign mini groups here; one for each type of study – family, twin, adopted) and neural. Students record their ideas on the A3 sheet as to the validity and/or reliability of research, real-life applications, issues and debates that relate specifically

to the explanation they have been assigned. You may also require students to add any information gained from independent research set as a homework.

Once the A3 sheets are annotated, students attempt the 16-mark question. The A3 sheets should be easily accessed enabling students to get up and visit the sheets to gather ideas/information to help them construct their answer.

Additional activities:

Before the completed essays are handed in to be marked, ask students

NO HANDOUT

P   H   S   **G**   T

Mixed-ability groups work well with this activity so a range of ideas is recorded showing different levels of thinking. This helps later visitors to the 'library' access a range of points for each topic.

to return to the group they were in when creating the A3 sheets. Divide the class essays between these groups. Students then peer assess the sections of the essay relating to the A3 sheet they created; adding any additional comments or making corrections where needed.

TOPIC: Family systems theory and anorexia nervosa

Exploded outline

When outlining the family systems theory, students need to include different components of the psychosomatic family that the theory identifies as contributing to the development of AN. Enmeshment is placed above autonomy and control on **Handout 93** as lack of autonomy and control are consequences of enmeshment. Rigidity and (lack of) conflict resolution are also included

as they have been suggested as contributory factors. Students use the suggested words at the bottom of each box to ensure each component is clearly outlined.

Additional activities:

If students have dramatic talents they could work in groups to create a still image representing each component. These could be photographed for

HANDOUT 93

P   H   S   G   T

Students can use a textbook for support or outline each component from memory as a revision exercise.

students to add a description of the scene below the photograph making a visual revision tool to be used nearer the exam period.

TOPIC: Family systems theory and anorexia nervosa

Developed evaluations

Handout 94 provides an opportunity to practice evaluation writing. The first paragraph models PEEL as a method of creating a clear and concise evaluation of family systems theory of AN. The second paragraph requires students to identify PEEL in a second evaluative comment. Having seen and identified the paragraphs' structure, students now create two further evaluations using the PEEL structure.

Additional activities:

Students could consider wider implications of family systems theory:

• Does the theory blame family members for the problem?

• How would biological explanations disagree with the theory?

• How can the nature / nurture debate be applied to theories of AN?

References

Gremillion, H. (2003). *Feeding Anorexia: Gender and Power at a Treatment Center*. Durham, NC: Duke University Press.

Kog, E. and Vandereycken, W. (1989). Family interaction in eating disordered patients and normal controls. *International Journal of Eating Disorders, 8*, 11–23.

HANDOUT 94

P   H   S   G   T

Less-able students may benefit from a set of sentence starters to help structure their paragraphs. For example, P: the success of family therapies suggests families are integral to the recovery process.

TOPIC: Social learning theory and anorexia nervosa

NO HANDOUT

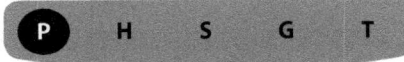

Making predictions

Students should have some knowledge of social learning theory from A Level Year 1, paper 2 Approaches where they are required to have knowledge of imitation, identification, modelling, vicarious reinforcement, role of mediational process and Bandura's research. Using this prior knowledge, students work alone or in pairs to create 10 statements about social learning theory. After sharing ideas with the class, students then create their own prediction of how the theory would explain the development of anorexia nervosa.

Students then refer to a textbook (*Complete Companion*, page 174) and answer the following questions about their prediction:

- I accurately predicted . . .
- I implied . . .
- I was incorrect about . . .
- I overlooked . . .

Additional activities:

The specification names 'modelling, reinforcement and media' specifically so students should ensure they have a clear understanding of these three

Students can conduct their own independent research into real-life applications of social learning theory. For example, in 2015, French MPs approved a law to ban cat walk models who were below a certain BMI and introduced a separate measure to tackle internet sites condoning anorexia.

concepts. Students can be set the homework task of creating a leaflet for parents explaining each concept and offering advice to reduce the risk of their child developing disordered eating.

TOPIC: Social learning theory and anorexia nervosa

HANDOUT 95

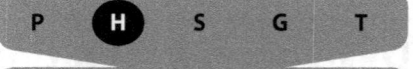

Complete the critique

Handout 95 shows the AO1 commentary and AO3 evaluation points in response to the question: Discuss social learning theory as an explanation for anorexia nervosa. (8 marks). Students use their textbook (*Complete Companion*, page 175) to complete the critique of the theory. As the AO1 focuses on the role of the mother as a model and the influence of the media, peer influences are not considered for AO3. The answer demonstrates how to address an 8-mark question as it is important students can discuss

explanations at a suitable length for 8- and 16-mark questions. For a 5-mark AO3 response, two well-constructed paragraphs are sufficient. **Handout 95** provides three options from which students may wish to address two. Alternatively, students could respond to all three before selecting the strongest two for their final answer.

Additional activities:

Once completed, the 8-mark answer can be used as a base to create a 16-mark response (AO1 – 6, AO3 – 10 marks) by

Less-able students may need specific studies presented on a separate piece of paper to match to the evaluative statements shown if they struggle to identify relevant research in their textbook.

adding peer influences and developing the depth at which maternal influence and media are considered.

TOPIC: Cognitive theory and anorexia nervosa

HANDOUT 96

A cognitive behavioural model

Although no specific model is named in the specification, students do need to understand the role of irrational beliefs and distortions in the development of AN. Garner and Bemis' (1982) explanation outlines how this faulty thinking applies to the disorder. Students use their textbook (*Complete Companion*, page 176) to summarise the model in a flow diagram to aid revision. Once completed, students apply their knowledge to Jessie's case. Teacher discretion is needed here as this is a sensitive topic and it may be that some students in the class would find it emotionally difficult to consider Jessie's case.

Additional activities:

Students can also be given the task of creating a visual diagram of the transdiagnostic model (Fairburn et al, 2015) representing 'core psychopathology', the influence of self-esteem and three mechanisms maintaining AN.

References

Fairburn, C.G., Cooper, Z. and Shafran, R. (2003). Cognitive behaviour therapy for eating disorders: a "transdiagnostic" theory and treatment. Behaviour Research and Therapy, *41*, 509–28.

Higher-order thinking questions can be set:

Where do the cognitive behavioural model and the transdiagnostic model originate from?

Can these models explain why higher incidents of AN are traditionally seen among the female population?

Evidence for distortions and irrational beliefs are often from self-reports. Why might this be a problem?

Garner, D. M. and Bemis, K. M. (1982). A cognitive-behavioral approach to anorexia nervosa. *Cognitive Therapy and Research, 6(2)*, 123–50.

TOPIC: Cognitive theory and anorexia nervosa

Cognitive chit-chat

Students move around the classroom asking their peers for opinions to complete each speech bubble. Students can use the textbook (*Complete Companion*, page 176) to identify points they can explain to their peers.

Each bubble provides a line for the speaker's name to be recorded should you decide to take in completed handouts to check student opinions. Adding names to comments also deters any silly or underdeveloped responses. Speech bubbles allow for different forms of evaluation from research evidence to issues and therapeutic interventions based on cognitive assumptions. Once complete,

the handouts can be taken in to assess learning of the whole class. For example, if one student appears on a number of sheets saying the same comment, it may suggest they need more help to broaden the scope of their evaluations. You could offer a reward for the student who appears on the most sheets making the widest range of comments.

Additional activities:

Once complete, **Handout 97** can be used as a writing frame to address the evaluative part of the question, 'Outline and evaluate the cognitive explanation of anorexia nervosa.' (16 marks) – AO1 – 6 marks, AO3 – 10 marks.

Students could be assigned specific evaluative points to research before the activity such as limitations, supporting evidence, impact of therapies derived from the theory. This suggestion provides a more structured way of organising the activity by assigning topics to students. The main activity gives students personal choice over what they wish to discuss with their peers.

TOPIC: Biological explanations for obesity

Exam marking

Candidate 1: This answer is accurate but lacks the detail needed to access mark band 3. The candidate shows they understand that the hypothalamus is involved but fails to mention the arcuate nucleus. They also seem unsure as to the actual role this brain area plays in producing a desire to eat. The evaluative comment is easy to identify but again, lacks the detail needed for the top mark band. The introduction (first two sentences) does not address the question and so cannot be credited.

Candidate 2: A more detailed account is given, this time for the role of leptin, and a case study of the use of leptin with an obese child has been used to

support the explanation. However, this criticism could be developed by stating research into obese children to support the role of leptin, thus demonstrating awareness of more than one study.

Additional activities:

After discussing the strengths and limitations of each candidate's response, students can apply the exam technique identified to the following question: Briefly explain and give **one** criticism of genetic explanations of obesity. (6 marks). These can be peer assessed using the mark scheme provided on **Handout 98**.

Students may find it useful to discuss each answer in small groups to develop a secure understanding of what a successful answer looks like.

TOPIC: Biological explanations for obesity

A-Z challenge

Ask students to form groups of four. On a sheet of A3 or sugar paper students write the alphabet horizontally down the left-hand side of the page. Using the textbooks, students record a word or phrase for each letter of the alphabet that relates to biological explanations of obesity. Some letters may need a little more creative thinking than others for example, D – determinism (gene/neural mechanisms cause obesity), Y (neuropeptide Y).

Once the alphabet is completed, students view each other's alphabets and replace any words with a better word and/or query the use of some words.

Additional activities:

Share news headlines of people suffering obesity. This could be statistics as well as sensational stories that are often reported in the media. Ask students to consider what they think causes obesity (their responses may fall under specific biological or psychological approaches). The discussion could then develop to consider the impact of taking a biological approach for how society views obesity and possible treatments. If you have a mature class, you could even ask them to consider how society reacts to someone who is

NO HANDOUT

| P | H | **S** | G | T |

Allow one 'scout' per group who is able to visit one other group to take back ideas to their group. One, one-minute visit usually does the trick.

obese compared to someone who is anorexic. Are these two eating disorders attributed to different causes? Who, if anyone, receives more sympathy? Why might different societal reactions exist?

TOPIC: Psychological explanations for obesity

Dangers of dieting

Handout 99 shows the start of a news article reporting how attempts to restrict eating can actually lead to overeating which increases the risk of obesity. Students could use the concepts of restraint theory, the boundary model (Herman and Polivy, 1984) and/or disinhibition to expand the explanation as to why restraint can lead to overeating.

Additional activities:

Before introducing the concept of restrained eating leading to obesity,

set students a homework web-hunt in which they are asked to bring three different pieces of internet research found when searching, 'dieting leads to weight gain'. Students should aim for different sources where possible, e.g. anecdotal evidence, research, news article. In lesson, students share the resources gathered to identify common themes/explanations. These can then be applied to the psychological explanations named on the specification: restraint theory, disinhibition and the boundary model.

HANDOUT 99

| **P** | H | S | G | T |

More-able students could add a counterargument to the article suggesting that biological explanations are more plausible.

References

Herman, C.P. and Polivy, J. (1984). A boundary model for the regulation of eating. In A.J. Stunkard & E. Stellar (Eds). *Eating and its Disorders*, pp. 141–56, New York, NY: Raven.

TOPIC: Psychological explanations for obesity

Exploring the evidence

Handout 100 provides students with an opportunity to revisit research methods while considering evidence for restrained eating leading to overeating.

Once research methods questions have been addressed, students should give a written summary explaining why these two studies provide evidence for restraint theory, disinhibition and the boundary model. Following this, evidence to challenge restraint theory can be introduced (Tomiyana et al. (2009) criticised the artificial nature of laboratory-based studies into eating.)

Additional activities:

In order to fully address evaluation questions, students will need more than two pieces of evidence. Using a textbook (*Complete Companion*, page 181) students can create a set of flash cards for relevant evaluative comments. On one side students summarise the evaluation in a single sentence, then on the reverse record a more detailed paragraph. These can then be used to test retention of evaluations nearer exam time.

HANDOUT 100

| **P** | H | S | G | T |

Students could be challenged to design their own study into the effects of restrained eating on food intake.

References

Herman, C. P. & Mack, D. (1975). Restrained and unrestrained eating. *Journal of Personality, 43,* 647–60.

Tomiyama, A. J., Mann, T. and Comer, L. (2009). Triggers of eating in everyday life. *Appetite, 52(1),* 72–82.

Wardle, J. and Beales, S. (1988). Control and loss of control over eating: An experimental investigation. *Journal of Abnormal Psychology, 97(1),* 35–40.

TOPIC: Explanations for the success and failure of diets

Daisy's diet club

Handout 101 introduces students to Daisy, who has produced a leaflet to help her diet club members stick to their eating regimes. Each tip is based on psychological explanations of the success or failure of diets. Students are asked to identify the psychology behind the tips and to include research evidence.

This activity can be used in conjunction with textbooks (*Complete Companion*, page 182) to introduce reasons for diets' success/failure or as a revision activity with tips cueing recall of different explanations.

Suggested links for each tip:

Focus on detail - Redden (2008)

Role of denial - Wegner (1994)

Pleasure - Stroebe et al. (2008)

Avoid triggers - Brunstrom et al. (2004)

Ironic process - Soetens et al. (2006)

Additional activities:

A simple plenary is to provide students with a Post-it® and ask them to create a fridge magnet giving a diet tip based on one psychological explanation. Display an image of a fridge on the class white board for students to stick their note to. Students then choose another 'magnet' and on the reverse, summarise the relevant explanation.

References

Brunstrom, J.M., Yates, H.M. and Witcomb, G.L. (2004). Dietary restraint and heightened reactivity to food. *Physiology & Behavior, 81(1)*, 85–90.

Redden, J.P. (2008). Reducing satiation: The role of categorization level. *Journal of Consumer Research, 34(5)*, 624–34.

Soetens, B., Braet, C., Dejonckheere, P. and Roets, A. (2006). 'When Suppression

> Students can practise higher-order thinking skills by ordering Daisy's diet tips from most to least successful; giving reasons for the decisions made.

Backfires': The ironic effects of suppressing eating-related thoughts. *Journal of Health Psychology, 11(5)*, 655–68.

Stroebe, W., Mensink, W., Aarts, H., Schut, H. and Kruglanski, A.W. (2008). Why dieters fail: Testing the goal conflict model of eating. *Journal of Experimental Social Psychology, 44(1)*, 26–36.

Wegner, D.M. (1994). Ironic processes of mental control. *Psychological Review, 101*, 34–52.

TOPIC: Explanations for the success and failure of diets

Discussing dieting writing frame

Students use their textbook (*Complete Companion*, page 183) or class notes to create an essay plan for the 16-mark question: Outline and evaluate one or more explanations for the success and/or failure of diets.

You may wish for students to work in pairs to complete **Handout 102** which can then be taken in, checked and photocopied so each student has their own copy to revise from (this cuts down on teacher marking and students benefit from being able to collaborate with a peer).

Additional activities:

Students could peer assess each other's writing frames once completed using the following tasks:

- In one colour highlight all key terms the author has included.

- In another colour highlight research evidence.

- On Post-it® notes add any missed detail.

- In green pen correct any inaccuracies.

> Less-able students may need support considering issues such as free will and determinism. Students who are confident in their understanding of issues and debates could be used as class experts for this section.

TOPIC: The physiology of stress

General adaptation syndrome

Handout 103 is divided into two sections. The first activity requires students to match the physiological changes and effects an individual experiences to each stage of the GAS. This consolidates knowledge (AO1) of the stress response. The second activity involves students applying (AO2) their understanding to a scenario.

Application: Tom initially experiences the alarm phase when he learns of his father's accident and races to the hospital. He will have had a raised heart rate as a result of the fight or flight response. When his father was recovering from his operation in hospital, Tom's body adapted to the stressor and he may have felt as if he was coping with the situation. However, his biochemical resources were being depleted. Long-term care of his father

has led to exhaustion. Tom's adrenal glands have become damaged due to over-activity and his immune system is unable to cope resulting in him suffering from a cold.

Additional activities:

Students who find visualising concepts useful for revision could create a cartoon strip depicting a stressor and the character's three reactions to the ongoing threat.

The body's response to stress involves a lot of biological terminology and so students may benefit from keeping a mini glossary for this topic. I (RG) find providing memory tips useful such as 'Adrenaline from adrenal glands', 'M for middle and medulla', 'cortisol is released from the cortex'.

HANDOUT 103

| P | H | S | G | **T** |

Some students may find it helpful to cut out the text boxes and physically manipulate them before deciding on the correct order. This activity could be turned into a group match-up task with students writing each GAS stage in their own words after cards are correctly matched.

TOPIC: The physiology of stress

Evaluating the GAS

Handout 104 relates to two evaluative comments: research support for the existence of a general response to different stressors and an alternative explanation for the stress-related illness seen in the exhaustion phase. Once completed the cloze exercise provides a model for the structure and level of detail needed when students write the second evaluation.

Refer to page 192 of the *Complete Companion*. The words provided for the second task refer to the suggestion that depletion of resources such as sugars and proteins are not the cause of stress-related illness. Rather it is the increased activity of hormones such as cortisol, also associated with the exhaustion phase, that are responsible for a decline in health.

Additional activities:

Once **Handout 103** and **104** are completed, students can use these to revise the GAS in preparation for a possible exam question: Discuss the physiology of stress. In your answer you should include the general adaptation syndrome, the hypothalamic pituitary-adrenal system and the sympathomedullary pathway. (16 marks).

Working in a triad, one student could write about GAS, one student could be responsible for short-term stress, the other taking long-term stress. Students can then check each other's contributions before combining all to form a complete answer. Students should be encouraged to focus of clarity of written work as well as the content.

HANDOUT 104

| P | H | S | **G** | T |

Organising students to work in pairs of similar abilities will give students the opportunity to think through their ideas to create a coherent paragraph. These could then be swapped with other pairs, for example, a lower-ability pair swop with a more-able pair to model how to construct clear, coherent and concise evaluations.

References

Selye, H. (1936). A syndrome produced by diverse nocuous agents. *Nature, 138*, 32.

TOPIC: The role of stress in illness

Developing the detail

P   H   **S**   G   T

I (RG) find students are able to recall general summaries of what was done and what was found, but often fail to add the data needed to produce accurate and detailed descriptions. The first candidate response on **Handout 105** outlines the Williams et al. (2000) study into anger. Students highlight the correct data from a choice of three at various points in the response.

Answers:

- 13,000 people
- 10 questions
- six years later
- 256 had suffered heart attacks
- over two-and-a-half times more likely
- 35% more likely

For the second section of **Handout 105**, students are required to use the items shown to create a concise description of the findings and procedures of Kiecolt-Glaser's et al. (1984) study of changes in NK cell activity during periods of low (one month prior to exams) and high (exam period) stress.

Additional activities:

Present students with short explanations for:

- How the activation of the sympathetic branch of the autonomic nervous system leading to increased adrenaline can lead to cardiovascular disorder.
- How the activation of the HPA system as a result of ongoing stress leads to production of cortisol which reduces immune response.

(*Complete Companion*, page 194)

Working individually, students pick the five most important words and record these on the classroom whiteboard. As a class they must agree on the five words that must appear in a description of the role of stress (short and long term) on the body. Students then use the words chosen to write a description in their own words.

This exercise can be used to create revision notes when introducing the two studies (*Complete Companion*, page 194) or can be used as a scaffolded test of recall for less-able students. More-able students could be asked to recall both studies unaided with the handout forming a feedback activity once their answers are marked.

References

Kiecolt-Glaser, J.K., Garner, W., Speicher, C.E., Penn, G.M., Holliday, J. and Glaser, R. (1984). Psychosocial modifiers of immunocompetence in medical students. *Psychosomatic Medicine, 46,* 7–14.

Williams, J.E., Paton, C.C., Siegler, I.C., Eigenbrodt, M.L., Nieto, F.J. and Tyroler, H.A. (2000). Anger proneness predicts coronary heart disease risk: Prospective analysis from the atherosclerosis risk in communities (ARIC) study. *Circulation, 101(17),* 2034–9.

TOPIC: The role of stress in illness

Putting stress on trial

P   H   S   G   **T**

A class debate may take some organisation but can help students develop their understanding of research into the effect of stress on the cardiovascular and immune system.

Stress is on trial accused of making people ill. Students take the role of prosecution (seeking evidence to convict stress) or defence (arguing that a causal link may not be possible between stress and illness, or that stress has benefits). Allow time in class to research and formulate arguments before the debate begins. You may wish to assign further roles such as jury, witnesses (someone taking on the role of a heart attack victim or medical professional explaining the link between stress and illness), judge and even courtroom typist to record key points in the case. If you have a large class, two smaller trials could be held: one for cardiovascular disorders, another for immunosuppression.

Additional activities:

Evaluation lucky dip – create strips of card each showing one of the following evaluation points:

- Research into stress and illness often use self-reports.
- Evidence supports the effects of stress on cardio-vascular disorders.
- People react differently to stress which may modify degree of illness experienced.
- Stress does not always have a negative effect on the immune system.
- A relationship between stress and illness is difficult to establish.

Create a second set of strips each showing one of the following:

- Email
- Post-it®
- Twitter post
- Facebook status
- Text message

Roles can be allocated based on students' abilities. For example, some students may relish the opportunity to hold court as the lead defence or prosecution barrister, others may enjoy a dramatic part as a witness such as recalling how after years in a high-powered career, a heart attack lead them to re-evaluate their life.

Place the strips in two separate envelopes. Students draw one strip from each envelope and must summarise the evaluation point in the method of communication selected. Once they have completed their own message, students share and record each other's points.

TOPIC: Sources of stress: life changes

Life changes: true or false?

This is a simple activity that provides space for students to develop their own judgements. First students identify whether the statement is true or false. If a statement is true, they can use the space provided to add further detail. If false, the space below offers an opportunity to correct the statement.

Additional activities:

When introducing the concept of life changes, ask students to work as a group to record as many life changes as possible on strips of paper. Challenge them to aim for 20 events. Once this is done, introduce the concept of

LCUs with marriage receiving 50 units. Groups then use the notion of marriage being assigned 50 life change units to order their events from highest to lowest. Students can suggest LCUs for each event as a reflection of the degree of readjustment needed should that event be experienced. When their lists are created, share the SRRS with the class for groups to compare their list to. At this point ask the class to consider strengths or limitations of the scale. For example, only Christmas is listed but this ignores festivals from other religions so may not apply to a multi-cultural society.

HANDOUT 106

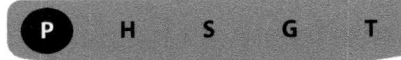

P   H   S   G   T

Develop students' research skills by asking them to complete the stretch box at the bottom of the handout.

References

Holmes, T.H. & Rahe, R.H. (1967). The social readjustment rating scale. *Journal of Psychosomatic Research, 11*, 213–8.

Rahe, R.H., Martin, J. and Arthur, R. (1970). Prediction of near-future health-change from subjects' preceding life changes. *Journal of Psychosomatic Research, 14*, 401–6.

TOPIC: Sources of stress: life changes

Creating concise evaluations

Handout 107 models how to create concise evaluations from textbook and/or class notes. This is an important skill for students to develop in terms of practising recording ideas in their own words (which deepens understanding) and building a bank of evaluations that can be realistically revised from in order to address 16-mark questions (10 marks awarded for AO3).

Once students have understood the modelled evaluative point and created a second summary using the extract shown, they should turn to their textbook (*Complete Companion*, pages 197 and 199) or class notes to create three more. You may wish to leave this activity until your students have studied daily hassles.

Additional activities:

Once students have studied daily hassles, provide an anonymous voting form asking them to decide which is more stressful: life changes or daily hassles. Students should justify their decision. Collect in the voting forms at the end of the lesson and type them up or display them in the classroom next lesson. If you have more than one class, it is interesting to see whether the overall judgement varies between classes. This also provides another opportunity to practice maths skills, e.g. in a class of 23 students, 7 students voted for life changes, what percentage voted daily hassles as a greater source of stress?

HANDOUT 107

P   H   S   G   T

Students who struggle with explaining comments in their own words should first explain what they have read to someone else who notes down the points made. They can then use this transcript to write their comments rather than looking at the extract provided.

References

DeLongis, A., Folkman, S. and Lazarus, R.S. (1988). The impact of daily stress on health and mood: Psychological and social resources as mediators. *Journal of Personality and Social Psychology, 54*, 486–95.

Lazarus, R. S. (1990). Theory based stress measurement and reply to commentators. *Psychological Inquiry, 1*, 3–51.

TOPIC: Sources of stress: Daily hassles

The six hats

After students have developed an understanding of daily hassles as a source of stress, this activity can be used to create the evaluation section of the following exam question: Describe and evaluate research on daily hassles as a source of stress. (16 marks)

Assign students to a hat. Students sit with other students of the same hat and work together to complete their section. Once finished, assign new hats to the groups. Students then complete the new section and share their ideas. Repeat this until students have completed the sections accessible to them according to their ability. I (RG) find that grouping students in two threes of different hats works better than one group of six, for sharing ideas.

Additional activities:

When evaluating research into daily hassles, a number of links can be made to research methods:

- The reliability of retrospective data (accuracy of memory).
- Problems of self-report (social desirability).
- Correlational research (no causal relationship established).
- Gender bias (assumption that the same things are seen as hassles for both genders).

Students could give a generic outline of each problem before creating a specific statement relating to daily hassles.

HANDOUT 108

P **H** S G T

Both the red and white hats should be accessible to most students, whereas the green and blue hats require higher-order thinking. Black and yellow hats target strengths and limitations so are useful practice for students who struggle to evaluate or often overlook evaluation in exam questions.

References

DeBono, E. (1985). *Six Thinking Hats*. Little, Brown and Company.

TOPIC: Sources of stress: Workplace stress

Apply your understanding

Handout 109 shows two candidates' responses to a possible exam question. Students are required to mark each answer and give a justification for the mark awarded.

Candidate 1: This response shows secure understanding of the job-strain model and has used appropriate terminology. Unfortunately, they cannot be awarded full marks as they have not fully applied this understanding to the question stem. Although references are made to Natasha, '... which Natasha has ... lack of predictability in her job ...' this is a weak attempt to engage with the stem.

Candidate 2: This response makes explicit links to Natasha's experience of work, but the answer lacks psychological knowledge; being able to identify why she experiences work overload and low control. However, they lose focus towards the end of the question and make assumptions that are not implied in the stem (her personality type). This will not lose the candidate marks but wastes time that could be spent answering other questions.

Additional activities:

Students create a research proposal to investigate workplace stress at Natasha's

HANDOUT 109

P H S **G** T

Allow students the opportunity to discuss their judgements of the exam responses to develop their understanding of what makes a successful answer.

company. Students could consider whether it would be better to compare different job roles within the company as a snap-shot or to conduct a longitudinal study. They should also consider how workplace stress and illness will be measured: self-report or physiological measures. Once created, students could critique each other's research proposals.

TOPIC: Sources of stress: Workplace stress

Improving the answer

Handout 110 shows an extract from an answer to the question: Describe and evaluate research into workplace stress. Include the effects of workload and control in your answer. (16 marks). Teacher comments are provided as a guide for improvement, covering common errors when writing extended answers: generic comments, studies lacking detail, repeating information. The handout could be photocopied onto the left-hand side of an A3 sheet to provide a blank space for students to add improvements or they may wish to re-write the whole extract.

Additional activities:

Students could conduct a mini research project into workplace stress experienced by students. A short questionnaire could be devised assessing work over- or underload and level of control experienced. Scores gained from the questionnaire could be correlated with number of illnesses experienced last term. Due to the potentially sensitive nature of this research students should be reminded of participants' right to withdraw and the importance of confidentiality.

References

Kivimäki, M., Leino-Arjas, P., Luukkonen, R., Riihimäki, H., Vahtera, J. and Kirjonen, J. (2002). Work stress and risk of cardiovascular mortality: Prospective cohort study of industrial employees. *BMJ, 325(7369)*, 857.

Lazarus, R.S. (1995). Vexing research problems inherent in cognitive-mediational theories of emotion, and some solutions. *Psychological Inquiry, 6*, 183–265.

Marmot, M., Bosma, H., Hemingway, H., Brunner, E. and Stansfield, S. (1997).

HANDOUT 110

| P | H | S | G | **T** |

The extract could be used to support students who struggle to produce 16-mark answers. Following on from this format, students could be set a series of questions to address to build their answer.

Contribution of job control and other risk factors to social variation in health disease incidence. *The Lancet, 350*, 235–9.

Schaubroeck, J., Jones, J.R. and Xie, J.L. (2001). Individual differences in utilizing control to cope with job demands: Effects on susceptibility to infectious disease. *Journal of Applied Psychology, 86(2)*, 262–78.

Shultz, K.S., Wang, M. and Olson, D.A. (2010). Role overload and underload in relation to occupational stress and health. *Stress and Health, 26*, 99–111.

TOPIC: Measuring stress: Self-report scales and physiological measures

Measuring stress is difficult!

Students use their memory (or class notes if needed) to recap the different stress measures used by researchers. This provides an opportunity to revise studies met earlier in the topic. They then match each evaluative comment to the relevant measurement. Clues are placed in evaluations deliberately to help students make matches. Students should be aware that some comments may relate to more than one measurement technique.

Additional activities:

Once completed, students can use **Handout 111** to revise for a formal assessment (timed, no notes) on the following question: Describe and evaluate ways that stress can be measured. In your answer make reference to self-report scales and physiological measurements. (16 marks)

HANDOUT 111

| P | **H** | S | G | T |

Once evaluations are assigned, students can order measurements from most to least useful (class needs to define what is meant by 'useful'), giving reasons for their decisions.

TOPIC: Measuring stress: Self-report scales and physiological measures

60-second summary

Once groups are formed, students are assigned one of four measurement tools:

- The Social Readjustment Rating Scale
- The Hassles and Uplifts Scale
- Skin conductance response
- Other physiological measures.

Students work together to create a 60-second summary in which they outline the measurement and give one or two evaluative comments regarding its use. Their summary needs to be scripted and practised before delivery to the class who will judge their performance. Groups are awarded points for accuracy (out of 10), clarity of written communication (out of 10) with one point deducted for each second over the 60 second limit. These summaries can be videoed and used later for revision.

Additional activities:

As an extension, each group could be asked to create two multiple choice questions. Questions from each group

NO HANDOUT

| P | H | S | **G** | T |

Assign roles to each member of the group based on ability. Speaker (clearly spoken, confident), script writer (good literacy skills), timer (ensures script is no longer than 60 seconds and offers feedback on where to slow down/speed up), editor (checks accuracy of the summary).

can be compiled to form a spot-check test after the speeches have been heard to check the class have understood the material presented.

TOPIC: Individual differences in stress: Personality

Reading race response sheet, Reading race Q and A

This activity takes the form of a competition between students in the class. Assign students to small mixed-ability groups and explain the rules of the race:

a) Students are given **Handout 112** and instructed to work as a team to ensure everyone has a detailed set of answers by the end of the task. The question master has a copy of **Handout 113** to read out questions one at a time to each group throughout the activity.

b) Question one is read out to the class. Once a group feels they have addressed the question in full, one member of the group approaches the question master with the group's handouts.

c) Once the question master has checked the accuracy and detail of the group's answer (by ticking or circling 'accurate' and 'detailed' in the response box) a new question, from **Handout 113**, is read to the group.

d) Each time a student approaches the question master for their group's answer to be checked and to receive the next question, they must form an orderly queue.

e) The first group to answer all questions is the winner - these students can then help the question master check responses from the remaining groups.

> Mixed-ability groups work well. Remind the class that everyone in the group needs to have an accurate and detailed answer recorded before the next question is given.

Additional activities:

Once completed, **Handout 112** can be used to address the following question: With reference to research evidence, discuss links between personality and stress. (8 marks) AO1 - 3 marks, AO3 - 5 marks. Students should answer the 8-mark question then use the mark scheme to self-assess their answer.

Level	Marks	Description.
4	7–8	Accurate and generally well detailed knowledge of links between stress and personality. Discussion is effective. The answer is clear, coherent and focused. Specialist terminology is used effectively. Minor detail and/or expansion of argument sometimes lacking.
3	5–6	Knowledge of links between stress and personality is evident. There are occasional inaccuracies. There is some effective discussion. The answer is mostly clear and organised. Specialist terminology mostly used effectively.
2	3–4	Knowledge of links between stress and personality is present. Focus is mainly on description. Any discussion is of limited effectiveness. The answer lacks clarity, accuracy and organisation in places. Specialist terminology used inappropriately on occasions.
1	1–2	Knowledge of links between stress and personality is limited. Discussion is limited, poorly focused or absent. The answer as a whole lacks clarity, has many inaccuracies and is poorly organised. Specialist terminology either absent or inappropriately used.
	0	No relevant content.

References

Friedman, M. & Rosenman, R.H. (1959). Association of specific over behaviour pattern with blood and cardiovascular findings. *Journal of the American Medical Association, 169*, 1286–96.

Giraldi, T., Rodani, M., Cartei, G. and Grassi, L. (1997). Psychosocial factors and breast cancer: a 6-year Italian follow-up study. *Psychotherapy and Psychosomatics, 66*, 229–36.

Morris, T., Greer, S., Pettingale, K.W. and Watson, M. (1981). Patterns of expression of anger and their psychological correlates in women with breast cancer. *Journal of Psychosomatic Research, 25(2)*, 111–17.

Myrtek, M. (2001). Meta-analysis of prospective studies on coronary heart disease, type A personality, and hostility. *International Journal of Cardiology, 79*, 245–51.

Ragland, D.R. & Brand, R.J. (1988). Type A behaviour and mortality from coronary heart disease. *New England Journal of Medicine, 318* (2), 65–9.

TOPIC: Individual differences in stress: Personality

Critical questioning

After reading the central passage, students work in mixed-ability pairs to fill in the surrounding boxes. Each box requires a different form of thinking. Some boxes are simple recall of knowledge, for example, 'Identify the facts: what happened in the study?' Other boxes demand a higher-order of thinking; 'How can hardiness reduce the likelihood of stress-related illness?' An alternative to mixed pairs would be to ask students to work individually for 10 minutes on boxes of their own choice then join with another student to work on one box together for 10 minutes. Following this, students form a new pair and share ideas until all boxes are completed.

Additional activities:

As a revision activity, students could identify one famous person they feel embodies the hardy personality and explain to the class why they feel the person shows control, commitment and challenge. This can be done for all personality types covered in this topic to create a personality gallery

HANDOUT 114

| P | **H** | S | **G** | T |

Students can support each other working in mixed-ability pairs, tackling specific questions then teaching each other. Some questions are more challenging than others.

displaying relevant research alongside the celebrity descriptions.

References

Kobasa, S.C. (1979). Stressful life events, personality, and health: An inquiry into hardiness. *Journal of Personality and Social Psychology, 37*, 1–11.

TOPIC: Managing and coping with stress: Drug therapies

Describing drug therapies

Handout 115 is divided into two activities describing the mode of action of BZs and BBs. First, students order the statements to produce a coherent account of the role of BZs in reducing the anxiety felt as a result of stress. Students may then wish to write their own 100-word summary using the ordered sentences for guidance.

Through answering questions in the second activity, students are elaborating the statements shown to produce an explanation of how beta blockers help people cope with stress.

Additional activities:

Crystal ball: working in pairs or small groups, students develop their own ideas regarding the strengths and limitations of drug therapies. In my (RG) experience students are often able to apply their general knowledge of drug therapy to this topic suggesting that prolonged use could lead to addiction (in the case of BBs, psychological but

HANDOUT 115

| P | H | S | G | **T** |

When sorting statements relating to BZs students may find it helpful to cut out each strip so they can physically sort sentences into a coherent summary.

not physical addiction) and questioning whether drugs treat symptoms rather than solve the problem. Once ideas have been shared, students use their textbook (*Complete Companion*, page 208) to identify and develop their predictions.

TOPIC: Managing and coping with stress: Drug therapies

Discussing drug therapies

Both activities on **Handout 116** require students to apply the strengths and/or limitations of drug therapies. Students could use the mark schemes provided to peer or self-assess the responses produced.

Additional activities:

Once **Handout 116** has been completed, students could be asked whether other stress management techniques may have been more suited to Tanya and Jay. A research task could be set for homework with students assigned either SIT or biofeedback to investigate. In the following lesson, after sharing their research with the class, students consider whether these methods may be more beneficial than drugs in treating Tanya and Jay.

HANDOUT 116

| P | H | **S** | G | T |

This activity could be completed from memory to check retention of knowledge. Students could then revisit their textbook (*Complete Companion*, page 209) to add any missed points in a different coloured ink to illustrate what aspects need further revision.

TOPIC: Managing and coping with stress: Stress Inoculation therapy

SIT revision record

Handout 117 provides a structured revision sheet for students who struggle to make detailed and/or organised revision notes. Using their textbook (*Complete Companion*, page 210) or class notes, students outline and evaluate SIT as a way to manage and cope with stress.

Students then use this record to revise for a formal assessment of the following exam question: Describe and evaluate the use of stress inoculation therapy in managing and coping with stress. (16 marks)

Additional activities:

More-able students can be challenged to complete a SWOT analysis on the use of SIT by the NHS.

Strengths – benefits SIT offers over other treatments, e.g. non-invasive, no side effects. Protection against future stress.

Weaknesses – time consuming, success dependent on client motivation.

Opportunities – creation of new jobs/training courses, long term cost saving.

Threats – short-term cost implications.

HANDOUT 117

P H S G T

On the handout key words are provided for each SIT phrase to highlight important aspects to support students' writing. Evaluative sentence starters are also added to help students structure their AO3 commentary.

TOPIC: Managing and coping with stress: Biofeedback

Biofeedback: fill in the blanks

By filling in the blanks, students produce a summary of the key components of biofeedback to answer the question: Explain how a therapist might use biofeedback to treat a person with stress. (6 marks)

A quick YouTube search produces a number of biofeedback videos that students may find useful to watch before attempting the activity. An extension task is provided at the bottom of **Handout 118**. Students should aim to provide a 50-word answer to the question: Explain **one** criticism of using biofeedback as a method of managing and coping with stress.

Additional activities:

Set students the task of finding a study to support each of the following claims:

- As monkeys can use biofeedback to raise and lower their body temperature the process must work on an unconscious level.
- Little evidence is provided for the success of biofeedback resulting from unconscious operant conditioning.
- Evidence suggests biofeedback is superior to relaxation alone.
- Biofeedback is non-invasive unlike drug therapies.
- Biofeedback does not provide immediate relief from stress.

HANDOUT 118

P H S G T

For more-able students the task can be made more difficult by removing the key words and instead providing the first letter at the start of each blank space (or you could even give no assistance at all).

TOPIC: Gender differences in coping with stress

Reading record: gender differences

Using their textbook (*Complete Companion*, page 214) or class notes, students summarise in their own words the different ways of coping with stress and reasons for these differences. Once completed, students should also consider how the stressor experienced may influence the method of coping seen.

After creating their reading record, students use the information to answer the exam question at the bottom of **Handout 119**.

Additional activities:

Once students have a secure understanding of the different physiological and psychological approaches to coping with stress, they could conduct a qualitative analysis of a reality TV show to determine whether gender differences can be seen in response to stressors. A suitable example may be the ITV show 'I'm a celebrity get me out of here' where competitors face a series of stressful trials as well as coping day to day in their environment.

HANDOUT 119

P H S G T

When completing this task, less-able students may benefit from a glossary of key terms to help them access the information, e.g. a definition of parental investment, adaptive response.

TOPIC: Gender differences in coping with stress

Creating commentaries

When evaluating gender differences in coping with stress it is not enough just to state evidence, students needs to use the research to address exam questions. They should be encouraged to analyse research, consider implications of findings and look at wider psychological issues. The boxes on the left-hand side of **Handout 120** contain evaluative points to be considered. All students are to attempt the two bold-edged boxes. Once these are complete they are free to stretch their thinking or challenge themselves by applying their knowledge to wider issues.

Additional activities:

Before completing **Handout 120**, display a continuum on the class whiteboard. Students decide where their opinion lies between the end points of, 'no gender differences' to 'men use problem-focused coping, females use emotion-focused coping'. Once they

HANDOUT 120

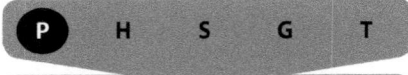

P   H   S   G   T

Students answer either bold, dashed or dotted boxes depending on their current level of understanding.

have recorded their ideas on a Post-it®, this is stuck at a suitable point along the continuum. Once the handout is completed, students re-visit their note and decide to either leave it in its original location or change its position along the scale.

TOPIC: The role of social support in coping with stress

Social support scenarios

For each scenario on **Handout 121**, students identify and define the type of social support accessed. Brenda is accessing instrumental support, Raj is being offered esteem support from his friends and Liam receives emotional support from his partner.

This activity provides a useful recap enabling students to address the exam question: What is meant by instrumental/emotional/esteem support? (2 marks)

The stretch activity at the bottom of **Handout 121** asks students to consider gender differences. For example, while women have been shown to be more likely to use social support when the type of support accessed is considered, men tend to use instrumental support with women using more emotional support.

Mark scheme:

1 mark awarded for a vague or muddled definition.
2 marks awarded for a clear and coherent definition.

HANDOUT 121

P   H   S   G   T

Students complete the stretch question once the kind of social support has been identified and defined for each scenario.

Additional activities:

As a homework activity, students could keep a log of the kinds of social support they have received over a two-day period. Logs could be analysed in class to identify whether a gender difference exists or whether different people (friends, family, teachers) are more likely to provide different kinds of support.

TOPIC: The role of social support in coping with stress

Speedy evaluations

Once students have a secure understanding of relevant research and issues regarding the role of social support, the class is ready to write speedy evaluations. This is a good activity to motivate a class who are reluctant to write or are struggling to write within a time limit.

Each student has five minutes to begin evaluating research into the role of social support in coping with stress (10 marks). Once this time limit expires, students pass their paper to someone else, making sure their name is written at the top to be returned to them later. They then have five minutes to read what has just been passed to them and plan what they will add. Students now have an additional five minutes to add to the evaluation in front of them. This continues until four rotations have taken place. As rotations progress, you may need to give students longer to read the previous evaluations before allocating five minutes for the student to add another evaluation. The evaluation is then returned to its original owner who crosses out repeated points and highlights key terms, research evidence, analysis of findings, issues and debates in different colours. They then mark the evaluation before using it as a model to write their own 10-mark answer.

Additional activities:

Working in groups, students are asked to create a summary of the stress unit.

NO HANDOUT

P   H   S   G   T

Students may benefit from a list of sentence starters and/or access to commentary in their textbook or class notes.

No notes are allowed and students have 10 minutes to record as much as they can remember. You may wish to provide headings from the aspects of stress named in the specification. Once the 10 minutes have ended, students rotate their summaries (the amount of rotations will depend upon how many groups you have). With each rotation, students identify points they missed in their summary. After rotations, students revisit their summary and add on any missed information.

TOPIC: Neural and hormonal influences

Aggression quintuplets

HANDOUT 122

P   H   S   G   T

Handout 122 would be a good activity to use once you have gone through the various neural and hormonal influences on aggression. Alternatively, you could give the students the information (*Complete Companion*, page 228) and ask the students to complete the activity by reading that information.

The students must sort the fifteen numbered statements into three groups using the handout (i.e. group A, B and C). Then, once they have done this, they should name the three groups. The group names should be 'The limbic system', 'Serotonin' and 'Testosterone'.

Once the students have grouped the statements, they should then write a brief summary of neural/hormonal influence on aggression by using the statements as part of the summary.

Answers

Group name: The limbic system

Numbers: 3, 5, 7, 9, 14

Group name: Serotonin

Numbers: 1, 2, 6, 12, 13

Group name: Testosterone

Numbers: 4, 8, 10, 11, 15

For less-able students it would be advisable to give them the group names before starting the activity as they may need this support to sort the statements into groups.

TOPIC: Genetic factors in aggression

Genetic factors – key details

HANDOUT 123

P   H   S   G   T

I (MG) am always looking for different ways to help students understand what is meant by 'detail' in AO1.

Handout 123 is entitled 'key details' and pulls out many of the numbers/ statistics/key terms that would be good to include in an answer outlining the genetic factors in aggression. All the students need to do is to write what that key detail refers to in the study of aggression. For example:

- MZ twins genes shared: 100%

- DZ twins genes shared: Around 50%

- Aggression variance: 50%

This could be used as a way to get students to read and assimilate the information (*Complete Companion*, page 230) or as a consolidating activity.

A key point to explain to the students is that they need to revise, retain and use as much of the information and statistics included on the sheet as possible.

A list of suggested answers could be given to less-able students to select from if you feel they will need extra support.

A follow-up activity could be to give students this completed sheet as scaffolding to write a 6-mark outline on this topic.

TOPIC: Genetic factors in aggression

Understanding twin studies

HANDOUT 77

P   H   S   G   T

See page 52

Although **Handout 77** is in the schizophrenia section, it can be easily adapted or used as it is to support students' understanding in this topic as well. See page 52 for the notes on this handout.

TOPIC: Genetic factors in aggression

Writing about twin studies

HANDOUTS 78 and 79

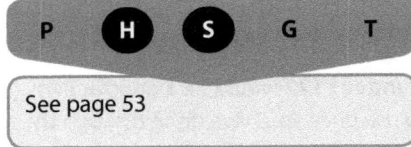

See page 53

The previous activity can be followed by a slightly adapted version of **Handouts 78** and **79**. All that really needs changing is to replace Joseph's (2004) study with something like Coccaro et al.'s (1997) study or similar. See page 53 for the notes on this handout.

References

Coccaro, E.F., Berman, M.E. and Kavoussi, R.J. (1997). Assessment of life history of aggression: development and psychometric characteristics. *Psychiatry Research, 73(3)*, 147–57.

TOPIC: Genetic factors in aggression

Debating the warrior gene

NO HANDOUT

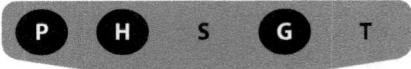

Arranging 'debates' can certainly be tricky. I (MG) once planned a lesson with a 30-minute debate in mind. It lasted about 5 minutes, followed by a 25-minute black hole in my lesson.

The mistake I made was not providing sufficient structure and guidance for the students. There are many different ways you could do this - there is no one-size-fits-all approach, since every debate is different in its requirements and characteristics. However, I'll describe some of the ways my colleagues have conducted debates with some success, and hopefully you will be able to adapt some of those ideas.

The idea of a 'warrior gene' for aggression provides plenty of scope for debate. An internet search for 'warrior gene' (*combine with 'in court' as well*) provides a treasure trove of fascinating reads. It is being used in court to defend people and to lower their sentences ('it was the gene that did it') and is also being used as evidence to convict people ('it must have been that person, they have the warrior gene!').

So the debate could centre around whether research about the warrior gene should be admissible in court.

Arranging a debate

Students could be assigned to debate teams, and given a position to defend. For example, 'Yes, research about the warrior gene should be admissible in court.'

Students should then be given time to prepare for the debate, perfect their arguments and prepare for rebuttals. It is often students' confidence that inhibits their participation in debates, so this period of reflection is quite important.

It might also be useful to formalise the debate by having a specific order to adhere to. For example, the debate should begin with one team presenting their arguments to support their position. The opposing team is them given the opportunity to rebut those arguments. Then, depending on the time available, the original team could answer those criticisms. There may also be opportunity to open the debate to the floor, with the teacher acting as facilitator.

House of Commons

An interesting variation to this would be contextualising the debate within

The method of differentiation will depend largely on how the debate is managed. Use of collaborative learning structures (see page 5) could be useful here. Alternatively, students could be assigned roles that reflect their ability.

The House of Commons, with one group presenting a bill with some relevance to the ethics debate, and the other team opposing the bill (for example, a bill which seeks to tighten the ethical rules within which psychologists have to operate). Students must also address each other in accordance with the proper parliamentary rule: "My Right Honourable Friend…"!

More informal

A more informal way to conduct a debate is to display a dimension line on the board and ask students to place a Post-it® with their initials on somewhere on the dimension line that reflects their view point.

The teacher can then ask for several students to justify why they have placed their note in that position on the line.

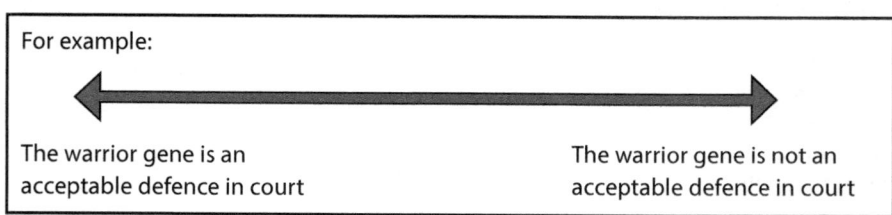

For example:

The warrior gene is an acceptable defence in court ← → The warrior gene is not an acceptable defence in court

TOPIC: The ethological explanation of aggression

Ethological spot the mistakes

Once you have taught your students the ethological explanation of aggression, you could test your students' knowledge and understanding by asking them to spot the deliberate mistakes on **Handout 124**. This can be a good activity to consolidate key terms or key principles.

The correct answers are shown in the version below, with words in bold replacing wrong ones on the handout.

The ethological explanation states that all members of the same species, (i.e. conspecifics) have a repertoire of stereotyped behaviours which occur in specific conditions and which **do not** require learning, i.e. are innate. Ethologist Niko Tinbergen called these innate behaviours **fixed** action patterns (FAPs). FAPs are produced by a neural mechanism known as an innate releasing mechanism (IRM) and are triggered by a very specific stimulus known as a sign stimulus. The IRM receives its input from sensory recognition circuits that are stimulated by the presence of the sign stimulus. The IRM then communicates with motor control circuits to **activate** the FAP associated with that sign stimulus.

Tinbergen's research with sticklebacks showed that a male stickleback fish will produce a fixed sequence of **aggressive** actions when another male enters its territory. The sign stimulus in this case is not the presence of the other male, but the sight of its distinctive red underbelly that acts as the sign stimulus. If this is covered up, the intruder is not attacked (Tinbergen, 1951).

The 'hydraulic model'

Each FAP has a reservoir of 'action-specific-energy'(ASE) that builds up over time. The appropriate sign stimulus causes the IRM to **release** this energy and the animal then performs the FAP. After performing the FAP, the reservoir of ASE is empty and the behaviour cannot be repeated until the ASE has built up again. This is sometimes called the **hydraulic** model of instinctive behaviour (Lorenz, 1950). Lorenz's model provides a way of visualising how these various hypothetical systems might work together to organise an animal's response to its internal and external environment. In the model, **ASE** is represented by fluid in a reservoir that, as it builds up, places pressure on a spring (the IRM), which is also being

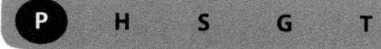

HANDOUT 124

P | H | S | G | T

> It might be necessary, for your less-able students, to give them more instruction as to where the mistakes might be. You could do this by highlighting the sentences where the mistakes are located.

pulled by weights (the sign stimulus). Together these lead to the release of the **FAP** when ASE is high enough and the appropriate sign stimulus is present. However, the FAP may also be produced in the absence of the sign stimulus if the level of ASE is sufficiently high, i.e. a behaviour can occur spontaneously.

References

Lorenz, K. (1950). The comparative method in studying innate behavior patterns. *Symposia of the Society for Experimental Biology, 4*, 221–68.

Tinbergen, N. (1951). The Study of Instinct. New York: Oxford University Press.

TOPIC: The ethological explanation of aggression

Ethological AO3: Brief summaries

This is a fantastic idea stolen (with permission!) from Jo Gotts at www.psychexchange.co.uk (now part of www.resourcd.com).

Essentially the activity involves students summarising information and as such, choosing the most important bits to retain in the synopsis. The information they need to summarise is on page 232 of the *Complete Companion*. Each 'brief' will be a summary of an evaluation point on the ethological explanation of aggression. One rule that should be maintained is that the students write full sentences. The idea here is that students have to read an evaluation,

process it, understand it and then write it back down in summarised form; this stops students simply copying text into their notes without actually thinking about what they are writing or understanding it.

Handout 125 therefore provides four briefs in which to write 'brief summaries' (do you see what Jo did?!) of evaluations of ethological explanations of aggression.

Beneath each 'brief' are some key words/studies which students should aim to include in their summary. You could change/adapt this sheet to suit your needs.

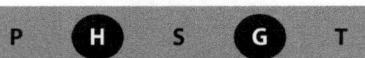

HANDOUT 125

P | H | S | G | T

> You could set up this activity so that more-able students are paired with less-able ones. The more-able student could have access to the full evaluations on page 233 of the *Complete Companion*. It is their job to articulate that evaluation and explain it to the less-able student. Then, without help from the more-able student, the less-able student must write their 'brief summary'.

TOPIC: Evolutionary explanations of human aggression

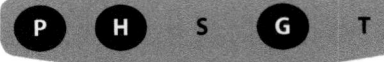

Evolutionary monsters

This is a really effective student activity designed to help them understand concepts such as the EEA (environment of evolutionary adaptation), genome lag, natural selection etc. Although the evolutionary approach seems quite straightforward, many students do struggle to get their heads around the different terms and how they relate to modern-day behaviour. I (MG) often find that students are disbelieving of evolutionary explanations because they do not make sense in a modern context.

As such, I think it is vital that you spend time teaching them about **genome lag**: the idea that the environments that species (including us) have adapted to have since changed, and continue to change. Evolution is a relatively slow process, environments can change overnight. This can result in behaviours that seemingly do not look adaptive in a modern-day context.

You can find the full instructions for the activity on page 27 of this book.

This activity lends itself to group activity and collaborative learning structures (see page 5) which ensure equal participation, stretch of the more-able and support for the less-able students.

The more-able student could also be set the task of explaining the features by sexual selection as well as natural selection.

TOPIC: Evolutionary explanations of human aggression

Evolution, aggression & now . . .

This activity follows on very nicely from 'evolutionary monsters' (see previous activity) and builds on students' understanding of the 'EEA', adaptation and genome lag. Hopefully **Handout 126** will help the students to understand why aggressive behaviours may have evolved in a different context and why they continue today despite the fact that the behaviours may be maladaptive in some circumstances.

For each of the three evolutionary explanations of human aggression included on page 234 of the *Complete Companion*, students are asked to consider three things:

- What the EEA was like in relation to the explanation.
- Why aggression evolved in that context; why aggression was adaptive.
- How our current environment could be seen as different to the EEA

and whether aggression is still an adaptive response.

For example (sexual jealousy):

- EEA: Paternal uncertainty . . . it was not possible for a male to know whether their partner is bearing their child or somebody else's offspring.

- Aggression as adaptive: It is adaptive to threaten violence or be violent towards female partners so that males can be more certain that a pregnant partner is carrying their offspring. This prevents wasting resources on another male's offspring.

- Current environment: Although it is still possible for men to be at risk of cuckoldry (having an unfaithful partner), technological advances mean that paternal uncertainty can be resolved by DNA tests. This means that aggression towards women is no longer necessary or adaptive (or indeed morally acceptable!).

The less-able students could be provided with the answers in a jumbled up order and their task is to identify which answers are required for each box.

Alternatively, collaborative learning structures (see page 5) could be utilised.

Personally though, for this activity, I (MG) would ask all students to attempt the handout to the best of their ability but I would be on hand to support those struggling with some of the boxes or the evolutionary concepts in general.

TOPIC: The frustration-aggression hypothesis

HANDOUTS 127 and 128

Feedforward marking

| P | H | S | G | **T** |

The concept of A B C and feedforward marking is outlined on page 2. I've (MG) found it to be a really effective marking and feedback technique that genuinely has an impact on student progress.

As a result, I've now started to use the concept to design handouts.

Handout 127 shows a fictitious student answer to the following exam question: Evaluate the frustration-aggression hypothesis. (10 marks)

In addition, in the grey boxes are some fictitious teacher comments and A B C . . . tasks. The students are therefore required on **Handout 128** to complete those tasks in order to improve the answer. It is always worth mentioning to the students during/after this task how small additions/sentences can have a huge impact on the quality of a piece of work.

Possible task improvements:

A: An individual *may* respond to frustration with aggression if it has been effective for them before (direct reinforcement) or they have observed it being effective for others (vicarious reinforcement). This alternative view suggests that individuals learn to produce aggressive behaviours if they are successful and that therefore aggression is not always an inevitable consequence of frustration.

B: Research has not always supported the central ideas proposed by the frustration-aggression hypothesis.

C: A revised frustration-aggression hypothesis is that aversive stimuli (such as high temperature, frustration) tend to make people angry which in turn increase the likelihood of aggression.

D: For example, following the First World War, many Germans blamed Jews for the loss of the war and the country's economic problems. This may have led to the German people condoning the violence committed against the Jewish people during this period.

E: One real-world application for this theory is the explanation of fan violence in sport.

F: These findings suggest that supporters become more aggressive when expectations of good performance are frustrated, thus supporting the frustration-aggression hypothesis.

References

Bandura, A. (1973). *Aggression: A Social Learning Analysis*. Englewood Cliffs, NJ: Prentice-Hall.

Bushman, B.J. (2002). Does venting anger feed or extinguish the flame? Catharsis, rumination, distraction, anger, and aggressive responding. *Personality and Social Psychology Bulletin, 28(6),* 724–731.

Priks, M. (2010). Does frustration lead to violence? Evidence from the Swedish hooligan scene. *Kyklos, 63(3),* 450–60.

Reifman, A., Larrick, R. and Fein, S. (1991). Temper and temperature on the diamond: The heat–aggression relationship in Major League Baseball. *Personality and Social Psychology Bulletin, 17,* 580–5.

Staub, E. (1996). Cultural-societal roots of violence: The examples of genocidal violence and of contemporary youth violence in the United States. *American Psychologist, 51(2),* 117.

> It is inevitable that some students will find the improvements harder to make than others – some students will need individual support during the activity in order to prompt the correct responses.
>
> You could ask the students to help each other in pairs/threes using a collaborative learning structure (see page 5) as long as it is set up in a way where all students are responsible and have to engage in the task.

TOPIC: Social learning theory

Making it relevant

There are a few topics in psychology that pop up quite a lot that students appear to remember well; social learning theory is one of them and they would have met this theory once or twice in Year 1.

The danger with this is that students remember the theory and its key concepts well but fail to apply them to the topic at hand – in this case aggression. I've (MG) seen my own students make this mistake myself and I have seen students across the country make this mistake in their examination papers.

Handout 129 is based on these experiences and was designed to show my own students how a very detailed and accurate description of social learning theory could actually only attract 2–3 marks if it lacks focus.

The student activity on **Handout 129** is to improve the description with brief examples, words and sentences to ensure that the description is focused on aggression and achieves closer to a 'level 4' mark band.

For example:

1. aggressive
2. aggressive
3. For example, observing an adult hitting a vending machine in frustration.
4. aggressive
5. aggressive
6. aggressive
7. For example, they may observe an older child acting aggressively towards another child in order to obtain their chocolate/sweets. If they are seen to be successful, this aggressive behaviour may be vicariously reinforced.
8. aggressive
9. such as when and how to be aggressive
10. A child who has a successful history of bullying other children may come to place a lot of value in aggressive behaviours.
11. aggressive
12. aggressive
13. (e.g. they weren't very good at being aggressive)

HANDOUT 129

The suggestions for improvements below could be given to less-able students. Although they should attempt the handout on their own first, they could be given the suggestions to select from as options for the parts they are finding difficult.

Once students have completed this activity, the powerful point to make is that with a few small tweaks, you could argue that this description has moved from a level 1/2 answer to a level 4 answer. *Focus and relevance in an answer is very important.* It's worth noting that the examples and further explanations are what truly help this answer to be 'more focused' from a marking point of view. However, adding the 'aggressive' wording also helps on a superficial level and serves to remind the reader (and writer!) what the answer is supposed to be about!'

References

Bandura, A. (1986) *Social Foundations of Thought and Action: A Social Cognitive Theory.* Englewood Cliffs, NJ: Prentice-Hall.

Bandura, A. and Walters, R.H. (1963). Social learning and personality development.

TOPIC: Social learning theory

Links – turning study evaluation into theory evaluation

Imagine that the following essay question comes up on the PSYA3 exam:

Outline and evaluate the social learning theory explanation for aggression. (16 marks)

Students would need to find 6 AO1 marks and 10 AO3 marks.

The 6 AO1 marks could include key concepts such as observation, imitation, mediational processes, vicarious reinforcement and identification. Part of the AO3 evaluation could include using the bobo dolls studies in support of social learning theory.

In order to gain more AO3 marks, it may be useful to include methodological evaluation of the evidence used to support social learning theory; this is a possible form of AO3 but students must be mindful to ensure that the focus

remains on the evaluation of social learning theory itself.

From past experience with my (MG) students, this skill is harder than it sounds. On the face of it, all students have to do is evaluate studies they have used to support or undermine the explanations. For example, they could evaluate Bandura's Bobo doll studies which they probably used to support Social Learning Theory.

However, I find that students forget that they are actually supposed to be evaluating Social Learning Theory, and instead spend most of their time 'vomiting' out their evaluations of the study (that is a phrase I use in the classroom . . .). As such, their essay loses focus and they forget to evaluate the theories with the studies.

HANDOUT 130

This handout provides scaffolding and structure for students' successful use of methodological evaluations in a theory essay.

Some students are likely to need one-to-one support so you need to make sure that you are on hand to help the students' understanding and to help them articulate their ideas in writing.

This 'links' activity aims to try and get students thinking about how they can turn their study evaluations into evaluations of the theory – rather than just blindly evaluating the study without any reference to the essay demands.

It includes a four-step process for doing this successfully as well as one completed example.

TOPIC: Social learning theory

Flipped learning: Bobo doll study

Flipped learning is an idea already explained on page 37.

It is a good idea to help save classroom time by not having to watch endless videos in lesson time. Choose the right internet search terms and a wealth of videos are available on Bandura's Bobo dolls studies.

Questions can be set for the students to answer, for example:

- Why do these studies support Social Learning Theory?
- How is aggression operationalised?
- What are the threats to internal validity in this study?
- What are the threats to external validity in this study?

NO HANDOUT

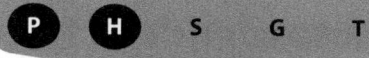

You could set different questions for different students – based on their ability level. Less-able students could be asked to recall details of the study and simple facts such as IV/DV etc. More-able students could be allocated higher-order questions such as why the study supports Social Learning Theory.

TOPIC: De-individuation

Photo rounds

This activity is a good way to introduce the concept of de-individuation. I (MG) would ask students to complete this activity before introducing the term and its meaning.

Show students a number of images/ photos which could be said to relate to the de-individuation explanation of human aggression (see examples on the right).

Ask the students to explain how each image could increase the likelihood of aggression.

For example:

A – Photo of James Bond or similar. Anonymity. 007 has no identifiable name.

B – Photo of a large crowd. Group pressure. Anonymity. Conformity.

C – Photo of someone or group of people wearing 'hoodies'. Obscures face. Anonymity.

D – Photo of police in full riot gear. Uniform gives legitimacy. Uniform makes people feel more part of a unit rather than themselves.

NO HANDOUT

P **H** S **G** T

This activity lends itself to group activity and collaborative learning structures (see page 5) which ensure equal participation, stretch of the more-able and support for the less-able students.

An extension activity for the higher-ability students could be to ask them to explain how they think the images are linked.

E – Photo of the night time. Night time makes antisocial behaviour easier to 'get away with'.

TOPIC: De-individuation

Linking crowds to aggression

There is a lot more to de-individuation than 'crowds lead to aggression', but sometimes this can be the superficial understanding that students take away from the topic.

Handout 132 is an attempt to illustrate the chain of psychology that links crowds to more aggressive behaviour. This activity could be completed with notes as a way to make students'

reading of the information more active. Alternatively, the handout could be used as a memory consolidation activity.

Answers:

1. state of de-individuation
2. anonymity
3. altered consciousness (interchangeable with 4)
4. uniform (interchangeable with 3)

HANDOUT 132

P H S G T

Less-able students could be provided with a list of possible answers for them to arrange correctly into the boxes.

5. unaccountable
6. own individuality
7. fear of evaluation
8. social norms.

TOPIC: Institutional aggression in prisons

Photo rounds

Rolling shows are a great idea to start lessons. Details on how to create a rolling show using PowerPoint are described on page 8.

There are many different examples and images of institutional aggression in prisons that you could include on the rolling show that would help orientate the students towards the content of the lesson and hopefully capture their interest.

Here are some examples you could search the internet for, but do be careful which images you select to show your students:

- Private Andrei Sychev's brutal beating by older soldiers at the Chelyabinsk Military School.
- Zimbardo's Prison Experiment.
- Abuse of Iraqi prisoners at Abu Ghraib.
- The Attica prison riot.

NO HANDOUT

P	H	S	G	T

This activity is not differentiated but could be followed by a discussion question using a collaborative learning structure (see page 5). For example, 'What factors increase the amount of aggression recorded in institutions such as prisons?'

TOPIC: Institutional aggression in prisons

Burgers

The 'burger' evaluation technique specifically aims to help students to use studies when evaluating theories/ explanations – an area where many students appear to lack confidence.

The principles of this technique are outlined earlier on page 7.

Handout 133 provides students with instructions on how to use this technique in order to evaluate explanations of institutional aggression in prisons.

Deconstruct this technique with your students, and then ask them to evaluate the importation and deprivation models using the studies provided at the bottom of the page.

References

DeLisi, M., Berg, M.T. and Hochstetler, A. (2004). Gang members, career criminals and prison violence: Further specification of the importation model of inmate behavior. *Criminal Justice Studies, 17(4)*, 369–83.

Harer, M.D. and Steffensmeier, D.J. (1996). Race and prison violence. *Criminology, 34(3)*, 323–55.

McCorkle, R.C., Miethe, T.D. and Drass, K.A. (1995). The roots of prison violence: A test of the deprivation, management, and 'not-so-total' institution models. *Crime and Delinquency, 41(3)*, 317–31.

Mears, D.P., Stewart, E.A., Siennick, S.E. and Simons, R.L. (2013). The code of the street and inmate violence: Investigating

HANDOUT 133

P	H	S	G	T

Handout 133 provides scaffolding for students' paragraphs which should support all students, particularly the less able. If students are finding this too hard, you could also instruct them on which model each study supports/undermines.

You can also make it an expectation that more-able students should attempt to provide extra commentary and/or counterarguments at the bottom of their 'burgers'.

the salience of imported belief systems. *Criminology, 51(3)*, 695–728.

Poole, E.D. and Regoli, R.M. (1983). Professionalism, role conflict, work alienation, and anomia: A look at prison management. *The Social Science Journal, 20(1)*, 63–70.

TOPIC: Media influences on aggression

Elaboration ladders

The idea behind, and the technique for, using elaboration ladders is outlined on page 7. In my (MG) experience, using the concept of 'ladders' has been one of the most successful visual 'gimmicks' in helping my students to understand the concept of evaluating in depth.

'Ladders' are a way to encourage students to write about their evaluative points in more depth and to avoid basic and superficial comments such as, "The problem with lab studies of the media's influence on aggression is that they are not like real life and so lack ecological validity". Remember that the mark schemes require students to be good at both description (AO1) and evaluation (AO3), and therefore, students will score

lower in the essay mark bands if their evaluation skills are not up to scratch (see page 7). The aim is to get students to levels 3 and 4.

Students start with an introductory evaluation comment at the bottom of the ladder and then gradually elaborate this comment further until they reach the top! The right-hand box prompts students to think of ways they could elaborate their evaluations (see page 7 for examples).

Handout 134 provides the framework and some starting points and hints for elaboration. Up the first ladder, the second rung could be: "This is because lab and field experiments manipulate an independent variable in order to

HANDOUT 134

P	H	S	G	T

Evaluating research in depth is undoubtedly a higher-order thinking skill that will stretch and challenge all learners. The 'ladder' handouts provide students with a scaffolded handout to help them increase the depth of their evaluative points.

observe the effect on a dependent variable." Third rung: "So for example, researchers can manipulate whether children play a violent or non-violent video game and then immediately measure their aggression afterwards." Final rung: "This is useful as it allows researchers to determine causal relationships between the media and aggressive behaviours."

TOPIC: Media influences on aggression

Columbine massacre – can we use this as evidence?

In 1999 Eric Harris and Dylan Kelbold walked into Columbine High School in Colorado where they were students and embarked on a massacre.

They killed 12 of their fellow students, 1 teacher, and injured another 21 before both committing suicide.

It was said that they were both obsessed by a violent video game called 'Doom'. Many hypothesised that their violence was influenced and encouraged by such games and the victims' families even tried to sue the makers of the game.

It is quite understandable that students will make references to such examples when considering the effects of violent video games on aggression – especially now that such games are more realistic than they were at the time of the Columbine massacre. The students are also likely to make comments such as, 'I play loads of video games and I don't consider myself to be violent or aggressive'.

However, we should probably be encouraging our students to develop a more scientific stance on this topic, rather than an anecdotal one.

Pose your students the following question:

Why should we never rely on one-off events as evidence for a link between violent video games and real-life violence?

NO HANDOUT

P **H** S **G** T

This activity lends itself to group activity and collaborative learning structures (see page 5) which ensure equal participation, stretch of the more-able and support for the less-able students.

Use a collaborative learning structure such as Random Numbers or Group Statements (see page 5) to ensure accountability and differentiation.

You can also lead this discussion in a way that considers the principles of science, e.g. replication, operationalisation, falsifiability, isolation of variables etc. All principles that anecdotal case studies are rarely able to uphold.

TOPIC: Media influences on aggression

Design your own experiment

The study of the media's effects on aggression is an ideal opportunity to get students to attempt designing their own studies.

Students could use **Handout 135** to structure their plans.

Try to get the students to pay special attention to the control of extraneous variables; for example, how long the participants watch a film clip for, standardised instructions etc.

HANDOUT 135

P H S G **T**

Some students will need your help with operationalising variables and controlling extraneous variables; ensure you are on hand to identify struggling students to help them consider their experiment planning.

TOPIC: Explanations of media influences

Application skills: The two-sentence technique

Application (AO2) skills need to be developed. It is the element of the examination where revision of content can only help to an extent . . . the ability to use that content in a new scenario is a skill that requires practice.

For the past few years, I (MG) have taught students the two-sentence technique (see page 6). This technique is outlined on **Handout 135** and students can read through a worked example which is relevant to the desensitisation explanation.

Essentially, the 'two-sentence technique' is a writing structure to help students illustrate both the appropriate selection of material, and then the appropriate application of that knowledge to a new scenario – both required by the AQA mark schemes to secure top level scores.

So, go through **Handout 135** with the students, and then ask them to complete **Handout 136** which requires them to select appropriate knowledge from the cognitive priming explanation.

HANDOUTS 135 and 136

P H **S** G T

Handouts 135 and **136** provide scaffolding for students attempting application questions.

The two-sentence technique is a little rigid in its structure and does not always lend itself easily to some application questions. However, it is an excellent teaching tool and scaffolded support for the students. More-able students may learn to use the technique in a more flexible way whilst the technique remains a good crutch for less-able students.

TOPIC: Defining and measuring crime

P   H   S   **G**   T

Group statements – Considering the nature of crime

The idea of group statements is outlined on page 6.

A good start for this topic might be to use team statements to provoke student thinking about what crime is and the changing nature of crime. So, for example, you could ask students to respond to the following discussion points:

- Before 1967, homosexual acts were illegal in the UK. In 1967 homosexual acts became legal. What does this suggest about 'crime'?

- Homosexual acts are now legal in the UK but considered to be illegal in more than 70 countries in the world. What does this suggest about crime?

- It is illegal to drive on the right-hand side of the road in the UK (there are some exceptions to that rule). In Germany, it is illegal to drive on the left-hand side of the road. What does that suggest about crime?

- Premeditated murder against other human beings is illegal in all countries with a government. What does this suggest about crime?

Using collaborative learning structures (see page 5) can help to ensure that your higher-ability students are stretched and that your lower-ability students are supported.

TOPIC: Defining and measuring crime

P   H   S   G   T

Defining and measuring crime: True/False

Handouts 137 and **138** provide an activity designed to encourage students to read textbook content carefully and a way to ensure that students are more likely to retain and understand that knowledge.

Various statements are included on the handouts and mirror the content from pages 256 and 257 in the *Complete Companion*. Students need to decide whether they think that statement is true or false. If the statement is true, they should develop that point with more detail. If the statement is false, the students should correct the statement.

Answers

1. False, 2. True, 3. True, 4. False, 5. False, 6. True, 7. True, 8. False, 9. True, 10. Actually… this one is open to debate and it is up to the student to justify their True/False selection.

This activity does not lend itself too easily to differentiation; students are more likely to differentiate themselves by the level of detail they include in their extensions and corrections.

However, you could separate the students into two groups: those that complete the activity with their textbook, and those that complete the activity after reading the relevant textbook page once only.

TOPIC: Offender profiling: The top-down approach

Offender profiling: Top-down flow chart

This activity would be best used as either an active way to read information on top-down offender profiling or as a consolidation/plenary activity.

If you have a lovely technician in your department, ask them to laminate enough copies of **Handout 139** for the class. Then, they should cut out the statements on **Handout 140** and place them into envelopes; there should be enough envelope 'sets' for each member of the class. If you don't have a lovely technician… consider setting it as a detention activity!

In essence, this is a very simple matching exercise. The grey boxes are for the name of the various stages in top-down offender profiling. The white boxes define what occurs during those stages.

Laminating the table mats and statement sets will save you cutting out the statements again the following year (and I'm sure you'll agree, we spend far too much time cutting up paper!).

Answers

Stage 1: Profiling inputs

- Data collected on the crime scene, background info on the victim and details of the crime itself.

Stage 2: Decision process models

- The profiler stars to organise the data into meaningful patterns.
  - Murder type – mass murder, spree or serial?
  - Time factors – did the crime take a long time, short time? Night or day?
  - Location factors – was the crime scene the same as the murder scene?

Stage 3: Crime assessment

- Crime and type of offender is classified as organised or disorganised.
  - (Organised) Crime is planned, victim targeted, body transported, weapon hidden, offender intelligent, competent, lives with partner.
  - (Disorganised). Crime is unplanned, random victim, little engagement with victim, crime scene contains clues, e.g. blood, semen.

HANDOUTS 139 and 140

You could use this activity to provide structure and scaffolding for an exam answer on offender profiling.

Less-able students could be told the order of the stages first in order to make the activity slightly easier.

Stage 4: Criminal profile

- Hypotheses are constructed about the background, habits and beliefs of offender. This informs investigation.

Stage 5: Crime assessment part 2

- Written report is given to the investigation agency and persons matching the profile are evaluated.

Stage 6: Apprehension

- If suspect is arrested, the profile-generating process is reviewed and checked for validity.

TOPIC: Offender profiling: The top-down approach

Exploring the 'Barnum Effect'

Snook et al. (2008) argue that profilers actually do little more than psychics. The process of top-down analysis is not based in any science or theory; in fact courts have been known to regard it as 'junk science'. The believability of such profiles might be explained in terms of the Barnum Effect – ambiguous descriptions can be made to fit any situation, such as in the case of horoscopes.

It might be worth demonstrating to students that horoscopes are written in such an ambiguous manner that they can really be applied to anyone - not an individual with a specific star sign. Following this you could ask students the relevance this might have to the evaluation of offender profiling.

- Cut up or print out horoscopes from the previous week.
- Ask students to identify their star sign.
- Give half of the students their correct horoscope and ask them to rate the accuracy of the horoscope out of 10.
- Give the other half of students the incorrect horoscope (but tell them it is the right horoscope) and ask them to rate the accuracy of the horoscope.
- Compare the two groups.

Unless you're unlucky (or horoscopes actually do work…), there is unlikely to be a difference between the two groups. You could do a stats test to make this point even clearer. You can then show students the research on the Barnum Effect and ask them to consider the relevance it might have

NO HANDOUT

This demonstration is difficult to differentiate but does involve higher-order thinking in order to apply to the evaluation of offender profiles. A collaborative learning structure can also be used to finish the activity (see page 5).

when considering the usefulness of offender profiles. (https://www.psychologytoday.com/blog/sideways-view/201411/weve-got-something-everyone-the-barnum-effect)

References

Snook, B., Cullen, R.M., Bennell, C., Taylor, P.J. and Gendreau, P. (2008). The criminal profiling illusion: what's behind the smoke and mirrors? *Criminal Justice and Behavior, 35(10)*, 1257–76.

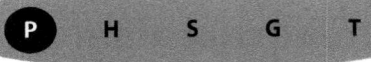
Spot the deliberate mistakes

Once you have taught the bottom-up approach to offender profiling, you could test your student's knowledge and understanding by asking them to spot the 14 deliberate mistakes on **Handout 141**. This can be a good activity to consolidate key terms of key principles, as well as build their confidence in using key terms related to offender profiling.

The correct answers are shown below.

Correct version: words in bold replace wrong ones on the handout.

*In the bottom-up approach, the profiles are driven from the **actual data** rather than from 'above' by the **judgement of the profiler**.*

Approach 1: Investigative Psychology

Canter proposed that profiling can and should be based on psychological theory and research.

- *Interpersonal coherence: People are **consistent** in their behaviour therefore there will be links (correlations) with elements of the crime and how people behave in everyday life. At the same time, people's behaviour **changes** over time and therefore looking at the differences in crimes over a four year period might offer further clues.*

- ***Forensic** awareness: Certain behaviours may reveal an awareness of particular police techniques and past experience, for example Davies et al. (1997) found that rapists who conceal fingerprints often had a previous conviction for burglary.*

- *Smallest space analysis: Data about many crime scenes and offender characteristics are correlated so that most common connections can be identified. For example Salfati and Canter (1999) analysed the co-occurrence of 48 crime scene and offender characteristics*

taken from 82 UK murder cases where the victim was a stranger. They identified three underlying themes:

- *Instrumental opportunistic – **'instrumental'** refers to using murder to obtain something or accomplish a goal, **'opportunistic'** means that the offender took the easiest chances*

- *Instrumental cognitive – a concern about being detected and therefore more **planned**.*

- *Expressive impulsive – **uncontrolled,** in the heat of strong emotions, feel provoked by victim.*

Approach 2: Geographical profiling

*Canter has also proposed that criminals reveal themselves through the locations they choose. Geographical profilers are concerned with **where** rather than **who**. Offenders are more likely to commit a crime near where they live or where habitually travel because it involves least effort.*

- *Circle theory: Canter and Larkin (1993) proposed that most offenders have a spatial mindset – they commit their crimes within a kind of imagined circle.*

  - ***Marauder** – offender's home is within the geographical area where crimes are committed.*

  - ***Commuter** – offender travels to another geographical area and commits crimes within a defined space around which a circle can be drawn.*

- *Criminal geographic targeting (CGT): This is a computerised system developed by Kim Rossmo. It produces a **three** dimensional map displaying spatial data related to time, distance and movement to and from crime scenes. The map is called a jeopardy surface.*

It might be necessary, for your less-able students, to give them more instruction as to where the mistakes might be (see page 260 of the *Complete Companion*). You could do this by highlighting the sentences where the mistakes are located. To challenge your more-able students, do not allow them to use the textbook.

References

Canter, D. and Larkin, P. (1993). The environmental range of serial rapists. *Journal of Environmental Psychology, 13,* 63–69.

Davies, A., Wittebrod, K. and Jackson, J.L. (1997). Predicting the antecedents of a stranger rapist from his offence behaviour. *Science and Justice, 37,* 161–170.

Rossmo, D.K. (1999). *Geographic profiling.* Boca Raton, FL: CRC Press.

Salfati, C.G. and Canter, D.V. (1999). Differentiating stranger murders: Profiling offender characteristics from behavioural styles. *Behavioural Science and the Law, 17,* 391–406.

TOPIC: Offender profiling: The bottom-up approach

NO HANDOUT

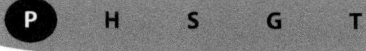

Flipped learning: Canter and/or Railway Murder documentary

Flipped learning is an idea already explained on page 37.

It is a good idea to help save classroom time by not having to watch endless videos in lesson time. There are a number of videos available on YouTube (at the time of writing) that could be very useful.

For example, *Following in the killers' footsteps* by David Canter, and documentaries on the 'Railway Rapist'

case mentioned on page 260 in the *Complete Companion* which involved David Canter.

Questions can be set for the students to answer, for example:

- The techniques used.
- Possible evaluations of the technique.
- How the techniques might be applied to help solve a current high-profile media crime (on the news or on a soap).

> You could set different questions for different students – based on their ability level. Less-able students could be asked to recall factual details about the techniques used. More-able students could be asked to consider strengths and weaknesses of the bottom-up technique.

TOPIC: Offender profiling: The bottom-up approach

NO HANDOUT

Dimension line

This is an adaptable idea based on the dimension line activity described on page 5.

The two extremes of the dimension for this activity would be 'the top-down approach is the most effective technique' versus 'the bottom-up approach is the most effective technique'.

Students would be required to place a Post-it® on the dimension line to indicate their viewpoint. They should either justify their opinion on the note or place their initials on the it and be ready to justify their opinion when asked.

Alternatively, you could offer two dimensions as shown below:

> This activity is ideally suited to the use of a collaborative learning structure (see page 5). Using collaborative learning structures can help to ensure that your higher-ability students are stretched and that your lower-ability students are supported.

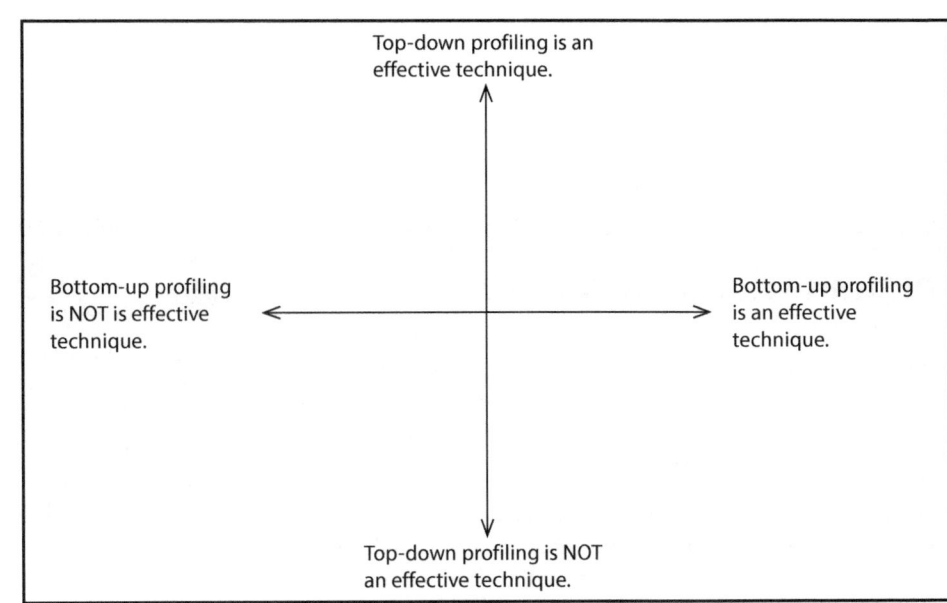

TOPIC: Biological explanations of offending behaviour: An historical perspective

NO HANDOUT

P	H	S	G	T

Draw a criminal

This activity might work well as a starter to this topic. Simply ask students to draw what they think a typical criminal might look like.

This would be designed to tease out their stereotypes on criminals and could lead to a discussion about where/how those stereotypes have developed. Is it the media? Is it because some people are more likely to commit crimes than others? Are criminals more likely to have some physical features than non-criminals? Before undertaking this activity, you should think carefully about your own class and whether this might prove a socially sensitive exercise. Think about the possible drawings that students might provide.

This activity is not differentiated. However, you could target more high-order questions at more-able students in the ensuing discussion.

TOPIC: Biological explanations of offending behaviour: An historical perspective

HANDOUT 142

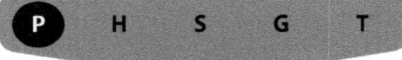

P	H	S	G	T

Historical approach crossword

A crossword may seem a little too juvenile for A Level students but, as an activity, it certainly has its merits (and in my (MG) experience, there is no such thing as *too* juvenile for A Level students!). This activity can be used to force students to engage with textbook material in more depth and to read for meaning; the clues on this crossword are designed to encourage this. The crossword would work well with page 262 of the *Complete Companion*.

The answers are as follows:

Across

2. athletic
5. atavisticform
10. face
11. dimensions
12. innate
13. three

Down

1. postmortems
3. environmental
4. deception
5. arms
6. somatotype
7. Lombroso
8. ears
9. insane

It is likely that some students will finish earlier than others. This is because some students will be able to work out the answers more easily and may read more quickly than others. As such, you may wish to have an extension activity up your sleeve. You could ask students to add two to three questions/answers to the crossword using the text provided.

TOPIC: Biological explanations of offending behaviour: Genetic and neural

HANDOUT 143

P	H	S	G	T

Biological explanations – key details

I (MG) am always looking for different ways to help students understanding what is meant by 'detail'.

Handout 143 is entitled 'key details' and pulls out many of the numbers/statistics/key terms that would be good to include in an answer outlining the genetic and neural explanations of offending behaviour. All the students need to do is to write what that key detail refers to in the study of offending behaviour.

This could be used as a way to get students to read and assimilate the information (page 264 of the *Complete Companion*) or as a consolidating activity.

A key point to explain to the students is that they need to revise, retain and use as much of the information and statistics included on the sheet as possible.

A list of options could be given to less-able students to select from if you feel they will need extra support.

A follow-up activity could be to allow students this completed sheet as scaffolding to write a 6-mark outline on this topic.

TOPIC: Biological explanations of offending behaviour: Genetic and neural

Understanding twin studies

Although **Handout 77** is in the schizophrenia section, it can be easily adapted or used as it is to support students' understanding in this topic as well. See page 52 for the notes on this handout.

HANDOUT 77

P H **S** G **T**

See page 52.

TOPIC: Biological explanations of offending behaviour: Genetic and neural

Writing about twin studies

The previous activity can be followed by a slightly adapted version of **Handouts 78** and **79**. All that really needs to be changed is to replace Joseph's (2004) study with something like Raine's (1993) study or similar. See page 53 for the notes on this handout.

References

Joseph, J. (2004). Schizophrenia and heredity: Why the emperor has no genes. In J. Read, L. Mosher and R. Bentall (eds), *Models of Madness: Psychological, Social and Biological Approaches to Schizophrenia*. Andover: Taylor & Francis.

HANDOUTS 78 and 79

P H **S** G **T**

See page 53.

Raine, A. (1993). *The Psychopathology of Crime*. San Diego, CA: Academic.

TOPIC: Psychological explanations of offending behaviour: Eysenck's theory

Completing the EPQ

Students like completing questionnaires/scales etc.

It might be worth asking students to complete the Eysenck Personality Questionnaire (EPQ) as a homework task before you start this topic (a short version is given on page 255 of the *Complete Companion*). There are plenty of places online where students can do this. For example:

http://similarminds.com/eysenck.html

http://www.trans4mind.com/personality/EPQ.html

However, it would be important to prepare students for the possible results; for example, explain that there are issues with validity and that any links to criminal behaviour are correlational and not causal. In addition, you might want to consider the students in your group and whether it is appropriate.

If you feel it is appropriate, it can be a useful discussion starting point for these questions:

- What did you think of the questions?
- What did you think about the results?

NO HANDOUT

P H S **G** T

The discussion element of this activity could utilise a collaborative learning structure (see page 5) to ensure the less-able students are supported and the more able are stretched.

- Do you think that personality can be measured using this technique?
- Do you think that personality is always consistent?
- Can you spot any potential problems with the validity of the study?
- How could the reliability of the research be assessed?

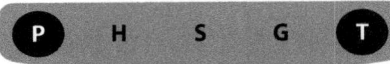
TOPIC: Psychological explanations of offending behaviour: Eysenck's theory

Eysenck: Evaluation 'signposts'

The rationale for **Handout 144** is included at the top of the page.

In summary, over the years of teaching and marking for AQA I (MG) have come to the conclusion that AO3/ evaluation signposts are actually crucial to successful evaluation for several reasons. As such, I work hard to develop students' skills in writing their own.

Here are some rough suggestions for **Handout 144** for your guidance (and based largely on page 267 of the *Complete Companion*). This activity should be completed without access to the *Complete Companion* as the paragraphs are lifted from the textbook; the purpose of this activity is for students to develop their own 'AO3 signposts' in order to hone their exam technique.

- There is mixed support for a key element of Eysenck's theory that personality types have a biological basis.

- One of the problems for Eysenck's personality theory is that it assumes that personality is consistent; there is a disagreement about whether this is the case.

- A further issue with any theory of personality is that the score or label given to any person depends on questionnaire tests – which may not be valid (validity is the key issue).

- There is research support for a link between personality and criminal behaviour.

- Eysenck's theory of personality may not actually be useful in the real world.

References

Dunlop, P.D., Morrison, D.L., Koenig, J. and Silcox, B. (2012). Comparing the Eysenck and HEXACO models of personality in the prediction of adult delinquency. *European Journal of Personality, 26(3)*, 194–202.

HANDOUT 144

P   H   S   G   T

This may prove to be a very difficult activity for some students.

To reduce the level of difficulty, the signposts below could be given to students who then have to choose which is the most appropriate for each paragraph.

Mischel, W. and Peake, P.K. (1982). Beyond deja vu in the search for cross-situational consistency. *Psychological Review, 89*, 730–55.

Zuckerman, M. (1987). All parents are environmentalists until they have their second child. *Behavioural and Brain Sciences, 10*, 42–3.

Zuckerman, M. (1987). All parents are environmentalists until they have their second child. *Behavioural and Brain Sciences, 10*, 42–3.

TOPIC: Psychological explanations of offending behaviour: Cognitive

Feedforward marking

The concept of A B C and feedforward marking is outlined on page 2. I've (MG) found it to be a really effective marking and feedback technique that genuinely has an impact on student progress.

As a result, I've now started to use the concept to design handouts.

Handout 145 shows a fictitious student answer to the following exam question: Outline the cognitive explanation of offending behaviour. (6 marks)

In addition, in the grey boxes are some fictitious teacher comments and A B C . . . tasks. The students are therefore required on **Handout 146** to complete those tasks in order to improve the answer. It is always worth mentioning to the students during/after this task how small additions/sentences can have a huge impact on the quality of a piece of work.

Possible task improvements:

A: These are a form of irrational thinking that might allow an offender to deny

or rationalise their behaviour due to a twisting of reality.

B: For example, seeing a smile but thinking that the person is actually thinking bad thoughts about you.

C: This is called magnification and minimalisation.

D: *E*ffect is a noun, *a*ffect is a verb. Effect is the result of something. Affect is to influence something.

E: Each stage describes a more advanced level of moral reasoning that is more logically consistent.

F: They believe that breaking the law is justified because the rewards outweigh the costs.

G: It is an evaluation point and the question only asked for an outline.

References

Hollin, C.R., Browne, D. and Palmer, E.J. (2002). *Delinquency and Young Offenders*. Oxford: Blackwell Publishing.

HANDOUTS 145 and 146

P   H   S   G   T

It is inevitable that some students will find the improvements harder to make than others – some students will need individual support during the activity in order to prompt the correct responses.

You could ask the students to help each other in pairs/threes using a collaborative learning structure (see page 5) as long as it is set up in a way where all students are responsible and have to engage in the task.

Krebs, D.L. and Denton, K. (2005). Toward a more pragmatic approach to morality: A critical evaluation of Kohlberg's model. *Psychological Review, 112*, 629–49.

Kohlberg, L. (1969). Stage and sequence: the cognitive-developmental approach to socialisation. In D.A. Goslin (ed.), Handbook of Socialisation Theory and Practice. Skokie, IL: Rand McNally.

TOPIC: Psychological explanations of offending behaviour:
Differential association

Evaluation elaboration

Handout 147 is designed to illustrate to students the level of depth required to achieve top AO3 marks.

Students should start by reading the boxes on the far left-hand side of the page, which outline simple evaluation points. Ask them to highlight (or shade in) each of the boxes in that column with a different colour.

The students should then read the boxes in the next column. Each represents further explanation/elaboration of one of the evaluation points, but they are not in the same order. Students should highlight (or shade in) those boxes with the correct, corresponding colour.

They should repeat this until all boxes in all columns are shaded in. This will require some thought from the students.

Purpose:

Explain to students that the more they can elaborate their original evaluation points, (e.g. 'A strength of the differential association explanation of offending is that it is supported by evidence'), the more AO3 marks they are likely to get. This is denoted at the top of the handout. The evaluation comments start at 'Level 1', and then increase in marks the further they are elaborated, through 'Level 2', 'Level 3' and 'Level 4'. These are loosely based on the AQA essay mark schemes.

Answers:

The correct answers are as follows:

"The major strength of this theory is that it changes people's views about the origins of criminal behaviour."

- The theory marked an important shift from 'blaming' individual factors to pointing to social factors. The theory suggested that crime did not have to be explained in terms of personality (mad or bad).

- Such an approach has important real-world implications because learning environments can be changed.

- Sutherland also shifted the emphasis away from 'bad' individuals by highlighting white-collar crime which is often committed by those otherwise seen as 'respectable'.

"Differential association theory is supported by evidence."

- Osborne and West (1982) found that, where there is a father with a criminal conviction, 40% of the sons had committed a crime by aged 18 compared to 13% of sons of non-criminal fathers.

- This evidence suggests that criminality appears to run in families and that therefore suggests that criminal behaviours and attitudes are the result of social learning.

- On the other hand, it could also be argued that the evidence could be explained in terms of genetic inheritance as well.

"There are methodological issues with this theory."

- This is because it is largely based on correlational analysis.

- The problem with this type of data is that it is not possible to determine the cause from the effect.

- In terms of peer influences, it could be that offenders seek out other offenders and this would explain why offenders are likely to have peers who are offenders.

"The absence of biological factors from this account is a drawback."

> To challenge your more able, you could decide to cut out the twenty boxes and instruct the students to match them up to make five evaluation points. Once they have cut out the boxes, they should mess the boxes up so it is no longer clear which boxes belonged to which columns. This is a more difficult activity because the students must decide on the order of the elaboration as well.

- The diathesis-stress model may offer a better account by combining social factors with vulnerability factors.

- Predisposing factors may be innate genetic ones or early experiences such as maltreatment.

- Indeed, attachment research suggests that emotional problems in childhood make a child vulnerable to deviant peer influences later in life. As such, the social approach on its own may be an insufficient explanation.

"The differential association explanation struggles to account for all kinds of crime."

- Social learning influences are probably confined to 'smaller' crimes rather than violent and impulsive ones such as rape and murder.

- On the other hand, in England and Wales in 2014 there were 500 murders and 400,000 burglaries; so the theory is able to explain a large proportion of the crime.

- A related criticism is that differential association also can't explain why most offences are committed by people under 21.

References

Osborn, S.G. and West, D.J. (1979). Conviction records of fathers and sons compared. *The British Journal of Criminology, 19(2)*, 120–33.

TOPIC: Psychological explanations of offending behaviour: Psychodynamic

Building the bigger picture

This activity may work particularly well if you used **Handout 106** in the AS/Year 1 *Teachers Companion* when teaching the psychodynamic approach. It is a very similar activity, but will require more understanding of the approach and application to offending behaviour.

Freud and the psychodynamic approach are really fun to teach but it can be tempting to go off on too many tangents because you know your students will want to hear about it!

Students tend to hold on to the 'shocking' elements they hear about the psychodynamic approach but do not always fully engage with the psychodynamic approach in the holistic way that it requires.

Freud was the first person to put forward an integrated and comprehensive explanation of all human behaviour. It could be argued that he is the only person to have done this.

Consequently, it is important that students see Freud's approach for what it is – like a jigsaw of interrelated parts.

The following activity is designed to help students to do this.

The bigger picture

Ask students to cut out the grey shapes on **Handout 148**. Then, using their notes or their textbook (page 270 in *The*

Complete Companion), ask them to define the terms and concepts, i.e. id, Oedipus Complex, Offending behaviour etc.

Then provide students with some A3 paper or larger. Ask the groups to stick the grey shapes onto their paper in a pattern which they feel reflects the links between the terms and concepts (this could literally be in any order, such is the interrelatedness of Freud, so reassure them this is not an activity with an objective outcome).

Once they have arranged their shapes, they should then draw a series of arrows/lines to illustrate the links between them. On those arrows/lines they should write explanations of how/ why these elements are linked.

If your students have done this properly, their A3 paper should look like a web of messy associations between various elements of the psychodynamic approach to explaining offending behaviour.

This hopefully will give students a better feel for the holistic nature of the psychodynamic approach, and reinforce the interrelated nature.

Students might be tempted to make the links too generic; make sure that they keep them tightly focused on forensic psychology and offending behaviour.

If you feel that some of your students will struggle with this activity, provide them with a sheet which suggests some of the concepts that they should attempt to connect. For example, the 'cheat sheet' could suggest that 'underdeveloped' and 'offending behaviour' should be connected. This could be accompanied by prompt clues such as 'explain why an underdeveloped superego might lead to antisocial behaviour'.

TOPIC: Dealing with offending behaviour: Custodial sentencing and recidivism

Considering the evidence

Students may have what you might call a 'tabloid' perspective on dealing with offenders: lock them up; throw away the key; longer sentences; take a life, lose a life etc.

There are, of course, some strong arguments for this to be the case. However, the fact is that the evidence for the effectiveness of custodial sentences isn't that great.

The activity on **Handout 149** may help to challenge students' pre-conceived ideas on this topic. It asks the students to sort the arguments/evidence into those that support or are against the use of increased custodial sentencing. They must also rate each fragment from 1 (very weak) to 5 (very strong) – they can decide how they do this.

An interesting discussion that may arise from this is the difference between social

arguments for custodial sentencing, e.g. retribution, recidivism, incapacitation, and the evidence for the effectiveness of sentencing in reducing crime rates. The former tends to support the use of sentencing and the latter tends to undermine the use of sentencing.

References

Calhoun, J.B. (1962). Population density and social pathology. *Scientific American, 206(2),* 139–48.

Klein, N.C., Alexander, J.F. and Parsons, B.V. (1977). Impact of family systems intervention on recidivism and sibling delinquency: A model of primary prevention and program evaluation. *Journal of Consulting and Clinical Psychology, 45,* 469–74.

HANDOUT 149

P H S G T

This is an activity that is ideally independent and requires all students to consider the evidence. On that basis, it is best that one-to-one support is offered to students who are struggling to deal with the evaluation and higher-order thinking.

However, it may be that task 4 on **Handout 149** could utilise the 'team statements' collaborative learning structure (see page 5).

TOPIC: Dealing with offending behaviour: Behaviour modification in custody

Hobbs and Holt (1976): Study deconstruction

Research methods is embedded throughout the examination papers; in fact, research methods questions are worth at least 25% of all marks. As such, research methods teaching and learning should be embedded throughout the course.

One way to encourage this is to ask your students to deconstruct psychological studies into their constituent parts. **Handout 150** provides students with a framework to do this, as well as an opportunity to consider reliability, validity etc.

If there is time, encourage students to contextualise the criticisms on the back of the handout because it is easier to just write generic evaluation statements.

Please remember that the purpose of this activity is for students to continue to explore research methods and practise their analysis of research studies.

In terms of an essay question of behaviour modification, students should not be lured into providing methodological criticisms in the exam unless it is linked to the explanation (not the study).

References

Hobbs, T.R. and Holt, M. (1976). The effects of token reinforcement on the behavior of delinquents in cottage settings. *Journal of Applied Behavioural Analysis, 9(2),* 189–98.

HANDOUT 150

P H S G T

For less-able students, you could provide them with definitions of the keys terms, (i.e. independent variable, dependent variable, research design etc), lists of types of experiment (lab, field, natural, quasi) etc.

In the feedback and progress-checking session, ensure that you target the highest-order questions to the most able (i.e. potential problems).

TOPIC: Dealing with offending behaviour: Behaviour modification in custody

Design your own token economy

As an introduction to this topic, you could ask the students to quickly design their own token economy within the context of a prison. Alternatively, you could ask them to choose a different context than prison to begin with, (e.g. behaviour in school, scouts, little brothers/sisters at home etc).

This activity could work by roughly going through the following steps (which could be displayed on the board):

- Pinpoint the behaviours that need to be changed – these should be specific, observable and measurable.
- Choose the types of tokens to be used, (e.g. plastic chips, gold stars, play money etc.).
- Choose the reinforcers that the tokens can be exchanged for, (e.g. TV time, chocolate).
- Set the reinforcement cost, (i.e. determine how many tokens are required for each reinforcer).

NO HANDOUT

P H S **G** T

Using collaborative learning structures (see page 5) can help to ensure that your higher-ability students are stretched and that your lower-ability students are supported.

TOPIC: Dealing with offending behaviour: Anger management

Moving up the levels

I (MG) have found myself in the last few years writing 'needs more detail' in some of my essay marking feedback. Of course, this is pretty useless feedback for students who genuinely do not understand what is meant by 'detail'. It is much easier to *show* them and *illustrate* to them what is meant by 'detail' and how this translates into examination marking.

It is feasible that within this topic the following question might be asked in an A Level examination: Outline anger management as a method for dealing with offending behaviour. (6 marks)

Suppose that you have taught your students this explanation and so they need to outline this study in good detail. This activity should help them to know what 'good detail' means. Try using **Handout 151** with your students after you have outlined the explanation to them in detail.

Handout 151 outlines the explanation accurately, but with some vague information in places or key examples/ ideas missing. The students should add details to the description by using the table at the bottom of the handout.

Suggested additions:

1. which focuses on how a prisoner actually thinks and aims to change how the person handles anger and aggression.
2. Cognitive restructuring
3. Regulation of arousal
4. Behavioural strategies
5. This approach aims to provide a kind of vaccination against future 'infections'.
6. and how anger can be both adaptive and non adaptive. They also analyse situations that provoke their anger.
7. such as self-regulation, cognitive flexibility and relaxation.

HANDOUT 151

P H **S** G **T**

This provides less-able students with a tangible example of what examiners mean by 'detail'. It could be given to less-able students in order to increase their examination skills and to structure their answers.

8. so they can resolve conflicts without being angry.
9. such as role plays
10. i.e. in the prison.

References

Novaco, R.W. (2011). Perspectives on anger treatment: Discussion and commentary. *Cognitive and behavioral practice, 18*, 251–55.

 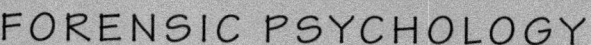
TOPIC: Dealing with offending behaviour: Restorative justice programmes

NO HANDOUT

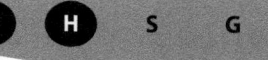

Proposal: Restorative justice in school

A nice idea for a classroom activity or homework might be to ask students to write a proposal to use restorative justice techniques to improve behaviour in school, (e.g. lower school or their previous secondary school).

To structure the activity, you could include the following instructions:

Write a report to a head teacher proposing the use of restorative justice to improve behaviour. The report should include the following:

- *Introduction section: Between 200–300 words outlining what restorative justice is and the evidence supporting its effectiveness.*

- *Proposal section: Four specific ideas to increase the use of restorative justice in school. Each must be justified with psychological principles and/or evidence. The proposals must consider rehabilitation, atonement, victim's perspective.*

- *Evaluation section: Between 200–300 words outlining the potential difficulties that may be encountered with by using restorative justice techniques.*

> You may need to provide some specific ideas to less-able students that they can build on (for example, use of 'reflection forms' for bad behaviour and restorative meetings between perpetrator/victims). However, these students should then be expected to think through the details and specifics of these ideas themselves.

TOPIC: Dealing with offending behaviour: Restorative justice programmes

HANDOUT 152

Plenary questions

Plenary Questions is a very simple and effective idea. It is a good way to end the lesson and ascertain the main themes, concepts and key words that the students have picked up on during the lessons. Essentially, the activity simply involves cutting up the plenary questions and asking the students to select one from the hat.

You can then have a feedback session with the students. Alternatively, if you have lots of time left, the students could answer as many questions as they can on the handout.

> You could pair the students so that there is a high-ability student and a low-ability student. The job of the high-ability student is to select the question and teach the answer to the low-ability student; in the whole-class feedback session, it is the low-ability student that must answer. Several of the questions do entail higher-order thinking (e.g. synoptic links) and therefore your higher-ability students are also being stretched.

TOPIC: Describing addiction

Tolerance and withdrawal

Two tasks are presented on **Handout 153**. Each task shows an example of what needs to be done in the other task. The 'tolerance' task requires students to read the outline and identify eight key terms from the passage that they would include were they to write the outline themselves. The 'withdrawal' task provides students with eight key terms to use in creating an outline of the concept. The 'tolerance' task provides a model for students when completing their withdrawal outline.

As a form of peer assessment for withdrawal outlines, students can swap handouts and highlight the key terms used in the outline: have they managed to use all eight terms?

Additional activities:

The 16 key terms identified on **Handout 153** (8 from tolerance and 8 from withdrawal) can be used to play bingo. Students create a 3×3 grid to record key terms associated with describing addiction. The teacher, or a confident student, gives a description of a term and if students think that term is on their grid they cross it off.

HANDOUT 153

| P | H | **S** | G | T |

Less-able students may require a set of questions to help them structure their outline. For example, 'When does acute withdrawal start?', 'How long does post withdrawal last?'

TOPIC: Describing addiction

Apply your addiction knowledge

Handout 154 presents the case of Terrance who has developed an addiction to prescription pain killers. Students apply their understanding of physical and psychological dependence, tolerance and withdrawal to explain Terrance's experience. If you wish to use this activity as a marked exercise, students could be advised there are 4 marks available and the mark scheme shared with the class.

Additional activities:

As an introduction to risk factors related to addiction, ask students to discuss why they think Terrance (and other people) developed an addiction to pain killers. Students could be prompted to think about genetic vulnerability, stress, personality, family influences and peers.

HANDOUT 154

| P | **H** | S | G | T |

Once completed, students could consider ethical implications of prescribing medication.

Level	Description
Level 2 3–4 marks	Knowledge of factors are clear and mostly accurate. Material is used appropriately to explain Terrance's situation. The answer is generally coherent with effective use of terminology.
Level 1 1–2 marks	Some knowledge of factors is evidence. Links to Terrance's behaviour are not always effective. The answer lacks accuracy and detail. Use of terminology is either absent or inappropriate.

TOPIC: Risk factors: Genetics, stress and personality

Single-sentence summary

HANDOUT 155

P   H   S   **G**   T

Students can work in pairs to draft and redraft sentences on a mini whiteboard before transferring the final sentence to their handout.

This activity requires students to strip down risk factors (*Complete Companion*, page 294) to their most basic point. Creating single sentence summaries ensures students understand the risk factor and can form a useful revision tool as the sentences can be used to cue further details for each explanation.

At the bottom of **Handout 155** an 'Apply your knowledge' question worth 4 marks is provided for students to check their understanding of the risk factors summarised above. Once students have answered the question on paper, the mark scheme shown below can be used to assess students' responses.

Additional activities:

Students can use the simple summaries to produce detailed outlines of risk factors or as cues to create a word search or crossword.

Level	Description
Level 2 3–4 marks	Knowledge of risk factors are clear and mostly accurate. Material is used appropriately to explain Lottie's situation. The answer is generally coherent with effective use of terminology.
Level 1 1–2 marks	Some knowledge of risk factors is evidence. Links to Lottie's behaviour are not always effective. The answer lacks accuracy and detail. Use of terminology is either absent or inappropriate.

TOPIC: Risk factors: Genetics, stress and personality

Ranking risks

NO HANDOUT

P   H   S   **G**   T

Mixed-ability pairs works well with this activity as more-able students consolidate their understanding when explaining to others and less-able students are supported to develop their understanding.

Students write each risk factor (Biological - genetic vulnerability, Biological - dopamine, Stress - self-medication, Stress - traumatic stress, Personality - key traits, Personality - addiction prone, Personality - personality disorder) on separate Post-it®. After considering evidence for these different risk factors (see page 294 of the *Complete Companion*), students rank the Post-it®, ordering them in a continuum from most to least evidence, or most to least common reason for addiction.

Additional activities:

However evaluations: On one side of their page students record an evaluative comment. For example, individuals who inherit the A1 variant of the dopamine-receptor gene have been associated with addictive behaviour because of their low dopamine levels. Drug taking may increase dopamine levels and activate the brain-reward pathway. On the right-hand side of their page students add the 'However'. See the example below for the left and right side.

←————————————————————————————→

A1 variant   Diathesis-stress

TOPIC: Risk factors: Family influences and peers

Team work

Family influences can be split into two topics: parental and sibling influences. Peers can be divided into three: social networks, social identity theory and indirect peer influences. Working in pairs assign one topic (presented on a strip of paper) to each pair to read, understand and explain in their own words. Students then form groups.

• Group 1: 'Family influence' will contain four students (a parental influence pair and a sibling pair).

• Group 2: 'Peer influence' will contain three students (one from each pair looking at networks, identity and indirect influence).

Working in their new groups, students address one of the following questions:

• Briefly outline the role of family influences as a risk factor in the development of addiction.

• Briefly outline the role of peer influences as a risk factor in the development of addiction.

NO HANDOUT

P   H   S   **G**   T

Students need to be placed in mixed-ability pairs to ensure groups formed have suitable information to work with to produce their final summary.

Additional activities:

To consolidate their knowledge of social risk factors students could produce, and maybe even deliver, a form/tutor-time presentation explaining the role of family and/or peers in increasing the risk of addiction either in general or for a specific addiction such as smoking.

TOPIC: Risk factors: Family influences and peers

Social risk factors match up

Handout 156 is designed to illustrate to students the level of depth required to create evaluations worthy of the top mark band when evaluating family and peer influences in the development of addictive behaviour. Students should start by reading the boxes on the far left-hand side of the handout, each of which gives a simple evaluation point. Ask them to highlight each box in a different colour. The students should then read the boxes in the next column. Each represents further explanation/elaboration of one the evaluative points, but they are not in the same order. Students should highlight those boxes with the correct corresponding colour. They should repeat this until all the boxes in all columns are matched.

Additional activities:

Rather than highlight each box, students may wish to use the handout

as a cut and stick activity to create fully formed evaluations that can be condensed to 50-word evaluations from which to revise.

A stretch activity is included at the bottom of **Handout 156** in which students use their understanding of how to create an effective evaluation (as model in the activity) to consider the real-world application of research into social risk factors.

References

Bahr, S. J., Hoff mann, J. P. and Yang, X. (2005). Parental and peer influences on the risk of adolescent drug use. *Journal of Primary Prevention, 26(6)*, 529–51.

De Vries, H., Candel, M., Engels, R. and Mercken, L. (2006). Challenges to the peer influence paradigm: results for 12–13 year olds from six European countries from the European Smoking

HANDOUT 156

P   H   S   G   T

Now effective evaluations have been modelled, students create their own evaluation to discuss real-life application of research into social risk factors.

Prevention Framework Approach study. *Tobacco Control, 15(2)*, 83–9.

Litt, D. M. and Stock, M. L. (2011). Adolescent alcohol-related risk cognitions: The roles of social norms and social networking sites. *Psychology of Addictive Behaviors, 25(4)*, 708–13.

Stattin, H. and Kerr, M. (2000). Parental monitoring: A reinterpretation. *Child Development, 71(4)*, 1072–85.

TOPIC: Explanations for nicotine addiction: Brain neurochemistry

Detailed descriptions

Handout 157 presents a very basic summary of the role of brain neurochemistry in addiction. This outline lacks the necessary expansion if asked to outline the explanation as part of a 16-mark question (AO1 = 6 marks) and so students need to develop the detail for each point made.

Additional activities:

The neurochemical explanation of nicotine addiction contains a lot of specialist terminology. Therefore, students may find it helpful to create a glossary of key terms containing biological terminology and where appropriate diagrams of brain areas to consolidate their understanding.

HANDOUT 157

P   H   **S**   G   T

Some sections are easier to develop than others, so allow students time to compare their responses with others to spot any missed concepts.

Key terms to include in the Glossary:

Dopamine, ventral tegmental area (VTA), nucleus accumbens (NAc), glutamate, GABA, monoamine oxidase (MAO).

TOPIC: Explanations for nicotine addiction: Brain neurochemistry

Save or steal?

Initially working alone, students record evidence and expansion comments beneath each evaluative category. Next, they are allowed time to 'steal' ideas from peers by reading others' evaluative comments and adding any missed information to their own handout. You could encourage students to visit as many peers as possible rather than just work as a pair. Alone, once again, students now 'save' the best comments from their own responses and their peers' to create 50-word summaries for each evaluative category. This requires students to consider the value of their own research and that of others when choosing what to include in each summary.

Additional activities:

For students who find visualising useful, once **Handout 158** is completed, students could create labelled pictures summarising each evaluation point. These can be displayed around the room and used later when revising the topic nearer exam time.

HANDOUT 158

P	H	S	G	T

You may wish to complete the top section of **Handout 158** yourself and make this available to less-able students when they complete the 'steal' section of the handout.

TOPIC: Explanations for nicotine addiction: Learning theory

Arty outlines

Allow students the choice of creating a role play with a small group of peers or a cartoon (either alone or with a friend works best) explaining the initiation, maintenance and relapse of smoking behaviour. Students should ensure that for the three areas specialist terminology associated with learning theory is clearly referred to.

Key terms to include:

Role models, vicarious reinforcement, positive consequences, operant conditioning and rewards, negative reinforcement, classical conditioning and associations.

The class could hold an art exhibition where cartoons and role plays are shared with each other.

Additional activities:

Keeping an approaches journal is an ongoing task but one that will help students make links across topics and consolidate their knowledge. As with other approaches, learning theory is found in a number of topics across Year 1 and 2 of the specification. Provide students with a small exercise book, or ask them to bring in their own note book, which is divided into the different approaches. Every time an approach is discussed, students record a brief summary of the explanations it provides for a specific aspect of human behaviour.

NO HANDOUT

P	H	S	G	T

Allowing students to use a medium that suits their own interests and talents (either drama or art) helps personalise learning.

TOPIC: Explanations for nicotine addiction: Learning theory

Examining evaluations

Two exam responses outlining criticisms of learning theory are presented on **Handout 159.** Students are required to record the strengths of the candidate's response as well as suggest any areas for development. Students should be reminded that 'criticism' can refer to strengths and/or limitations, whereas if the question just called for limitations, then only negative commentary would be credited.

Candidate 1: The first criticism is structured using PEEL and so provides a detailed outline of one strength of the theory. The second criticism is less detailed but does make a valuable point about gender differences: we cannot adopt a 'one theory fits all' approach. The candidate could have concluded that the learning theory cannot explain these gender differences so is an incomplete explanation of smoking addiction.

Candidate 2: The first criticism is concise but underdeveloped. The reader is never really sure if the author understands what is meant by an 'approach bias' as the research evidence lacks detail. The second criticism is more successful, although they failed to use paragraphs correctly.

As an extension activity, students could be asked to improve either Candidate 1's gender paragraph and/or Candidate 2's classically conditioned cue paragraph.

Additional activities:

Handout 159 does not consider research support for mood manipulation and explanations of smoking initiation. Students could be asked to create their own evaluations for these points following the advice identified in **Handout 159**.

HANDOUT 159

| P | H | S | G | **T** |

Students can be supported by modelling how to examine Candidate 1's response then allow students to tackle Candidate 2 alone.

References

Karcher, M. J., and Finn, L. (2005). How connectedness contributes to experimental smoking among rural youth: Developmental and ecological analyses. *Journal of Primary Prevention, 26(1)*, 25–36.

Unrod, M., Drobes, D. J., Stasiewicz, P. R., Ditre, J. W., Heckman, B., Miller, R. R. and Brandon, T. H. (2014). Decline in cue-provoked craving during cue exposure therapy for smoking cessation. *Nicotine and Tobacco Research, 16(3)*, 306–15.

TOPIC: Explanations for gambling addiction: Learning theory

Slot machine addiction

Handout 160 describes Charlie's addiction to playing slot machines. Students use their knowledge of schedules of reinforcement, the concepts of 'big win' and 'near miss', as well as the gambling environment to explain why Charlie is addicted.

Partial/variable reinforcement: Charlie wins sometimes but not others. This uncertainty keeps him playing for longer. Variable reinforcement refers to the occasional supply of rewards – long periods without a win are reinforced by the occasional pay-out.

Big-win hypothesis: Charlie's early win of £150 has shaped his long-term behaviour; he continues to gamble in the hope of repeating this large pay-out.

Near-miss: Occasionally Charlie nearly reaches the maximum prize. This 'near-miss' creates a brief period of excitement which encourages further gambling.

Gambling environment: The bright lights and sounds of the casino lure Charlie into further gambling as it is an exciting environment. The environment cues thinking about gambling.

HANDOUT 160

| P | H | **S** | G | T |

Students could be asked to explain Charlie's gambling using their memory of learning theory as a revision exercise. Once completed, students use their textbook to add any missed details.

Additional activities:

Students could be asked to explain the popularity of the National Lottery using concepts relevant to learning theory's explanation of gambling.

TOPIC: Explanations for gambling addiction: Learning theory

Improve the evaluation

Often students create evaluations that are a list of points rather than an effective evaluation of a theory. **Handout 161** shows an example of this (and once again paragraphs have been forgotten!). First, students need to split the evaluation into different sections (paragraphs) by highlighting each comment in a different colour.

Students then improve each section using their textbook (*Complete Companion*, page 303) or class notes. Students may find it helpful to use PEEL structure to develop the depth of their commentary.

Additional activities:

Once completed, allow time for students to view each other's

HANDOUT 161

| P | H | S | G | **T** |

Students may need one of the points modelled to show how to expand the detail before attempting others on their own.

evaluations. If you allow mobile phones in class, any paragraphs students feel are particularly effective can be photographed and added to their own notes for homework.

TOPIC: Explanations for gambling addiction: Cognitive theory

Cognitive biases match up

Students match the cognitive bias to the definition and example of thinking resulting from this bias. Once matches have been made, students could complete the AO1 section of a 16-mark question: Discuss the role of cognitive biases in explaining gambling addiction. (AO1 = 6 marks). Once written, this outline can be peer assessed before students carry out individual research to gather evaluative commentary needed to address the remaining 10 marks of the exam question.

Additional activities:

Students can create a gambling questionnaire to identify different cognitive biases. Students swap their questionnaire with others who identify which bias each of the questions is targeting. This provides useful revision of the design and use of self-report methods, e.g. question order, filler/checking questions, question wording, open and closed questions. They can then use the questionnaire for some research.

HANDOUT 162

P **H** S G T

Deepen students' thinking by asking them:

Which bias do you feel is most influential?

Do biases differ with the type of gambling?

What causes biases to occur?

TOPIC: Explanations for gambling addiction: Cognitive theory

Traffic lights

Forced choice traffic lights: Provide students with an image of a traffic light with space to record ideas next to each coloured light. Students have to decide which theory they feel offers the best explanation of gambling: learning theory (conditioning and reinforcement), cognitive theory (biased thinking) or biological psychology (mentioned as an AO3 point and students can apply knowledge gained from studying nicotine addiction). By

the green light they name the theory they feel offers the best explanation and justify their decision. The amber light reflects the theory they feel contributes to addiction but is not the sole cause. The red light is reserved for the theory they feel is least likely and/or faces the most problems and so cannot explain addiction fully.

NO HANDOUT

P H **S** G T

Once completed, allow students time to read each other's traffic lights to amend their traffic light comments.

TOPIC: Reducing addiction: drug therapy

Market place

Divide the class into four groups (if you have a large class, eight groups may be needed with two groups per topic). Each group is assigned one form of drug therapy: Nicotine replacement therapy (NRT), prescription medication (varenicine, bupropion) for smoking and opioid antagonistics, antidepressants for gambling addiction. Using a sheet of A3 paper, the group creates a poster outlining how the drug works. You can set restrictions here, e.g. maximum of 20 words and at least two diagrams, to prevent students simply copying out passages from the textbook (*Complete*

Companion, page 306). Once complete, one student stays with the poster while other group members disperse to visit other posters. The student remaining with the poster then teaches visitors about their drug. On reuniting with their original group, students who visited other posters need to teach the student who stayed behind about the other drugs.

Additional activities:

Following this market place activity, the class can be set a quiz which each student completes without conferring.

NO HANDOUT

P H S **G** T

Place students in groups so a range of skills are covered: confidence with biological knowledge, creativity, speaking and listening abilities will create effective groups.

Students' marks for each group are then added together to identify the group who were best at teaching each other about each drug. You could also identify which type of drug was best understood by the class (had the most correct answers) to identify the most successful teacher and poster.

TOPIC: Reducing addiction: drug therapy

Making links

Using their textbook (*Complete Companion*, page 307) or class notes, students have to apply their knowledge of research into drug therapy to form effective evaluations (following the PEEL paragraph structure). For example,

Point – NRT trials are not truly blind.

Evidence – This is because patients receiving nicotine have a different experience than those given a placebo.

Expansion – In 73 double-blind placebo trials only 17 had blind assessments. In the 17 studies 2/3rds of participants in the placebo condition were confidence they were not using a real nicotine patch.

Link – The lack of effective blinding in trials means conclusions about NRT therapy are more uncertain than previously claimed.

Additional activities:

Students could be asked to consider whether drug therapy alone is sufficient to manage addictive behaviour. This

HANDOUT 163

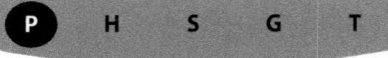

Less-able students may benefit from sentence starters in the evidence box to guide their thinking. Alternatively, research could be given to students to place in the relevant textboxes; transforming the information into their own words.

could generate discussion of the social cues triggering addictive behaviours, through processes etc.

TOPIC: Reducing addiction: Behavioural interventions

Behavioural interventions

Using their textbook (*Complete Companion*, page 308) or class notes, students address the questions displayed on **Handout 164.** Earlier questions require students to report AO1 knowledge of classical conditioning and outline covert sensitisation. Later questions demand evaluative commentary in considering the ethical implications of inflicting unpleasant stimuli on clients and research evidence supporting the use of therapies. When answering the final question, students can also consider whether behavioural interventions only treat symptoms rather than the causes of addiction.

Additional activities:

For homework, students could create an aversion therapy for either a smoke or an internet gambler. They should consider:

- What aversive stimuli would be ethically acceptable to use in the treatment?
- How would the stimuli be administered?
- What potential problems may reduce the effectiveness of the therapy?

HANDOUT 164

P	H	S	G	T

Working in groups allow students the choice of working through all questions together or assigning one question each then teaching each other.

TOPIC: Reducing addiction: Behavioural interventions

Word games

As a conclusion to the behavioural intervention topic, students could create a class crossword. To do this, project a grid onto the class whiteboard into which students should write key words relating to the topic. This can be a team game with points being awarded for length of word and/or number of letters used from other words.

Once the grid is complete, this can be photographed and shared with students. A suitable revision activity would be to produce a crossword clue for each of the words in the grid.

Additional activities:

Alternatively, once words are placed on the grid a game of taboo can be played. Split the class into two groups. One student from each team is given a word to describe to the class. The first team that guesses correctly wins a point.

NO HANDOUT

P	H	S	G	T

If playing as a team, mixed-ability groups work well as students can produce central words (aversion, association) and peripheral words (sickness-inducing).

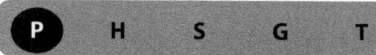

TOPIC: Reducing addiction: Cognitive behavioural therapy

CBT summary

If asked to outline the use of CBT to reduce addiction, students who give a generic outline of the aims and aspects of CBT will receive few marks. **Handout 165** provides thinking prompts to encourage students to tailor their outline of CBT specifically to the treatment of addiction. A stretch activity is included for students to apply their understanding of CBT to the treatment of nicotine addiction.

Additional activities:

As a revision activity or plenary, students could be provided with statements relating to different aspects of CBT and asked to identify which part of CBT they refer to. For example,

- Clients are not always aware of their cognitive biases.
- Client is asked to identify and avoid risky situations.
- During this time students are encouraged to keep a diary.

HANDOUT 165

P H S G T

Once completed, more-able students can be asked to predict potential strengths and limitations of using CBT to treat addiction. Prior knowledge of drug and behavioural therapies can be used to help form opinions.

TOPIC: Reducing addiction: Cognitive behavioural therapy

Adding it up

This activity requires higher-order thinking as students are required to make judgements as to the strength of the evaluative comments relating to CBT. Students begin by folding their page in half. On the left-hand side they summarise supporting research and positive aspects of the treatment. On the right-hand side, students summarise any limitations (this could also include more favourable research for other forms of therapy). Once all ideas have been recorded, students assign a score to each evaluative point, 5 = convincing strength/limitation, 1 = weak strength/limitation. Students then total the scores for each side of the page to identify whether, on the whole, they feel CBT is a helpful or unhelpful therapy. Students can then summarise their opinion.

Additional activities:

To conclude the consideration of different attempts to reduce addiction (drug therapy, behavioural interventions, CBT) students can be

NO HANDOUT

P H S G T

Students are asked to consider the value of evidence/issues provided as evaluative comments. This could be considering methodological issues and comparison to other forms of therapy.

given a range of scenarios (examples of personal experience of various addictions can be found on the internet) and asked to suggest a suitable treatment for the individual.

TOPIC: The theory of planned behaviour

The theory of planned behaviour

The theory of planned behaviour (TPB) emphasises the belief that behaviour is under the conscious control of the individual. For example, it would assume that if the individual *intended* to give up smoking, then they would be able to do so. Ajzen (1989) also stated that the extent to which the individual believes they are able to perform the behaviour in question (perceived behaviour control) acts on the intention to behave in a particular way or directly on the behaviour itself, as well as attitudes about that behaviour and their awareness of social norms surrounding that behaviour.

Handout 166 contains a diagrammatic representation of this model (taken from *Complete Companion*, page 312). After reading about the diagram, students try to recreate it on **Handout 166** from memory. Once complete, using their class notes and a different coloured ink, students add any missed details or make any necessary corrections to their diagram. Once students have completed the diagram their understanding can be used to explain Lucy's current attitude and behaviour regarding smoking and possibly suggest strategies to reduce her addiction.

Additional activities:

Students could conduct internet research into the various smoking prevention programmes available. For example, the NHS quit smoking campaign https://quitnow.smokefree.nhs.uk/?gclid=CLey3u6i9MkCFUQUwwodnKEBCA

Students could identify elements of the theory of planned behaviour in these campaigns. For example, the NHS site

HANDOUT 166

P H S G T

Less-able students may need teacher support to understand the model so working together in a small group may be helpful while other students apply their knowledge to Lucy's case.

has 'Why quit?' (changing behavioural attitude), 'Successful stories' (changing subjective norms – lots of people can and do quit, perceived behavioural control – the stories emphasise effort is needed to change behaviour).

References

Ajzen, I. (1989). Attitude, structure and behaviour. In A.R. Pratkins, S.J. Beckler & A.G. Greenwald (eds). *Attitude, structure and function*. Hilsdale, NJ: Lawrence Erlbaum Associates, 241–74.

TOPIC: The theory of planned behaviour

TPB evaluation

Provide students with the following claims:

- Theory of planned behaviour (TPB) is too rational – it fails to take into account emotions and compulsions.
- TPB ignores other mediating factors – for example peer influence.
- TPB research has methodological problems – researchers often rely on questionnaires.
- TPB predicts intentions - rather than actual behaviour change.
- TPB ignores the influence of substances – alcohol and drugs can promote risky behaviour.

Students work in small groups to predict what each evaluative claim refers to. For example, TPB ignores other mediating factors - for example 'peer influence' might lead students to suggest this refers to the role of friends in supporting the person in their attempts to quit or tempt them back into old habits. Once all predictions have been made, students compare their ideas to textbook evaluations (*Complete Companion*, page 313) adding any missed information and correcting any errors in thinking.

NO HANDOUT

| P | H | S | **G** | T |

This is a tricky task and so students benefit from working in mixed-ability groups. Some claims are more obvious than others, e.g. evaluation of questionnaires allows students to use previously acquired knowledge of research methods.

Additional activities:

Once **Handout 166** and this activity is completed, students address the exam question: Outline and evaluate the theory of planned behaviour in relation to the reduction of addiction. (16 marks)

TOPIC: Prochaska's six-stage model of behaviour change

Sort out the stages

Handout 167 involves a simple match up task to present the six stages of behaviour change. Students should be able predict the order through reasoning skills rather than relying on a textbook to help them order the stages.

The model represents WHEN the person progresses but doesn't explain HOW an individual moves from one stage to the next. As an extension to this activity, students could be asked to consider what support/strategies are needed for progression to occur.

Additional activities:

An alternative use of **Handout 167** would be to cut out each stage description and assign one stage to each student. On an A4 page or mini whiteboard, students represent their stage in symbols and key terms only. Students then form groups of six (one student per stage) and describe their stage using their image. Once all have been explained, students work together to order their images into a timeline.

HANDOUT 167

| P | **H** | S | G | T |

Once ordered, ask students to hypothesise why only 1 in 5 people are thought to reach the final stage. Could reasons differ depending on the type of addition and/or person?

References

Prochaska, J. O. and DiClemente, C. C. (1992). Stages of change in the modification of problem behaviors. *Progress in Behavior Modification, 28,* 183–218.

TOPIC: Prochaska's six-stage model of behaviour change

Taking turns

Provide students with one card from a deck of playing cards; this could be drawn at random or cards deliberately assigned to students. Students are given 15 minutes to read evaluations relating to the six-stage model. They are allowed to make any brief notes needed as they read. Once the evaluations have been read, students place this information face down on their desk. They are now asked to create a 10-mark evaluation of Prochaska's model. The number of the playing card they have been assigned denotes the amount of times they are allowed to turn over their reading

material to recap the evaluative points presented, e.g. 2 = 2 turns allowed, ace = could be one or 11 turns. Less-able students could be given a picture card enabling them to have unlimited turns.

Additional activities:

Once they have completed their evaluations, students form groups of four. They now cut up their evaluations and stick effective comments from all four essays onto a new sheet of paper to create a final evaluation. This can then be photocopied for all members of the group.

NO HANDOUT

| P | H | S | G | **T** |

The number of turns allocated can reflect students' needs. For example, less-able students are allocated more turns than those with better retention of material just read.

References

Prochaska, J. O. and DiClemente, C. C. (1992). Stages of change in the modification of problem behaviors. *Progress in Behavior Modification, 28,* 183–218.

Refer to the appropriate skills for the question set.

MARKING GRID

Question:

Skill⮯	AO1: Knowledge & understanding	AO2: Application to the question stem	AO3: Evaluation	Structure and specialist terminology
Level 4 **7–8 marks**	Knowledge is accurate and generally well detailed. Minor detail and/or expansion of argument sometimes lacking.	Appropriate application and links made between research and question stem. Clear and effective comments.	Evaluations are effective.	Answer is clear, coherent and explicitly focused on the question. Effective use of a range of specialist terminology.
Level 3 **5–6 marks**	Knowledge is accurate and generally well detailed.	Appropriate application and links made between research and question stem. Most comments are clear and effective.	Evaluations are often effective/evaluation is effective.	Answer is clear, coherent and focused on the question. Effective use of specialist terminology.
Level 2 **3–4 marks**	Knowledge is of the concept/research is evident.	Some effective application seen but research (theory/study) links to stem not always explained.	Any evaluations present are apparent but have limited effectiveness.	Answer is mostly clear and organised but may lack focus in places. Specialist terminology mostly used appropriately.
Level 1 **1–2 marks**	Knowledge is limited. Answer is mainly description focused.	Application to the question stem is absent or inappropriate.	Evaluative comments are very limited, poorly focused or absent.	The whole answer lacks clarity, accuracy and organisation in places. Specialist terminology used inappropriately or is absent from the answer.

Markers' comments:

Author's next steps:

▶ Lesson notes p.1

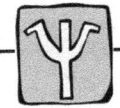

Refer to the appropriate skills for the question set.

EXTENDED ANSWER MARKING GRID

Question:

Skill ⮌	AO1: Knowledge & understanding	AO2: Application to the question stem	AO3: Evaluation	Structure and specialist terminology
Level 4 13–16 marks	Knowledge is accurate and generally well detailed.	Appropriate application and links made between research and question stem.	Evaluations are effective.	Answer is clear, coherent and focused on the question. Effective use of specialist terminology.
Level 3 9–12 marks	Knowledge of the concept/research is evident. There may be occasional inaccuracies.	Appropriate application but research (theory/study) links to stem not always explained.	Evaluations are often effective/evaluation is effective.	Answer is mostly clear and organised but may lack focus in places. Specialist terminology mostly used effectively.
Level 2 5–8 marks	Knowledge is vague and/or inaccurate or partial performance in relation to question*. Answer is mainly description focused.	Only partial application is seen.	Any evaluations present are apparent but have limited effectiveness.	Answer lacks clarity, accuracy and organisation in places. Specialist terminology used appropriately on occasion.
Level 1 1–4 marks	Knowledge is limited and/or or partial performance in relation to question*.	Application to question stem is limited or absent.	Evaluative comments are very limited, poorly focused or absent.	The whole answer lacks clarity, shows many inaccuracies and is poorly organised. Specialist terminology is either absent or inappropriately used.

*partial performance, e.g. questions states, 'discuss two explanations' and answer only considers one.

If only one explanation (or study) outlined at level 3 or 4 then candidate cannot score above level 2.

If only one explanation (or study) outlined at level 2 then candidate cannot score above level 1.

Markers' comments:

Author's next steps:

▶ Lesson notes p.1

EXTENDED ANSWER MARKING GRID VERSION 2

Terminology

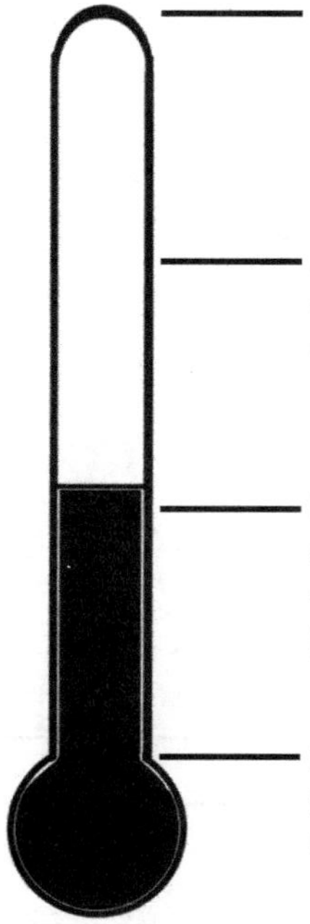

- L4: Coherent. Focused. Effective.
- L3: Mostly clear, focused, effective.
- L2: Lacks clarity, accuracy, organisation in places.
- L1: Lacks clarity, accuracy, organisation.

Evaluation

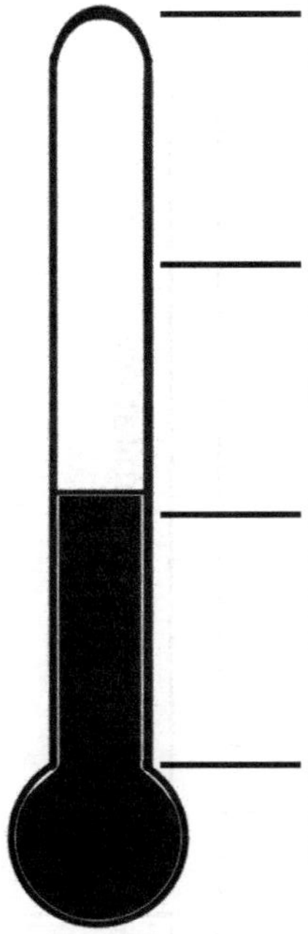

- L4: Thorough and effective
- L3: Mostly effective. Occasionally inaccurate
- L2: Partly effective. (Focus mainly on description)
- L1: Limited, absent or lacks focus.

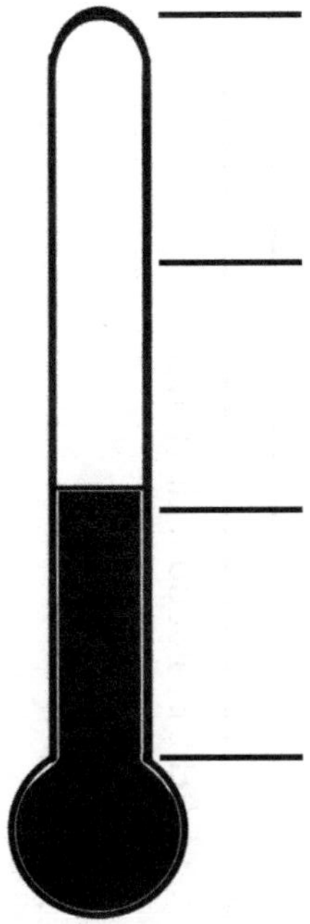

Knowledge & Understanding

- L4: Accurate/ Detailed
- L3: Present, occasionally inaccurate
- L2: Present but vague/ inaccurate
- L1: Limited

LEVEL 4: A Level... 13-16 marks

LEVEL 3: A Level... 9-12 marks

LEVEL 2: A Level... 5-8 marks

LEVEL 1: A Level... 1-4 marks

Target:

Marks/ GRADE AWARDED:

Overall level awarded / Comments:

▶ Lesson notes p.1

REVISION RECORD

| TOPIC: | SECTION:
PAPER: |

Six sentence summary:

1.

2.

3.

4.

5.

6.

Topic glossary (including definitions):

PEEL Evaluation: Strength

PEEL Evaluation: Limitation

PEEL Evaluation: Strength

PEEL Evaluation: Limitation

▶ Lesson notes p.1

ASSESSMENT: FEEDBACK AND FEEDFORWARD

Date:

Type of question: Knowledge / Evaluation / Essay / Application / How Science Works / Maths

Total Marks: out of   **Grade Equivalent:**   Over Target/ On Target/ Under Target

Improvements/Amendments/Responses:

A:

B:

C:

Improved mark if resubmitted:

▶ Lesson notes p.2

PEER ASSESSMENT GRID

Write down four key words that the student has used. **Suggest one key word that they could have used but didn't.**	
Write down the best sentence/quote from their piece of work and explain why you chose that, i.e. what is good about it?	
Write down one sentence/quote which doesn't make sense to you, i.e. it lacks clarity, or accuracy, isn't fully explained.	
Add one complete sentence which improves the essay. **On the essay, write *1 to show where the sentence should go.**	*1 –

AO2: APPLICATION OF KNOWLEDGE

Question:

Stem sentence	Concept/research	Application

▶ Lesson notes p.7

ELABORATION LADDERS

Why does that matter?

How would that affect the results/validity?

Can I explain my point with an example?

Have I got evidence?

How could it be improved?

Have I got a counter argument?

How does this affect the main argument?

Use the prompts above to help you **elaborate** the evaluative arguments on the bottom rung of the ladders.

The more you elaborate your points (without repeating yourself), the more marks you get – hence the smiley face at the top!

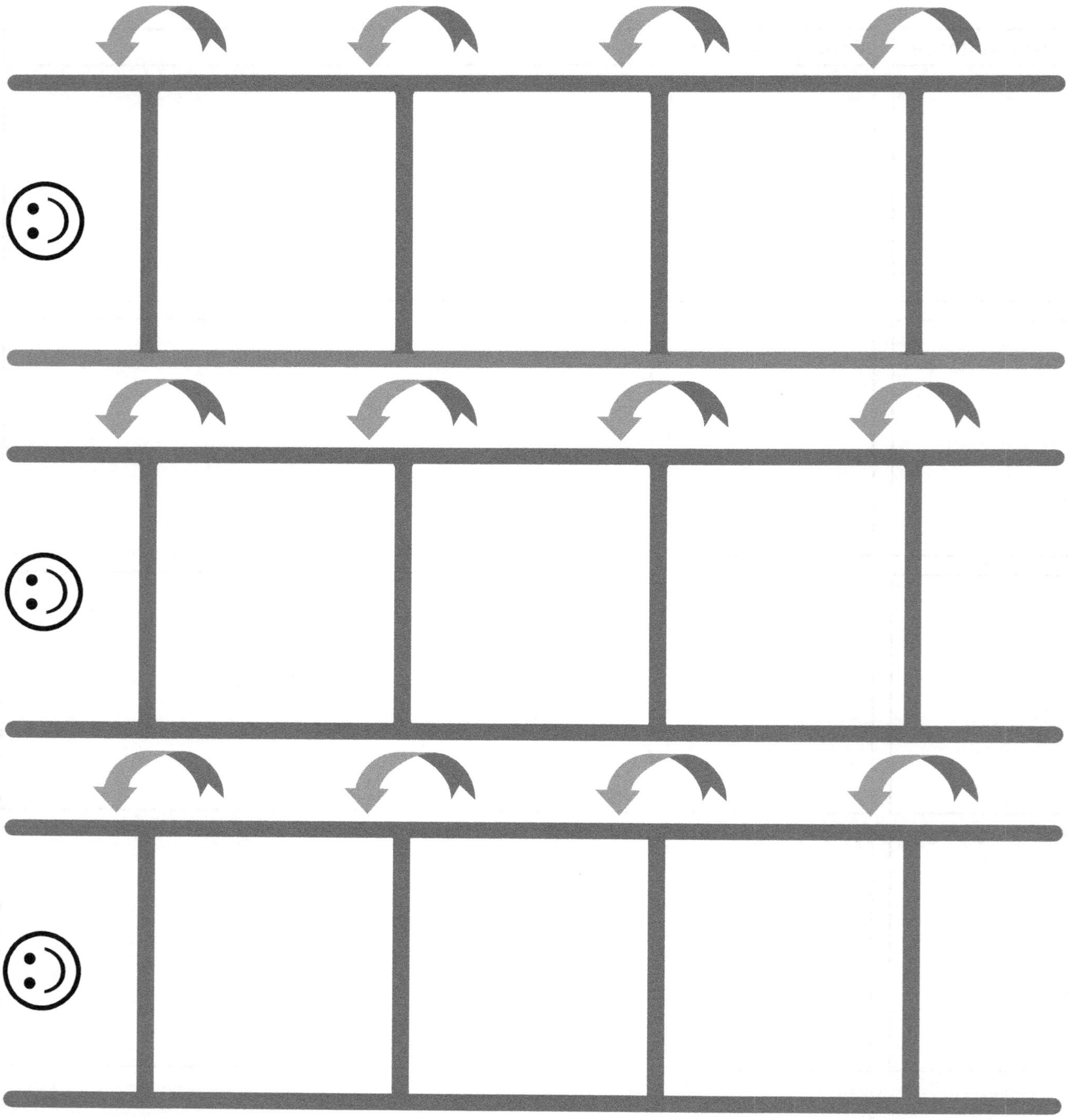

:)

:)

:)

▶ Lesson notes p.7

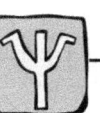

BURGER EVALUATION SKILLS

The 'burger technique' is a way for you to structure an evaluation paragraph where you use a study to support or undermine a theory/explanation. The most important point of the process is the bottom of the burger where you explain how and why that study is relevant. This is where you can really demonstrate your understanding of a) what the theory/explanation would predict, and b) whether or not we should accept that theory based on the research evidence.

Example

A study that supports/undermines the [insert name of theory/explanation here] is . . .

Describe procedure and findings of a relevant study.

supports/undermines the [insert name of theory/explanation here] theory because . . .

A study that undermines the learning theory explanation of attachment is Harlow's (1959) study of rhesus monkeys.

Harlow separated rhesus monkeys from their mothers at birth and placed them in a cage with a wire monkey with a feeding bottle attached and a wire monkey wrapped in soft cloth. The monkeys spent most of their time clinging to the cloth monkey, especially in times of distress.

This undermines the learning theory view of attachment because, according to the explanation, the young monkeys should have attached to the wire monkey which dispensed food because they would associate it with a sense of pleasure and the reduction of their hunger drive. However, the infants tended to cling more to a mother which offered them comfort.

▶ Lesson notes p.7

BURGER EVALUATION SKILLS

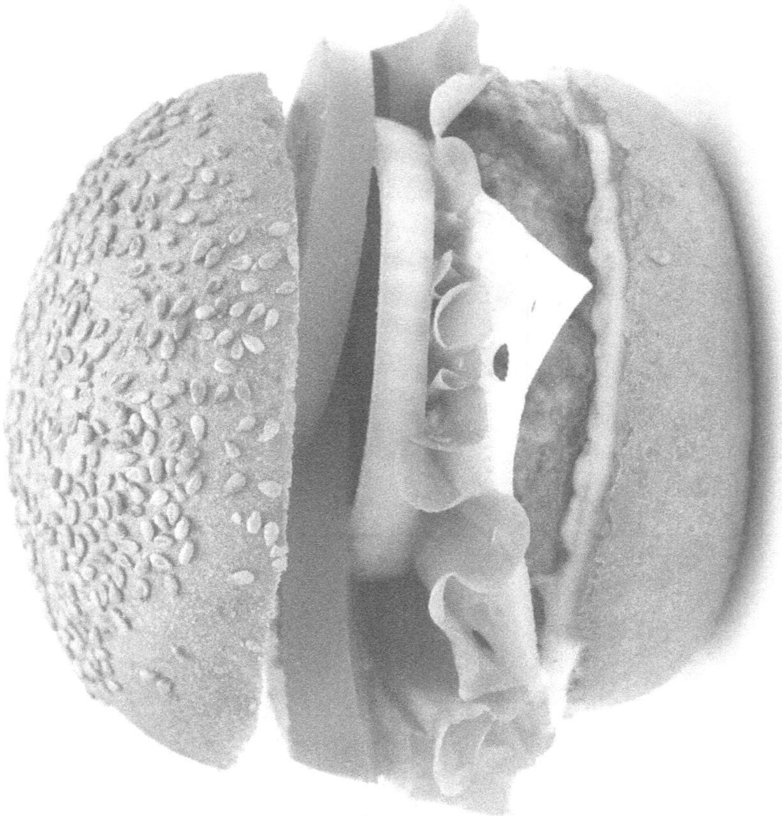

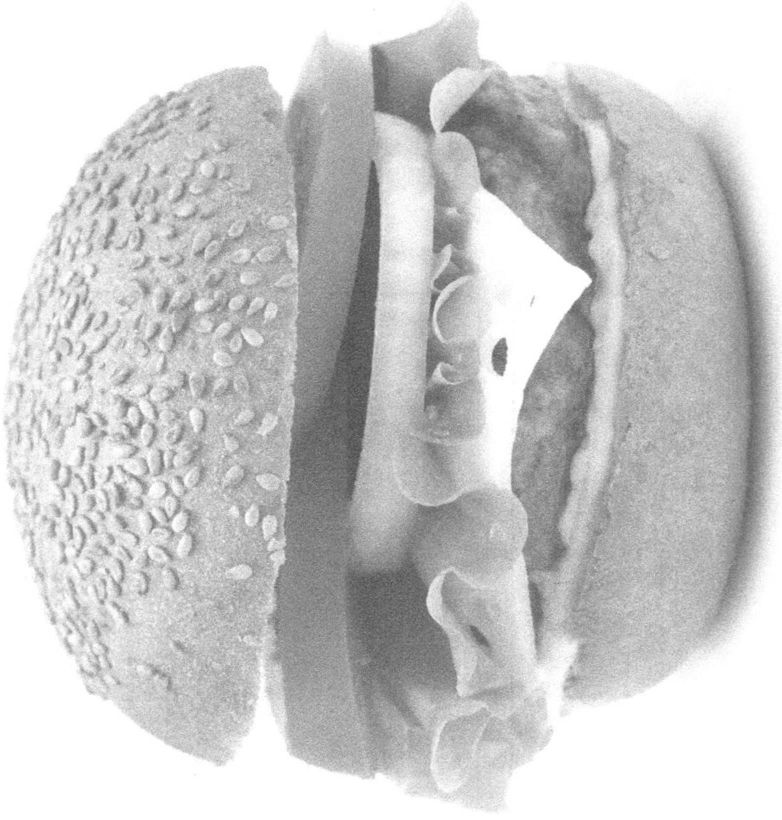

▶ Lesson notes p.7

CONSIDERING CONTENT ANALYSIS

In the scenario below highlight the following components in different colours:

- How data was collected (the sampling method)
- How data was coded (placing data into categories)
- How data was represented (quantitative or qualitative analysis).

> Researchers asked A Level students to keep a diary for the Spring term (February to April). The students were asked to record, on a daily basis, positive and negative events and experiences that occurred during the school day. On the last day of the Spring term students handed in their diary for analysis.
>
> Each diary page was numbered which allowed researchers to use a random number generator to select five pages per diary for analysis. On each page of the diary individual statements were given an identifier code. Statements with similar content were then placed together and a category was identified. This lead to the identification of repeated themes in the entries: homework, peer relations, extra-curricular commitments, coursework, teachers, form time, study periods, assessments and break/lunchtime. These categories were grouped into larger units to produce three main themes: time pressures, relationships and attainment.

Give **one** strength of using content analysis for this study. (2 marks)

_____

_____

_____

_____

Give **one** limitation of using content analysis for this study. (2 marks)

_____

_____

_____

_____

STRETCH: Create your own diary entries and try to code them.

_____

_____

_____

_____

_____

▶ Lesson notes p.11

CASE STUDY MATCH UP

You may well have met a number of case studies when studying other areas of the specification. Test your retention of information by matching the individual to the description and knowledge gained.

Individual	Description	Knowledge gained
Henry Molaison (HM)	A five-year-old boy with a phobia of horses questioned by his father following psychologist's instruction.	The little boy's inability to accept himself as female and resulting emotional damage suggests gender identity is a result of nature not nurture.
Clive Wearing	Surgical accident lead to a little boy losing his penis. He was raised as a girl using surgical, hormonal and psychological treatments.	Subsequent changes to his personality now thought to be temporary. Suggests parts of brain can be removed without being fatal.
Little Hans	Surgery to remove the hippocampus resulted in an inability to form new memories.	Suggested separate brain areas are involved in procedural and episodic memories.
Phineas Gage	Contracted a virus that resulted in severe damage to long-term memory.	Demonstrated the Oedipus complex. The horse represented the father and threat of castration.
David Reimer	American railroad worker who experienced severe brain trauma as a result of a metal rod passing through his skull.	Helped identify areas of the brain involved in the formation of memories.

▶ Lesson notes p.12

EXPLAIN YOURSELF

"The case study method offers rich, in-depth data."

"Case studies can be used to investigate rare behaviour and experiences."

"It is difficult to generalise insights gained from a case study."

"Case studies require consideration of important ethical issues."

▶ Lesson notes p.12

APPLYING DEFINITIONS

The following scenarios demonstrate concepts relating to reliability. For each scenario identify the concept from the list below and define that concept in the space provided. The first one has been done for you.

Reliability	Improving observer reliability	Test-retest reliability	Inter-observer reliability	Improving self-report reliability

Scenario	Concept definition
Researchers interested in the effects of stress on physical health used questionnaires to measure the level of stress participants had experienced in the previous six months. The questionnaire chosen was an established measurement tool frequently used by other psychologists. Researchers repeatedly found those who scored highly on the stress questionnaire reported increased rates of illness.	Reliability – this concept refers to consistency of measurement. If the measurement is repeated, and the same results are found, the measurement is said to be consistent. If results are inconsistent then the measurement is unreliable.
Psychologists were interested in the eating behaviour of people who were following a programme of restricted eating (dieting) compared to people who were unrestrained eaters (those not on a diet). Participants completed a questionnaire about what foods they consumed frequently, occasionally or never. One week later they were asked to complete the questionnaire again. The responses participants gave from both questionnaires were then compared.	
Two psychologists observed the behaviour of an infant interacting with its mother. They were asked to record the number of times the infant displayed the following behaviours: smiling, tongue protrusion, sucking, fixed gaze, laughing, crying and grasping with hands. The data collected by the two researchers was then correlated to determine whether observations were consistent in their measurement of each of the behaviours listed.	
Before carrying out an investigation into aggression in the playground, researchers decided to train the people who would be observing the children. Behavioural categories, such as hitting and pushing, were clearly defined and examples given to help observers identify which actions would be considered an example of that behaviour. Watching videos of playground behaviour gave observers the opportunity of practising identifying behaviours before the actual study took place.	
Before participants were asked to complete a questionnaire about their gambling behaviour, researchers decided to test whether items on the questionnaire were unambiguous. A small group of people, similar to those who would be involved in the actual study, were asked to identify any questions they felt were unclear or could be interpreted in different ways. These were then rewritten before the questionnaire was given to participants.	

▶ Lesson notes p.12

ROLL WITH IT

Below is a set of questions relating to validity. Take it in turns to roll two dice to identify the question you have to answer and teach to the rest of the group. Either take the number shown on one die, or add the two numbers together (e.g. 2 + 3 = 5).

1. What is meant by the term validity?

2. What is the difference between internal and external validity?

3. Why do demand characteristics reduce internal validity?

4. What is meant by the term temporal validity?

5. Why does the presence of confounding variables reduce internal validity?

6. Explain how face validity can be used to assess validity of a measurement.

7. How does social desirability bias differ from demand characteristics?

8. Why does social desirability bias reduce internal validity?

9. Explain how concurrent validity can be used to confirm validity of a measurement.

10. Why is mundane realism important when considering the extent to which a study has ecologically validity?

11. Give an example of an investigator effect that risks reducing internal validity.

12. How can psychologists improve the validity of questionnaires?

► Lesson notes p.13

UNJUMBLE THE JUMBLE

A student has been making revision notes regarding validity in psychological research. Unfortunately, they have become very muddled: points are all jumbled together with no subheadings or specialist terminology. Use their comments to create a more orderly set of notes to revise from.

Validity is concerned with data. Do the data represent reality or are they just the result of the research? Psychologists are concerned with what occurs inside a study as well as after a study. Inside a study, problems can reduce validity for example, the investigator's behaviour, participants' reactions to the investigator and the presence of other variables that may differ across the conditions of the independent variable. Psychologists also need to look beyond the immediate investigation and consider other groups of people, time periods and situations. How natural the task participants perform needs to be considered and it shouldn't be assumed that just because a natural experiment was conducted the tasks within that study were natural.

When using questionnaires there are a number of things psychologists can do to check validity. One way is to simply look at the questionnaire to determine whether the questions seem to be asking about the topic being investigated. Any 'problem' questions would need to be reworded or removed. Another way is to get participants to complete a second, established questionnaire. If the first questionnaire is valid then participants should show similar scores on both measurements. If using other methods of investigation, then research could be set up so that neither the participant or person collecting the data are aware of the aims of the investigation. This would improve validity.

Subheadings you can use to structure your own revision notes include:

- **Internal validity**
  - Investigator effects
  - Demand characteristics
  - Confounding variables
  - Social desirability bias

- **External validity**
  - Population validity
  - Temporal validity
  - Ecological validity (and mundane realism)

- **Assessing validity**
  - Face validity
  - Concurrent validity

- **Improving validity**
  - Double blind

▶ Lesson notes p.13

FEATURES OF SCIENCE

Label the following information boxes with the features of science shown here.

Empirical methods	Objectivity	Replicability	Theory construction	Hypothesis testing
Inductive model	Deductive model	Falsifiability	Paradigm	Paradigm shift

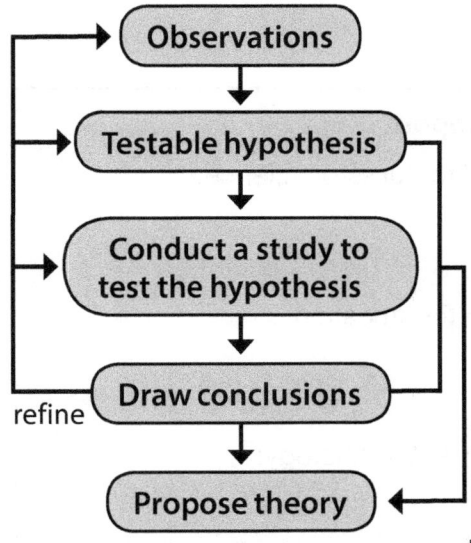

Observations → Testable hypothesis → Conduct a study to test the hypothesis → Draw conclusions → Propose theory

refine

Information is gained through direct observation or experiment rather than from unfounded beliefs or reasoned argument.

A unified set of assumptions and methods. Kuhn argued that rather than continual fine tuning of theories, science has two main phases: 'normal science' where a dominant theory holds and 'revolution' where the normal view is overthrown.

A collection of general principles that explain observations and facts that help us understand and predict natural phenomena.

Data are unaffected by the expectations of the researcher. Carefully controlled conditions and systematic collection of measurable data is required.

To demonstrate validity, psychologists usually test a different group of people and often use a slightly different task to see if the same behaviour is observed. In order to do this the original study needs to be recorded carefully, giving full details of what was done and what was found.

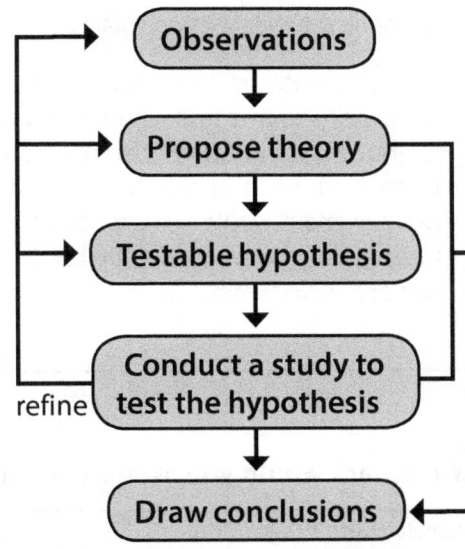

Observations → Propose theory → Testable hypothesis → Conduct a study to test the hypothesis → Draw conclusions

refine

Popper argues it is not possible to confirm a theory, it is only possible to disconfirm it. The only way to prove a theory correct is to actually seek to disprove it. Therefore, all research starts with a null hypothesis which can either be accepted or rejected once data have been collected.

General testable expectations. If these predictions are found to be correct the theory is supported. If predictions are not fulfilled, then the theory from which it was derived requires modification.

Gradually disconfirming evidence accumulates and the dominant theory is overthrown. One example of this revolution is the work of Copernicus who overthrew the belief that the earth was the centre of the universe.

▶ Lesson notes p.14

EXAMINING ANSWERS

Harriet's mother is always telling her that blondes have more fun. Harriet is studying psychology and explains to her mother that something isn't true just because you believe it to be so.

Outline how Harriet could use her knowledge of the features of science to explain what is wrong with her mother's argument.
(6 marks).

Harriet's mother is being subjective as she is basing her theory on personal experience rather than objective observations of a number of blonde people.

She has also failed to operationalise the variable 'blonde'. For example, does she mean natural or dyed blondes? If she does not give a clear definition of what she means by blonde then she may be at risk of bias when assigning people to the category of 'blonde' or 'not blonde'. Furthermore, other researchers would not be able to replicate the research exactly to check reliability of her claim.

Harriet's mother is not able to measure 'fun' empirically as it is not a physical entity unlike height or weight. Therefore, how can she measure fun accurately? Any questionnaire or measurement scale she creates to assess fun may be biased by her own opinion of what 'fun' is.

Examiner's report.

Knowledge of features of science:

Application to the question:

Use of specialist terminology:

Clarity and organisation:

What mark would you award this answer?

Level / mark	Description
3 5–6 marks	Knowledge of features of science is clear and generally well detailed. Application to the claims made by Harriet's mother is clear and effective. The answer is coherent with appropriate use of terminology.
2 3–4 marks	Knowledge of features of science is evident. There is some effective application to the claims made by Harriet's mother. The answer is organised but may lack clarity in places. Specialist terminology is mostly used effectively.
1 1–2 marks	Limited knowledge demonstrated for features of science. Application to the claims made by Harriet's mother lack clarity, accuracy or be inappropriate. The answer may lack accuracy and be poorly organised. Specialist terminology is used inappropriately on occasions.
0	No relevant content.

▶ Lesson notes p.14

RESEARCH REMINDER

Complete the questions relating to the research shown below to refresh your knowledge of Year 1 research methods.

A psychology teacher was interested in whether colour improves recall of information. One of his psychology classes was given all resources on coloured paper and PowerPoints using brightly coloured fonts and backgrounds. Another of his psychology classes received the same resources and slides but in the traditional black font on a white background. At the end of the topic each class sat a multiple choice quiz to test their recall of information. He then randomly selected ten students from each class to carry out a statistical analysis of their quiz scores to determine whether a difference was seen between coloured or traditional resources. He set a probability level of 95% ($p \leq 0.05$).

The quiz scores (max. score 20) for the ten students selected from each class are shown below.

Class A Coloured resources	Class B Traditional resources
9	12
10	4
3	16
15	17
18	20
7	6
11	14
5	8
10	16
19	11

Statistical testing suggested a significant difference in quiz scores did not exist between students from class A and those from class B. The psychology teacher therefore accepted the null hypothesis.

Identify the population and sample in this study.

State the operationalised independent variable.

State the operationalised dependent variable.

Create the alternative hypothesis.

Create the null hypothesis.

Explain what is meant by $p \leq 0.05$.

▶ Lesson notes p.15

STATISTICAL TESTING TERMS

Type of test used when the study has a non-directional hypothesis.

Inferential statistics

Data grouped into separate categories such as smoker, non-smoker.

Parametric tests

Non-parametric tests

Term for data that could not have arisen by chance, or is extremely unlikely to have arisen by chance.

The observed value calculated using a specific inferential statistic to analyse the data collected.

Significant

Accepting a null hypothesis that should have been rejected.

Nominal level

Ordinal level

Rejecting a null hypothesis that should have been accepted.

Interval level

Calculation that allows conclusions to be drawn based on the probability that a particular pattern of results could have arisen by chance.

Test statistic

Data that are ordered in some way where the difference between each interval is not the same, for example, the height of participants.

Significance level

Value a test statistic must reach in order for the null hypothesis to be rejected.

Critical value

One-tailed test

Data that are measured using units of equal intervals, for example, number of correct answers on an IQ test.

Two-tailed test

Type of test used when the study has a directional hypothesis.

Type I error

A category of statistical test used to analyse data that is at nominal or ordinal level.

Type II error

Usually set at 0.05, meaning there is a 5% possibility results did occur by chance.

A category of statistical tests that make calculations using the mean and standard deviation of a data set, making them a more powerful test.

► Lesson notes p.16

NON-PARAMETRIC TESTING 1

For the following examples, work out what statistical test should be used, whether the observed value is greater or less than the critical value (see **Handout 22** for critical values tables) and state if data are significant or not significant.

Smokers and non-smokers were approached in a town centre and asked whether they agreed with the current smoking ban. It was hypothesised that more smokers would be against the ban than non-smokers. The following data were recorded:

	Smoker	Non-smoker
Against ban	34	12
For ban	16	38

Using a statistical test the observed value of 19.48 was calculated.
The degrees of freedom was 1
Probability was set at p ≤ 0.05

- The statistical test used was:

  because . . .

- The critical value is:
- Data are significant / Data are not significant (circle correct statement).

An investigation was carried out to determine whether a relationship exists between the average number of cigarettes smoked in a day and score on a smoking attitudes scale. The following data were recorded:

Pt.	Average cigarettes	Smoking attitude score
1	5	27
2	8	16
3	0	5
4	25	35
5	20	28
6	1	14
7	10	23
8	15	32

Using a statistical test the observed value of 0.952 was calculated.
The number of participants was 8 (n = 8)
Probability was set at p ≤ 0.05
A directional hypothesis was used.

- The test used was:

  because . . .

- The critical value was:
- Data are significant / Data are not significant (circle correct statement).

An investigation was carried out into students' ability to concentrate in morning and afternoon lessons. It was hypothesised that a difference will be seen in concentration (as rated on a scale of 1–20) between students in morning lessons and students in afternoon lessons. The following data were recorded:

Pt.	Morning group	Afternoon group
1	13	5
2	8	9
3	16	9
4	12	6
5	12	12
6	8	9
7	12	4
8	14	12
9	18	14
10	15	6

Using a statistical test the observed value of 19.5 was calculated.
Probability was set at p ≤ 0.05

- The test used was:

  because . . .

- The critical value was:
- Data are significant / Data are not significant (circle correct statement).

► Lesson notes p.17

NON-PARAMETRIC TESTING 2

Critical value tables to help you. You **DO NOT** NEED TO REVISE THESE NUMBERS.

The exam will give you a table if they ask you to decide if data are significant or not significant.

Sign test

N	One-tailed test	
	0.05	0.025
	Two-tailed test	
	0.10	0.05
5	0	1
6	-	0
7	0	1
8	0	1
9	0	1
10	0	1

Wilcoxon

N	One-tailed test	
	0.05	0.025
	Two-tailed test	
	0.10	0.05
5	0	5
6	-	3
7	2	8
8	0	11
9	3	8
10	2	1

Chi-Squared

df	One-tailed test	
	0.05	0.025
	Two-tailed test	
	0.10	0.05
1	2.71	7.78
2	3.84	9.49
3	4.60	9.24
4	5.99	11.07
5	6.25	10.64
6	7.82	12.59

Spearman's Rho.

N	One-tailed test	
	0.05	0.025
	Two-tailed test	
	0.10	0.05
5	0.900	0.634
6	1.000	0.738
7	0.829	0.600
8	0.886	0.700
9	0.714	0.564
10	0.786	0.648

Mann-Whitney. One-tailed test (0.05)

		N_A					
		5	6	7	8	9	10
N_B	5	4	5	6	8	9	11
	6	5	7	8	10	12	14
	7	6	8	11	13	15	17
	8	8	10	13	15	18	20
	9	9	12	15	18	21	24
	10	11	14	17	20	24	27

Mann-Whitney. Two-tailed test (0.05)

		N_A					
		5	6	7	8	9	10
N_B	5	2	3	5	6	7	8
	6	3	5	6	8	10	11
	7	5	6	8	10	12	14
	8	6	8	10	13	15	17
	9	7	10	12	15	17	20
	10	8	11	14	17	20	23

Remember:

Some tests are significant when the observed value is equal to or exceeds the critical value, for others it is the reverse.

One way to remember is to see if there is a letter R in the name of the test.

If there is an **R** then the observed value should be **gReateR** than the critical value, (e.g. for Spearman's and Chi-Squared).

If there is no R (e.g. Mann-Whitney and Wilcoxon) then the observed value should be less than the critical value.

- Test/observed value = the value calculated by the inferential statistic.
- N = number of participants.
- df = degrees of freedom (for tests that do not use N).
- Critical value = value the test/observed value is compared to.
- Significant = data occurred due to action of IV/ relationship between variables.
- Insignificant = data occurred due to chance.
- $p < 0.05$ = 5% risk data occurred due to chance.
- Type 1 error = rejecting a null hypothesis that is actually true.
- Type 2 error = accepting a null hypothesis that is not actually true.

▶ Lesson notes p.17

PARAMETRIC TESTS OF DIFFERENCE

Section 1

Participants took part in a driving simulation where a number of hazards were presented such as a child running across the road. Reaction times were recorded when participants were sober and on another instance when they had consumed enough alcohol to be over the legal drink drive limit.

a. Identify a suitable statistical test. (1 mark)

b. Justify your choice of test. (3 marks)

c. State the non-directional hypothesis. (2 marks)

Which answers are better? Why?

Candidate 1.

a. The psychologist could use a related t-test to investigate the reaction times for alcohol and non-alcohol conditions.

b. The reason for using this test is that data are related, the psychologist is looking for a difference and the data are above an ordinal level of measurement.

c. Reaction time is faster when participants are sober than when they are over the drink drive limit.

Candidate 2.

a. Related t-test.

b. Looking for a difference between drunk and sober reaction times. The data are related as participants take part in both conditions. Reaction times are an interval level of measurement.

c. There is a difference between reaction times to driving hazards when participants are sober compared to when they are under the influence of alcohol.

Section 2

Participants either read newspapers for a week or watched televised news programmes, covering the same news stories as the newspapers. At the end of the week participants were given a current affairs test to determine whether reading or watching the news lead to greater retention of knowledge.

a. Identify a suitable statistical test. (1 mark)

_____

b. Justify your choice of test. (3 marks)

_____

_____

_____

_____

_____

c. State the directional hypothesis. (2 marks)

_____

_____

_____

▶ Lesson notes p.17

TESTING CORRELATIONS

Developmental psychologists are interested in the effects of institutionalisation on children's development. A team of researchers studied 27 children who had been placed in an institution from birth before being adopted. For each child, the length of time spent in the institute (measured by months) was correlated with their score on the 11 plus exam (an intelligence test commonly used by grammar schools).

a. Identify the statistical test used to analyse the data. (1 mark)

_____

_____

b. Justify your choice of test. (3 marks)

_____

_____

_____

_____

c. Write a suitable directional hypothesis. (2 marks)

_____

_____

_____

d. Sketch a graph to represent expected data if the directional hypothesis were to be accepted. (3 marks)

	One tailed test	
	0.05	0.01
	Two tailed test	
df = N-2	0.10	0.02
19	.369	.433
20	.360	.423
25	.323	.381
30	.296	.349

e. The test value calculated was −.127. Significance level was set at $p \leq 0.05$. Identify the critical value (1 mark) and explain whether the directional hypothesis was accepted or rejected. (1 mark)

_____

_____

_____

_____

▶ Lesson notes p.18

CHI-SQUARED TEST

Use your knowledge of the Chi-Squared test to answer the following questions.

Psychologists conducted research into how parents and their children viewed childrens' bedtime. Parents and their children aged 10 were asked a number of simple questions to identify whether they felt a strict bedtime should be enforced for children, with responses being categorised into YES: a strict bedtime is needed and NO: a strict bedtime is not needed.

Explain why researchers chose a Chi-Squared test to analyse the data collected.

_____

_____

_____

_____

_____

	Female	Male	Totals
Pets increase stress		11	14
Pets reduce stress	16		23
Totals		18	

Work out data for the shaded cells.

Write a directional hypothesis for this study.

_____

_____

_____

_____

Extension: What percentage of men reported pets reduced their stress levels? Show your workings out. _____

Participants completed a questionnaire regarding belief in luck and gambling behaviour. Researchers hypothesised that there will be a difference in frequency of lottery play between those who believe in luck and those who do not.

The following data were recorded:

	Reported believing in luck	Reported not believing in luck	Totals
Played lottery every week	10	0	10
Played lottery once/twice a month	7	5	12
Never played lottery	1	13	14
Totals	18	18	36

Using the Chi-Squared test the test value $X^2 = 20.647$ was calculated. For a probability of $p \le 0,05$ can researchers accept the non-directional hypothesis? Explain why.

_____

_____

One tailed	0.10	0.05	0.025
Two tailed	0.20	0.10	0.05
df = 1	1.64	2.71	3.84
df = 2	3.22	4.60	5.99
df = 3	4.64	6.25	7.82
df = 4	5.99	7.78	9.49

▶ Lesson notes p.18

REPORTING INVESTIGATIONS

Highlight which section of the report each item shown below should be mentioned in.

| Abstract | Introduction | Method | Results | Discussion | References |

Full details of any journal articles or books that are mentioned in the report.

A 150–200 word summary of the whole investigation.

Ethical issues and how they will be dealt with are explained.

Researcher/s explain/s the origins of the current research study.

Data presented in tables and/or graphs.

Details of descriptive statistics (measures of central tendency and dispersion).

Summary of results and brief explanation of what they show.

Information about the sample and sampling technique are given.

Results from the study are discussed in reference to previous research in the area.

All apparatus/materials are described and procedure is reported in full detail.

Suggestions for future research are given.

If using qualitative data, categories and themes with examples are provided.

Methodological choices such as research design and method of investigation are justified.

A review of previous research is provided.

The methodology is evaluated and suggestions for improvements given.

Inferential statistics identified, calculated values and significance level reported.

▶ Lesson notes p.19

Gender and alpha bias

A student made notes on alpha bias in preparation for their paper 3 exam. Read their revision passage carefully then decide which sections can be used to address the exam questions shown below.

Treating or representing men and women differently based on stereotypes rather than actual differences is known as gender bias. This distorts the view of what behaviours we might see as typical and atypical for each gender. Alpha and beta bias refer to the different ways in which theories might be biased. Alpha bias occurs when theories exaggerate the differences between the genders which can lead to one gender being devalued in comparison to the other. This differs from beta bias which is the tendency to diminish gender differences by ignoring questions about the lives of one gender,
usually women, or assuming what is true for men also applies to women.

An example of alpha bias can be seen in Freud's psychoanalytic theory. Freud theorised that because women cannot undergo the same Oedipus conflict as men, their superego, which develops from this conflict, is inferior to men's. For Freud, resolving the Oedipus conflict involves the child identifying with their parent of the same sex. He claims, women form a weaker identification with their mothers compared to men's connection to their fathers and so are less moral than men.

Possible exam questions.

a) Explain what is meant by the term gender bias in psychology. (2 marks)   ☐ key colour

b) Explain the difference between alpha and beta bias. (4 marks)   ☐ key colour

c) Outline an example of alpha bias in psychological research. (3 marks)   ☐ key colour

Extension task.
When creating their revision notes the student failed to include a comment on androcentrism.
How would you explain this term and the effect it has on psychological research?

▶ Lesson notes p.20

Gender and beta bias

Basic definition: A tendency to ignore or minimise differences between men and women.

Beta bias can occur though ignoring questions about the lives of women.

Beta bias can occur by assuming that insights derived from studies of men will apply equally well to women.

Martha Mednick (1978) outlined four areas in which she felt women are neglected in psychology:

- issues of power in women's lives
- research into the life cycle of women
- interpersonal issues women face in their life
- the study of women of colour.

She also felt psychology should examine sex roles and the change in sex roles, with a focus on cross cultural perspectives. She further proposed that male psychologists should begin studying their own sexism and misogyny.

In 1984 Carolyn R. Payton was awarded the American Psychological Association's Award for public services. She took this opportunity to criticise the APA for its reluctance to comment on social issues affecting women and different ethnicities. She called for these neglected social groups to be represented in all areas of the APA to ensure issues in the lives of these people received adequate attention and consideration.

Androcenticism can result in people assuming that what is true for men is also true for women. This can minimise gender differences and lead to the needs of one gender (often women) being ignored.

Examples of this include . . .

Cultural bias crossword

Across

2. _____ (4) is the term used to describe the belief that perceptions, behaviours etc. are shared by all cultural groups.

5. _____ (4) bias occurs when theories ignore or minimise cultural differences.

6. Smith & Bond's (1998) review of textbooks found only _____ (3) percent of studies were from countries outside of America and Europe.

7. _____ (12) is a movement that disputes the view that European values are unviersal, arguing that theories should reflect that all black people have their roots in Africa.

8. Takano & Osaka (1999) review concluded the individualism - _____ (12) dimension may be an example of alpha bias.

9. The term _____ (10) is used to explain psychologies that result in the development of different groups of theories in different countries.

11. Approaches that emphasise the uniqueness of every culture are called _____ (4).

12. Culture consists of rules, customs, _____ (6) that bind individuals together to form a society.

Down

1. Evaluating other groups of people using the standards and customs of one's own culture is referred to as _____ (13).

3. Tests such as the IQ test used by Western psychologists which are then used with other groups are described as an _____ (7) etic.

4. The view that behaviour cannot by judged properly unless it is viewed in the context of the culture in which it originates is know as cultural _____ (10).

10. _____ (5) bias occurs when theoreis assume there are real and last differences between cultures.

▶ Lesson notes p.21

Cultural bias commentary

Students were asked to 'Discuss cultural bias in psychology' (16 marks). Read the three paragraphs taken from different students' responses to this question. For each extract record how you feel about their evaluative comment. Make sure you can explain the judgements you made about each paragraph.

Candidate 1.

One example of this is the use of the IQ test by the American army in WWI. White Americans scored highly but African-Americans performed poorly. This contributed to negative stereotyping of this ethnic group.

Commentary

Candidate 2.

One approach to counter ethnocentrism is to take an emic approach to research. For example, Afrocentrism emphasises the uniqueness of the African culture arguing that as all black people have their roots in Africa, the theories should express African values. Assuming European values apply equally to all produces explanations that are irrelevant to those of African descent and may even devalue non-European people.

Commentary

Candidate 3.

A researcher's choice of sample can inadvertently lead to cultural bias. Sears (1986) reported that 82% of studies drew samples from undergraduate populations with 51% studying psychology. This means findings are unrepresentative not only globally but also within Western culture.

Commentary

▶ Lesson notes p.21

Free will and determinism sound bites

Students can sometimes oversimplify their exam responses meaning that while they are accurate they lack the detail required to access the higher levels of the mark scheme. Expand each sound bite to produce an effective commentary of the free will / determinism debate.

The importance of emphasising determinism …	The importance of emphasising free will …
Scientific research seeks causal relationships with the aim of predicting future behaviour.	Only when an individual takes responsibility for their actions is personal growth possible.
Issues concerning the concept of determinism.	**Issues concerning the concept of free will.**
Science now accepts there is no such thing as total determinism.	Recordings of brain activity suggest seemingly conscious decisions are predetermined.
Determinism can over simplify complex behaviours.	The concept of free will may only be relevant to individualist societies.

► Lesson notes p.22

Table mat – Nature versus Nurture

Nature (heredity):

Nature influence 1:	Explanation:	Evidence/ example:	Nature influence 2:	Explanation:	Evidence/ example:

Nurture (environment):

Nurture influence 1:	Explanation:	Evidence/ example:	Nurture influence 2:	Explanation:	Evidence/ example:

▶ Lesson notes p.23

Table mat – Nature versus Nurture

The closer two individuals are genetically, the more likely that both of them will develop the same behaviours.
Genetic
A child may have the biological urge to occasionally act aggressively but the way they express that anger may be imitated as a result of the observation of models.
A behaviour or characteristic that promotes survival and reproduction will be naturally selected and passed on to future generations.
Assumes that all behaviour can be explained in terms of experience using the principles of classical and operant conditioning.
Evolutionary
For example, the concordance rate for a mental disorder such as schizophrenia is 40% for MZ twins (identical genes) and 7% for DZ twins (share 50% of their genes).
Social learning
Attachment could be explained by infants associating their mothers with food.
Behaviour is acquired through direct learning and indirect learning (vicarious reinforcement).
Behaviourism
Bowlby's attachment theory suggests that attachment is adaptive because it meant an infant was more likely to be protected.

▶ Lesson notes p.23

Interactionist approach
(Nature vs Nuture revisited)

At one time nature and nurture were seen as largely independent factors. However, for many years now no one has supported this view. It is accepted that the two processes do not just interact but are impossible to separate. Pick a characteristic/talent/skills of your own, (e.g. ability to play the piano) and consider how you might explain that skill in the context of the interactions below.

Nature affects nurture

Your examples:

Reactive influence

Genetic factors create an infant's microenvironment. The predisposition for a particular skill/behaviour has an influence on how people react to the infant.

Reactive influence example

A child who is genetically more aggressive might provoke aggression in others in their environment.

Passive influence

Parents' genes are passed onto the infant. Those same parents' genes also have an influence on the infant's environment.

Passive influence example

A child may inherit a genetic vulnerability for depression which is triggered by an unsettled/sad home environment due to the parent's depression.

Active influence

As children grow older they seek out experiences and environments that suit their genes.

Active influence example

A child genetically suited to playing musical instruments is more likely to ask to play more instruments and join bands/orchestras etc.

Nurture affects nature

Your examples:

Neural plasticity

Life experiences shape biology. Increased use of a neural pathway strengthens the neural connections in that pathway.

Neural plasticity example

Maguire et al. showed that the region associated with spatial memory in London taxi drivers was larger than in controls.

▶ Lesson notes p.23

Exploring experimental reductionism

It could be argued that the use of the experimental reductionism is extremely useful in the study of (1). This is because the experimental method is able to isolate individual variables and observe their effect on behaviour. For example, in (2) study, the independent variable of (3) is manipulated in order to see the effect on (4). As such, a clear cause and effect relationship was found between (3) and (4) because (5). This amount of control in the procedure allows psychologists to reduce complex situations in order to identify individual factors such as (3) that determine outcomes such as (4).

However, the counter argument to this is that the experimental reductionism used to productively study areas such as (1) means that the results do not actually reflect real behaviour in the real world. The operationalisation of variables such as (3/4) may result in something measurable and quantifiable but may not actually bear resemblance to the real thing. For example, in (2) study, the procedure is so controlled that the results may ignore important factors not taken into account such as (6). As such, it could be argued that experimental reductionism produces findings that are not actually useful for explaining behaviour.

TASK 1

The material on experimental reductionism in the grey box could be used in any essay if you add contextual details. You can do this by replacing the numbers with the following information:

1. The topic area, (e.g. eyewitness testimony).
2. The name of the research, (e.g. Loftus and Palmer).
3. The independent variable in the study, (e.g. verbs used in question).
4. The dependent variable in the study, (e.g. witnesses' speed estimation).
5. The results of the study ('smashed' witnesses' estimation of speed by up to 10mph).
6. Factors the study may have neglected to take into account due to the simplicity of the procedure (the fact that the study was meaningless to the witnesses because no real crime took place, the fact that the witnesses were asked to watch a video whereas in a real crime there may have been more distractions).

See if you can fit these examples (from Year 1) into the format given above.

A A relevant study on eyewitness testimony (leading questions or anxiety).

B Peterson and Peterson's research discovered that information in STM was lost after about 18 seconds. They had prevented their participants from using verbal rehearsal to keep the information in STM. Information stays in STM for as long as you like if you use rehearsal to keep it there. Of course that would mean that nothing else would be able to be coded into STM during that time so it isn't a particularly effective technique. This type of rehearsal is also known as maintenance rehearsal, because it maintains items in STM.

C Milgram's famous studies on obedience tested the idea that normal people are capable of evil acts due to blind obedience. In these studies, the 'teacher' (participant) was asked by the scientists' authority figure (the experimenter) to give electric shocks to the learner in the next room (confederate) when he answered questions incorrectly. He found that 66% of the participants administered a lethal 450 volt shock to the learner when instructed to do so by the experimenter. In a variation of this study, the learner and teacher were placed in the same room and obedience levels dropped to 40% suggesting that 'buffers' can increase obedience to authority figures.

▶ Lesson notes p.24

Connect 3 – Idiographic and Nomothetic

| Idiographic approach... | Nomothetic approach... |

Link...

Link...

| Qualitative methods... | Quantitative methods... |

Link...

Link...

| Humanistic approach... | Biological approach... |

▶ Lesson notes p.25

A trauma I'd forgotten…

From *The Times,* 4 April 2000.

Peter Moss was unaware he was a disturbed child – until he took part in research 35 years later. Then his hair fell out . . .

I am very persistent, and usually get what I want – even if I regret it afterwards. This, in about as many words, is what I told Julia Fabricius, the director of the Anna Freud Centre for Analytical Study and Treatment of Children.

What I got from Fabricius that I so badly wanted, and which she gave me against her better judgement, was access to my childhood file — an inch-thick catalogue of 'disruptive and antisocial behaviour, aggression, regression and chronic under-achievement', the result, it would seem, of a transparently disturbed mind.

That I knew such a file existed arose only from a letter that dropped on my doorstep more than two years ago. It was from the Department of Clinical Psychology at University College London, inviting me to participate in a research study at the Anna Freud Centre in Hampstead, North London, to assess 'the psychological and social adjustment, from childhood to adulthood, in a number of people who were referred as children for help with psychological problems'.

So I was a kid with psychological problems? Says who?

A troubled adulthood, certainly. But a troubled childhood, deeply traumatic and riddled with misery it turns out, I simply did not remember. And until the letter arrived I had no idea that I was ever referred for assessment, to say nothing of 'intensive and urgent treatment, individually and within a delinquency group', all those years ago.

For 35 years, since the closing of my file, aged ten, I had lived in blissful ignorance that such an episode ever existed. So deep was it buried — call it denial — that even three years of psychiatric treatment for severe depression in my mid-thirties failed to shed any light on this period of my life. Until that letter.

This was Cold Comfort Farm, and what began, I have to admit, with a frisson of anticipation — for the letter was surely bound to stimulate curiosity in an inquisitive soul like me — wound up unearthing something very nasty indeed in this particular woodshed.

It is only now, two years after a series of often painful interviews — yes, I could have withdrawn at any time, but I was in too deep to pull back — and the unveiling of 'the file', that I can understand why my parents denied me the treatment I so badly needed. They were in denial. What parents want to hear that their child is anything less than perfect, never mind depressed and highly neurotic?

Meeting Fabricius recently, two years after my first meeting with her, and three decades after the official end of my childhood (though the Anna Freud Centre, it would seem, was keen to restart it), revealed little to me, beyond the distinct feeling that some clinical psychologists are as tightly buttoned as the patients they treat.

I was, she advised me, one of 100, perhaps 150, former 'cases' who agreed to take part in the research study. 'I'm not sure of the exact numbers,' she said. 'It isn't strictly my department.'

How, I asked, was I selected? 'It was a random cross-section of those on our files.' And the purpose of the research? 'One purpose is to compare those who were referred, but not treated, with those who actually received treatment. Also, we wanted to speak with siblings of some of those we treated. The overall purpose, of course, is to assess the value of our treatment in the broadest sense.'

What, I mused, did they learn from me? 'I cannot really say,' Fabricius replied. 'As I said, this is not my department. Let me refer you to a colleague who is in overall charge of this particular research.'

I questioned such belated contact with people like me and the possibility — in my case, the actuality — of the subsequent distress such contact might cause. Again, I was referred to a 'higher authority', someone more authoritative even than the director of the centre at which I was both assessed in childhood and 'researched' in adulthood.

Peter Fonagy is the director of research at the Anna Freud Centre. We met at University College London, where he is also

▶ Lesson notes p.26

A trauma I'd forgotten…

director of the sub-department of Clinical Psychology. I jumped in feet first — the letter, the interviews, the flooding back of buried memories. 'And three weeks later,' I revealed, 'I descended into a deep depression and lost all my hair, before winding up back in therapy.'

Dr Fonagy was unmoved. 'There is no scientific evidence,' he claimed, 'of any risks in these research studies. Indeed we are not allowed to take risks in our research. Furthermore, I and my department are answerable to an ethics committee.'

In that case, I replied, I suggest you refer me to your ethics committee. I'm living proof of the risks involved, I'm concrete evidence of the damage that can be done by contacting the highly susceptible. Look at my head, where the hair used to be. Speak to the psychotherapist I saw for nearly six months following my involvement in your attempts to further your own education. The fact is, you guys lifted the lid on something I chose to bury, and I fell in head first.

The doctor was not for turning. 'The recovered memory debate is a major one,' he said. 'There are countless articles and papers that claim such phenomenon does not exist. Most scientists contend that early experiences cannot be forgotten. Furthermore, we have absolutely no evidence that the recollection of childhood experiences can be harmful.'

Surely I'm all the evidence they need? 'Look,' he said. 'I believe you, but most scientists would not.' I could see where Dr Fonagy's priorities lay, and it was clearly with the researchers rather than the researched. Equally clearly, I was now becoming something of an irritant to the good doctor, who claimed that I was the only person his department had heard from with any negative feedback. To Dr Fonagy, this is evidence of success. To me, it is evidence of British reserve, the 'why complain, we just won't come here again' syndrome.

Either way, it's an irrelevance. One person adversely affected is one person too many, surely.

Having cold-called childhood patients out of the blue in their middle years, I asked, might it not be a good idea to round off the research process by inviting them to give their reactions to their involvement, some sort of feedback, a sort of 'how was it for you' letter?

'Absolutely not,' he replied. 'We must protect people's privacy at all costs.'

I see. So it's OK to get people to open a can of worms in the interests of research, but it's not OK to ask them how they feel after peering inside. In other words, don't call us, and we won't call you. The morals of using an unsuspecting, and often vulnerable, public in research studies — particularly where mental health is concerned — are at best questionable, and need to come under the closest possible scrutiny.

My own participation left me with scars both emotional and physical, some of which I still bear. I am none too pleased, either, to be told that my reaction flies in the face of perceived scientific wisdom, as though I could not possibly have suffered such distress as I am claiming. And to add insult to injury, the research study cannot even be completed owing to 'lack of funding'. Is it the same lack of funding, I wonder, that necessitates a child waiting until middle age before being 'followed up' — and then only for research purposes?

Research is all well and good. But is it, in so far as it uses an obviously impressionable public, so vital that it is worth the risk of waking the slumbering giant of depression in some of the patients? 'Frankly,' said Dr Fonagy, 'we were not aware of any risks.'

Mental health remains a fudged issue in Britain. Even the mental health charity MIND, which I contacted some while ago for an exchange of views on the matter, has failed to respond, despite my spelling out the debilitating effects of my involvement in the research. Lack of funding, I wonder, or lack of concern? Either way, at least it has a certain consistency at the time when the words 'care in the community' have rarely had a more hollow ring.

'Your case will be referred to the ethics committee,' Dr Fonagy assured me. 'Who knows, it may even prompt an overhaul of the nature of our research. Do you mind if they contact you?'

I'm still waiting.

▶ Lesson notes p.26

6 key points – 25 words

Essays are typically worth 16 marks each. Of the 16 marks available for an essay question, 6 are assigned to AO1 and 10 to AO3. Assuming most students would write about 400 words in response to a 16-mark question, that would mean writing about 150 words on AO1; 25 words each for the 6 points.

We've picked 'six key things' you could explain in AO1 for this essay. Try to use around 25 words for each point and ensure that the total words used is around 150 words.

- Darwin's theory of sexual selection can be used to explain mate preference.

- In intrasexual selection…

- In intersexual selection…

- An example of this is the peacock's tail…

- In mating, it pays to be choosy…

- Buss's research suggests sex differences in mate choice.

► Lesson notes p.29

Application skills – Two-sentence technique

Use **Handout 135** to help you complete this application examination-style question.

> In Danny's wedding speech he talked about how much he loves Elena, his new wife: "She is not just my partner, she is my best friend; we share everything and tell each other everything." Danny's best man, John, remarked that "they are made for each other; they are both as attractive as one another!"
>
> Explain, using factors affecting attraction in romantic relationships, why Danny and Elena may have become attracted to each other. *(4 marks)*

KNOWLEDGE	*The matching hypothesis suggests that…*
APPLIED	*In this case…*
KNOWLEDGE	*Self-disclosure…*
APPLIED	*In this example…*

▶ Lesson notes p.30

Filtering Filter theory

**Early stages
of courtship**

**As the relationship
develops**

**Final relationship
assessment**

Sort these key words and phrases into a relevant place on the diagram above: Similarity in attitudes, complementarity of needs, social demography, mutual satisfaction, age/location/background, realistically available, harmonious, basic values, best predictor of stable relationships.

▶ Lesson notes p.30

Feedforward marking

Outline the social exchange theory of romantic relationships. (6 marks)

At the centre of **social exchange theory** (Thibaut and Kelley, 1959) is the assumption that all social behaviour is a series of exchanges – individuals attempt to maximise there rewards and minimise there costs for a 'profit'.

A: *Good simple intro to social exchange theory but needs to be made relevant to relationships. What are the costs/ benefits in relationships?*

B: *Explain why this is the wrong 'there'.*

In order to judge whether one person offers something better or worse than we might expect from another, Thibaut and Kelley proposed that we develop a comparison level (CL) – a standard against which all our relationships are judged. If we judge that the potential profit in a new relationship exceeds our CL, then that relationship will be judged as worthwhile and the other person will be seen as attractive as a partner. Vice versa if the final result is negative, (i.e. the profit is less than our CL).

C: *How is this comparison level for relationships developed?*

Someone who has previously had unpleasant or unsatisfying relationships may well have a very low CL. In contrast, someone who has previously had very rewarding relationships (and therefore a high CL) would have high expectations for the quality of any future relationships.

D: *What are the potential consequences for both? What impact might this have on other relationships?*

E: *Correct this grammatical error.*

Although an individuals' satisfaction with a relationship depends on the assessed profit received from that relationship relative to the comparison level, this is not the only factor that determines the likelihood of them staying in that relationship. A related concept is the comparison level for alternatives (CLA). A new relationship can take the place of the current one if its anticipated profit level is significantly higher.

F: *Explain what this is.*

► Lesson notes p.31

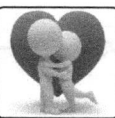

Feedforward marking

Teacher Comments:

> *This is a very good attempt at outlining the social exchange theory and has included all of the key elements. There are occasions when you haven't made the outline directly relevant to relationships. There are other areas where concepts could be explained and/or examples used to illustrate your understanding. Lastly, there are a couple of grammatical errors to look at.*

Improvements/Amendments/Responses:

A:

....

B:

....

C:

....

D:

....

E:

....

F:

► Lesson notes p.31

Q&A: Equity theory dominoes

Answer: Positive correlation	Central assumption of equity theory

Answer: Feelings of anger, sadness and resentment	Equitable relationship

Answer: Where one partner's benefits minus their costs is equal to the other partner's benefits minus their costs	Consequences of over-benefitted relationship

Answer: People are most comfortable when they perceive that they are getting roughly what they deserve from a relationship	Consequences of under-benefitted relationship

Answer: Restoration of actual equity by voluntarily setting things right or by urging partners to do so	Stage of marriage equity at highest

▶ Lesson notes p.31

Q&A: Equity theory dominoes

Answer: According to Schafer and Keith (1980), the honeymoon period and empty-nest stages	**Reason for marital satisfaction dip**

Answer: According to Schafer and Keith (1980), the child-rearing years can lead to a feeling of unfair division of domestic responsibilities	**Method for dealing with inequity**

Answer: Feelings of pity, guilt and shame	**Relationship between inequity and dissatisfaction**

▶ Lesson notes p.31

Investment model: Annotation

SATISFACTION

ALTERNATIVES

INVESTMENT SIZE

COMMITMENT LEVELS

FUTURE STAY OR LEAVE DECISIONS

- *Influenced extent to which other person fulfils individual's needs.*
- *Positive versus negative emotions experienced within relationship.*
- *Likelihood that an involvement will persist.*
- *High in romantic partners who are happy (high satisfaction, low quality of alternatives, high investment).*
- *This is based primarily on commitment levels, which in turn is based on satisfaction, alternatives and investment.*
- *A measure of the resources that would be lost if the relationship ended.*
- *For example, time, energy, friendships, possessions etc.*
- *An individual may persist with a relationship due to lack of options.*
- *Increase the dependency on the relationship and inducement to persist with the relationship.*
- *Extent to which individual's needs might be fulfilled outside relationship.*

▶ Lesson notes p.31

Investment model scale

A short version of the investment model scale-adapted from Rusbult et al. (1998)

1. **My relationship with my partner is much better than others' relationships.**

   0   1   2   3   4   5
   (Do not agree at all)   *(Agree somewhat)*   *(Agree completely)*

2. **I am very happy with my current relationship.**

   0   1   2   3   4   5
   (Do not agree at all)   *(Agree somewhat)*   *(Agree completely)*

3. **My relationship with my partner fulfils my needs for intimacy, companionship etc.**

   0   1   2   3   4   5
   (Do not agree at all)   *(Agree somewhat)*   *(Agree completely)*

4. **My intimacy needs (e.g. talking, sharing secrets) could be met in other relationships.**

   0   1   2   3   4   5
   (Do not agree at all)   *(Agree somewhat)*   *(Agree completely)*

5. **My companionship needs (e.g. enjoying time together) could be met in other relationships.**

   0   1   2   3   4   5
   (Do not agree at all)   *(Agree somewhat)*   *(Agree completely)*

6. **My security needs (e.g. being able to trust, stability in the relationship) could be met in other relationships.**

   0   1   2   3   4   5
   (Do not agree at all)   *(Agree somewhat)*   *(Agree completely)*

▶ Lesson notes p.32

Investment model scale

7. My sense of who I am is linked to my partner and our relationship.

0	1	2	3	4	5
(Do not agree at all)			*(Agree somewhat)*		*(Agree completely)*

8. I have told my partner many secrets about myself.

0	1	2	3	4	5
(Do not agree at all)			*(Agree somewhat)*		*(Agree completely)*

9. I have devoted a great deal of time to our relationship.

0	1	2	3	4	5
(Do not agree at all)			*(Agree somewhat)*		*(Agree completely)*

10. I want my relationship with my partner to last for a very long time.

0	1	2	3	4	5
(Do not agree at all)			*(Agree somewhat)*		*(Agree completely)*

11. It is likely that I will have a relationship with someone else within the next year.

0	1	2	3	4	5
(Do not agree at all)			*(Agree somewhat)*		*(Agree completely)*

12. I will work hard to make sure that my relationship with my partner is strong and secure.

0	1	2	3	4	5
(Do not agree at all)			*(Agree somewhat)*		*(Agree completely)*

▶ Lesson notes p.32

Report: Relationship breakdown

Report

Think of an example of a relationship breakdown which interests you. This could be from something in the news, from a soap, or one of your favourite films.

Using your psychology textbook to help you, write a report on the factors and process of that relationship breakdown.

Your report must include the following:

- Factors which lead to the breakdown (e.g. lack of skills, stimulation, maintenance difficulties).

- Examples to illustrate your points above, (e.g. quotations from interviews, film dialogue etc).

- Psychological evidence that this can lead to relationship breakdown (use studies from a textbook).

- A drawn diagram illustrating the model of the breakdown using Rollie and Duck's (2006) model (see right). Make it specific to your case study.

- Potential intervention techniques that could be (or should have been) used and their rationale.

BREAKDOWN
Dissatisfaction with relationship
Threshold: I can't stand this anymore

INTRAPSYCHIC PROCESSES
Social withdrawal; 'rumination' resentment
Brooding on partner's 'faults' and relational 'costs'
Re-evaluation of alternatives to relationship
Threshold: I'd be justified in withdrawing

DYADIC PROCESSES
Uncertainty, anxiety, hostility, complaints
Discussion of discontents
Talk about 'our relationship'; equity, roles
Reassessment of goals, possibilities, commitments
Threshold: I mean it

SOCIAL PROCESSES
Going public; support seeking from third parties
Denigration of partner, alliance building
Social commitment, outside forces create cohesion
Threshold: It's now inevitable

GRAVE-DRESSING PROCESSES
Tidying up memories; making relational histories
Stories prepared for different audiences
Saving face
Threshold: Time to get a new life

RESURRECTION PROCESSES
Recreating sense of own social value
Defining what to get out of future relationships
Preparation for a different sort of relational future
Reframing of past relational life.
What I learned and how things will be different

► Lesson notes p.32

Reasons why virtual relationships are better!

	Reason	Evidence and/or psychology
1		
2		
3		
4		
5		
6		
7		
8		

▶ Lesson notes p.33

Celebrity attitude scale

1	If I were to meet my favourite celebrity in person, he/she would already somehow know that I am his/her biggest fan.	SA A ? D SD
2	I share with my favourite celebrity a special bond that cannot be described in words.	SA A ? D SD
3	I am obsessed by details of my favourite celebrity's life.	SA A ? D SD
4	I would gladly die in order to save the life of my favourite celebrity.	SA A ? D SD
5	My friends and I like to discuss what my favourite celebrity has done.	SA A ? D SD
6	When something good happens to my favourite celebrity I feel like it has happened to me.	SA A ? D SD
7	My favourite celebrity and I have our own code so we can communicate with each other secretly (such as over the TV car or special words on the radio).	SA A ? D SD
8	One of the main reasons I maintain an interest in my favourite celebrity is that doing so gives me a temporary escape from life's problems.	SA A ? D SD
9	I have pictures and/or souvenirs of my favourite celebrity which I always keep in exactly the same place.	SA A ? D SD
10	If my favourite celebrity endorsed a legal but possibly unsafe drug designed to make someone feel good, I would try it.	SA A ? D SD
11	My favourite celebrity is practically perfect in every way.	SA A ? D SD
12	The success of my favourite celebrity are my successes also.	SA A ? D SD
13	I enjoy watching, reading, or listening to my favourite celebrity because it means a good time.	SA A ? D SD
14	I consider my favourite celebrity to be my soulmate.	SA A ? D SD
15	I have frequent thoughts about my favourite celebrity, even when I don't want to.	SA A ? D SD
16	When my favourite celebrity dies (or died) I will feel (or I felt) like dying too.	SA A ? D SD
17	I love to talk with others who admire my favourite celebrity.	SA A ? D SD
18	When something bad happens to my favourite celebrity I feel like it happened to me.	SA A ? D SD
19	Learning the life story of my favourite celebrity is a lot of fun.	SA A ? D SD
20	My favourite celebrity would immediately come to my rescue if I needed help.	SA A ? D SD
21	I often feel compelled to learn the personal habits of my favourite celebrity.	SA A ? D SD
22	If I were lucky enough to meet my favourite celebrity, and he/she asked me to do something illegal as a favour, I would like to probably do it.	SA A ? D SD
23	It is enjoyable to be with others who like my favourite celebrity.	SA A ? D SD
24	When my favourite celebrity fails or loses at something I feel like a failure myself.	SA A ? D SD
25	If I walk through the door of my favourite celebrity's home without an invitation he/she would be happy to see me.	SA A ? D SD
26	If my favourite celebrity saw me in a restaurant he/she would ask me to sit down and talk.	SA A ? D SD
27	If my favourite celebrity found me sitting in his/her car he/she would be upset.	SA A ? D SD
28	If someone gave me several thousand pounds to do with as I please, I would consider spending it on a personal possession (like a napkin or paper plate) once used by my favourite celebrity.	SA A ? D SD
29	I like watching and hearing about my favourite celebrity when I am in a large group of people.	SA A ? D SD
30	If my favourite celebrity was accused of committing a crime that accusation would have to be false.	SA A ? D SD
31	Keeping up with news about my favourite celebrity is an entertaining pastime.	SA A ? D SD
32	News about my favourite celebrity is a pleasant break from a harsh world.	SA A ? D SD
33	To know my favourite celebrity is to love him/her.	SA A ? D SD
34	It would be great if my favourite celebrity and I were locked in a room for a few days.	SA A ? D SD

▶ Lesson notes p.33

Connect 4

TV personalities

Link...

Parasocial relationships

Link...

Anxious ambivalent attachment

Link...

Secure-base

▶ Lesson notes p.34

Bem Sex-Role Inventory (BSRI)

How are masculine/ feminine/ androgyny/ undifferentiated operationalised?

What method did Bem use to conduct her research?

What is a major issue with this research method, especially for the nature of this research?

What potential threat is there to the external validity of the BSRI?

What is the potential threat to the internal validity of the BSRI and how did Bem attempt to reduce this threat?

How could the internal reliability of this scale be assessed?

How could the external reliability of this scale be assessed?

Bem introduced the concept of psychological **androgyny** in proposing that a person can be both masculine and feminine, an idea that contrasted with the traditional view that masculine *and* feminine behaviours are two separate clusters. She argued that it was actually psychologically more healthy to *avoid* fixed sex-role stereotypes. Instead, men and women should feel free to adopt a variety of masculine- and feminine-type behaviours as suits their personality.

Bem tested her ideas by creating a psychological test to measure androgyny, the Bem Sex Role Inventory (BSRI). This inventory was developed by asking 100 American undergraduates which personality traits they thought were desirable for men or women. The original list of 200 items was narrowed down to 40 (20 masculine and 20 feminine traits), and 20 neutral items were added as distractors.

Each person rates themselves on a 7-point Likert scale ranging from never or almost never true to almost always true. Numerical scores for all masculine items are added up and the same for all feminine items, and then a person is given a score for femininity, masculinity and androgyny. Bem designed the inventory to make it possible to test for masculinity and femininity independently rather than setting them against each other. Individuals were categorised as masculine (high masculine score, low feminine), feminine (low masculine score, high feminine) and androgynous (high ratio of masculine to feminine traits).

A fourth category of undifferentiated (low scores for both masculine and feminine) was added after criticisms by Spence et al. (1975), who pointed out a different kind of androgyny, where a person is neither masculine nor feminine (low in both). This is the undifferentiated type.

Identify and explain one ethical issue in using the BSRI.

Explain how the ethical issue above could be dealt with.

► Lesson notes p.35

Spot the deliberate mistakes

In the following passage about **the role of chromosomes in gender development** there are 11 deliberate mistakes, see if you can spot them and correct them…

Each person has 25 pairs of chromosomes (in each cell of the body). Each of these chromosomes carries hundreds of genes containing instructions about physical and behavioural characteristics such as eye colour and predisposition to certain mental illnesses.

One pair of chromosomes is called the sex chromosomes because they determine an individual's gender. In the case of a male this pair is called XX because both chromosomes are shaped like Xs. The female chromosome pair is described as XY. The Y chromosome carried very little genetic material although it does determine the sex of a child.

There is usually a direct link between an individual's chromosomal sex (XX and XY) and their internal genitalia (vagina or penis) and external genitalia (ovaries or testes). During prenatal development all individuals start out the same – a few weeks after conception both male and female embryos have external genitalia that look essentially masculine. When the foetus is about three months old, if it is to develop as a male, the testes normally produce the male hormone oestrogen which causes male external genitalia to develop.

Genetic transmission explains how individuals acquire their sex. It may also explain some aspects of gender (a person's sense of whether they are male or female) because of the link between genes, genitalia and hormones.

Genes/chromosomes initially determine a person's sex and they also determine which hormones are produced. Most gender development is actually governed by neurotransmitters. The hormone testosterone is produced in greater quantities in males, and the hormones oestocin and oxyrogen are mainly female hormones.

▶ Lesson notes p.36

Hormone quadruplets

1. Called the 'love' hormone as it promotes feelings of bonding.	2. Triggers the development of male genitalia.	3. Berenbaum and Bailey (2003) found that females exposed prenatally to large doses develop more tomboyish behaviour.	4. Produced in the pituitary gland.
5. Shi et al. (2015) found prenatal exposure can lead to smaller brain size.	6. Surge during puberty responsible for secondary sexual characteristics, e.g. facial hair.	7. Surge during puberty responsible for secondary sexual characteristics, e.g. breast development.	8. Important in breast feeding as it causes the milk to flow in a lactating mother.
9. Responsible for directing the menstrual cycle.	10. Causes 'default' female gender to be overridden.	11. Does NOT direct genitalia development prenatally.	12. Dampens the 'fight or flight' response and triggers alternative 'tend and befriend' response in females.

Group A: __ __ __ __   Title of Group:..

Brief Summary:...

....

....

....

....

Group B: __ __ __ __   Title of Group:..

Brief Summary:...

....

....

....

Group C: __ __ __ __   Title of Group:..

Brief Summary:...

....

....

....

► Lesson notes p.37

Gender constancy theory

Kohlberg's (1966) concept of **gender constancy** derives from Piaget's suggestion that young children cannot distinguish between appearance and reality (which is related to **conservation skills**).

Kohlberg's gender constancy theory holds that changes in gender thinking are solely the outcome of changes in a child's cognitive abilities as the child gets older. Children naturally progress from one stage to the next as they mature.

Task: *Illustrate the limitations children have in their gender thinking at each stage using the cartoon grid below. You could use stick people, speech marks and speech bubbles to do this.*

Stage 1: Gender labelling (2–3 years)

Stage 2: Gender stability (4 years)

Stage 3: Gender constancy (6 years)

► Lesson notes p.38

Gender schema theory: AO3 signposts

'AO3 signposts' are essentially the first sentences of every AO3/evaluation paragraph for the following reasons:

- They 'signpost' your evaluation to the examiner, i.e. they make it clear to the examiner that the paragraph they are about to read should be marked as AO3!
- They ensure that evidence is *used* as AO3 rather than just irrelevant description of studies. Sometimes, without the signpost, the paragraph may not gain any marks.
- They help form a 'line of argument' in your essay and show that the evaluation is 'clear, coherent and focused'… a level 4 descriptor.

Add a 'clear, coherent and focused' AO3 signpost below where you see the symbol.

Martin and Little (1990) found that children under the age of four showed no signs of gender stability, let alone signs of constancy (which, according to Kohlberg, appears around the age of six). Despite a lack of constancy, the children did display strong gender stereotypes about what boys and girls were permitted to do. This shows that they have acquired information about gender roles before Kohlberg suggested, in line with GST.

Zosuls et al. (2009) recorded samples of children's language and observed them at play in order to identify when they first started labelling themselves as a boy or girl. They concluded that children were using gender labels by the age of 19 months. However, there is more recent evidence that children show gender-typed preferences even earlier than this, (i.e. before gender identity), which was seen as a challenge to gender schema theory (Bandura and Bussey, 2004).

Martin and Halverson (1983) found that when children were asked to recall pictures of people, children under six recalled more of the gender consistent ones (such as a male firefighter or female teacher) than gender inconsistent ones (such as a male nurse or female chemist). Furthermore, children appear to pay greatest attention to ingroup rather than outgroup schemas. Bradbard et al. (1986) told 4–9-year-olds that certain gender neutral items, (e.g. burglar alarms, pizza cutters) were either boy or girl items. Participants took a greater interest in toys labelled as ingroup, (i.e. a boy was more interested in a toy labelled as a boy's toy).

In Martin and Halverson's study, when children were shown consistent or inconsistent (counter-stereotypical) pictures, they distorted the information. For example, when shown a boy holding a gun (consistent) or a boy holding a doll (inconsistent), children then described what they saw as a girl holding the doll. Such distorted memories search to maintain ingroup schemas and support GST because they show how behaviour can be explained in terms of schema-related behaviour.

Hoffman (1998) reports that children whose mothers work have less stereotyped views of what men do, suggesting that children are not entirely fixed in their views but are receptive to some gender-inconsistent ideas. The fact that gender schemas lead to misremembering or even distorting information has important implications for efforts to reduce gender stereotypes. It means that even when children are exposed to counter-stereotypes they don't remember them accurately. This suggests that the use of counter-stereotypes may not be the best way to reduce children's gender schemas.

▶ Lesson notes p.38

Choose the right word

Freud's theory of personality development (psychoanalysis) includes an explanation of gender development. The theory includes the structure of the personality (id, ego and superego) and defence mechanisms such as repression – these mechanisms are required to protect the **[id / ego / superego]** (the conscious self) from anxiety provoking thoughts. Such thoughts are **[regressed / repressed / displaced]** into the unconscious mind. Freud also described psychosexual stages when the life force (libido) is focused on different body parts. According to Freud, gender development occurs during the third stage – the **[oral / anal / phallic]** stage when a child is between the ages of three and six years. At this time a child's libido is focused on his/her genitals. The child's **[sex / gender]** identity is resolved during this stage either through the Oedipus complex or the Electra complex.

Freud (1905) proposed that, during this genital stage, boys experience the **[Oedipus Complex / Electra Complex]** which has three key components:

1. At the age of **[three or four / nine or ten / seventeen or eighteen]**, a young boy becomes aware of his sexuality and desires his mother, wanting her sole attention.

2. Boys then see their fathers as a rival for their mother's love and, as a result wish their father were dead. This wish creates anxiety and a fear of **[grounding / castration]**. Such fears are repressed.

3. The complex is eventually resolved because the boy begins to **[fight with / identify with / turn away from]** his father. It is through this that a boy *internalises* his father's gender identity and takes this as his own gender identity.

This gender identity leads to masculine behaviour and attitudes.

The **[Oedipus Complex / Electra Complex]** is used to explain why girls develop feminine behaviours. It is concerned with a conflict between a child and same-sex parent because they are competition for the opposite-sex parent. The basic concept is:

1. A young girl is initially **[disgusted by / intrigued by / attracted to]** her mother but this ends when the girl discovers that her mother doesn't have a penis. The girl blames her mother for her own lack of a penis, believing she was castrated, and so as a result she experiences penis envy.

2. The girl's sexual desires are transferred to the **[mother / father / brother / sister]**.

3. The complex is resolved when the girl converts her penis envy to a **[fear of having/ wish to have]** a baby, and this reduces her anger towards her mother. The girl can now identify with her mother and take on gender behaviours.

The end resolution is **[more / less]** satisfactory for girls because their identification with the same-sex parent is less strong – Freud believed there was little reason for anyone to identify with a woman because of her **[higher / lower]** status.

▶ Lesson notes p.38

Social learning: Making it relevant

Bandura (1991) proposed that gender role development is the result of learning from social agents who model and reinforce *1 behaviours.

Children observe the behaviour of others and learn the consequences of the behaviour (vicarious reinforcement). *2. Thus they learn the behaviours (through observation), and they also learn whether and when such behaviours are worth repeating (through vicarious reinforcement) *3. In addition, children are most likely to repeat behaviours of people they identify with. *4.

Information about reinforcements is stored as an expectancy of future outcome. Thus Bandura's theory moved from behaviourism to a kind of cognitive behaviourism because mental representations are involved (he later called his explanation 'social cognitive theory'). When appropriate opportunities arise in the future, children will display behaviours they have observed *provided* that the expectation of reward is greater than the expectation of punishment. This display of such behaviours is called imitation or modelling – but it depends on indirect reinforcement and opportunity.

If a child is rewarded, (i.e. gets what he or she wants or is praised by others) for certain *5 behaviours, they are likely to repeat the same action in similar situations in the future. This direct reinforcement then influences the value or usefulness of that *6 for that child. This direct reinforcement is also vital because a child may see a same-sex individual behaving in a way that is not usual for that gender and being rewarded for it *7. But if the boy tries it himself he may be 'punished' by disparaging remarks, which reduces the likelihood that this behaviour will be repeated.

Children learn through indirect and direct reinforcement but also learn through explicit (direct) instructions about appropriate gender behaviour. Direct tuition begins when children acquire linguistic skills. It serves as a convenient way of informing children about appropriate or inappropriate styles of conduct.

Bandura believes that people are not just shaped by environmental forces but also have the capacity to direct themselves, a process he called *environmental determinism*. This means that once children have internalised *8 behaviours, their own behaviour is no longer dependent on external rewards or punishments. They then direct their own behaviour. This is regarded as a key element of the social learning approach – the active role of children in their observational learning.

*1	
*2	
*3	
*4	
*5	
*6	
*7	
*8	

▶ Lesson notes p.39

Feedforward marking

Evaluate the influence of culture and the media on gender roles. (10 marks)

The evidence for cultural differences shows how culture influences gender roles, but there is contrasting evidence that shows that biology is at least as important. For example, social role theory (Eagly and Wood, 1999) argues that the biologically based physical differences between men and women allow them to perform certain tasks more efficiently.

A: Why? Give an example or two to provide evidence for this point.

Observers from one culture may record behaviours in another culture and 'see' things differently to the indigenous population. Another problem is that indigenous people may tell researchers what they want to hear. In fact this was the criticism Freeman (1984) made of Mead's research, suggesting that the data were not valid. Freeman himself worked with native Samoans who told him that they had created a false picture of their behaviour – but his version has also been criticised for being inaccurate, (e.g. Appell, 1984)!

Mead subsequently changed her conclusion and decided that there were more similarities between males and females than there are differences – though it does not detract from the fact that there are differences.

B: Write a clear AO3/evaluation signpost sentence. Make it clear to the examiner what this paragraph will be about and how it is relevant to the evaluation of the influence of culture on gender roles.

It is difficult to demonstrate the effects of media stereotypes because almost all children watch some television and therefore there are no control groups for comparison.

C: What does this mean? Explain the point.

D: Are there any studies that <u>do</u> have a control group? What does that evidence suggest?

A study that looked at the effects of TV on a community previously without it (Charlton et al., 2000) found no changes in aggressive behaviour and concluded that this was because of pre-existing community values that reduced the effect of exposure to the media.

In general, it seems that the media's effect is simply to reinforce the status quo. For example, Signorelli and Bacue (1999) examined the effects of over 30 years of TV programming and found very little change in gender stereotypes.

E: Why is study on aggression relevant to gender roles? Why might you expect male behaviour to change as a result of the introduction of TV?

There is research that has shown that exposure to non-stereotypical information in the media can change expectations. However, not all research has supported the effectiveness of this approach. Pingree found that pre-adolescent boys displayed *stronger* stereotypes after exposure to the non-traditional models.

F: Why might that be the case?

▶ Lesson notes p.40

Feedforward marking

Teacher Comments:

> *This is a very good answer and with small additions/tweaks it could be superb. All the building blocks are in place for an excellent answer. In places, you need to explain the evaluation in more depth, either by including examples or by making sure that the point being made is clear and obvious. In addition, you need to make sure that the focus is always on the evaluation of the influence of culture/media on gender roles; occasionally this focus is not clear.*

Improvements/Amendments/Responses:

A:

B:

C:

D:

E:

F:

▶ Lesson notes p.40

Atypical gender development crossword

ACROSS

2 The location of the BSTc (bed nucleus of the stria terminalis) which is twice as large in heterosexual men and women compared to transexuals' brains (8).

5 Zucker (2004) suggested that females identify as males because of severe paternal _____ (9) in early childhood.

6 A social explanation which suggests that childhood trauma can lead to mental _____ (7) which leads to gender issues.

8 A psychiatric disorder where a person feels uncomfortable with the gender assigned to them at birth: _____ _____ (6, 8) disorder.

9 BSTc is said to correlate with _____ (9) sex, not biological sex.

DOWN

1 Cross-wiring may mean that some males feel they should not have a penis and some females feel they should have one. Ramanchandran claims that the image of the sex organs is _____ (8) hardwired in the brain in a manner opposite to the person's biological sex.

3 This area of research is difficult to study because it is socially _____ (9), i.e. the outcome of the research may have social consequences.

4 The effect of the 'transexual gene' may be reduced action of the male sex hormone _____ which may under-masculinise the brain in the womb (12).

7 Hare et al. (2009) found that people with gender identity disorder were more likely to have a _____ (6) version of the androgen receptor gene.

10 Name of pesticide that contains oestrogens which may mean males prenatally exposed to high levels develop feminine behaviours (3).

▶ Lesson notes p.42

Applying Piaget's theory

Grace's family have a pet budgerigar named Yorkie. Grace likes to sit next to his cage to watch him flap his wings and crack seed pods with his beak. Grace knows that Yorkie is a bird as he has wings, a beak and feathers. She can now identify other birds who come into her garden and use the bird feeder as they share similar features and behaviours to Yorkie. She calls out 'birdie' whenever she spots one in the garden. One day, Grace's grandparents take her to the zoo. She is fascinated by the penguins but doesn't call out birdie when she seems them. Her granddad explained that they are birds as they also have feathers and a form of wings but that they are suited to the water. The next time they visit the zoo, Grace shouts "birdie" when she sees the penguins.

Use your understanding of Piaget's theory of cognitive development to explain how Grace's thinking has developed. (4 marks)

▶ Lesson notes p.43

Support or refute?

Many psychologists have conducted research into Piaget's theory of cognitive development. Read each study carefully before deciding the extent to which the research findings either support or cast doubt on the theory.

Fantz (1961) found infants as young as four days old spent longer looking at the image that most closely resembled a face than images with jumbled features or shading representing the amount of light and dark seen on the other faces. This suggests infants have an innate preference for faces.

Support ◄─────────────────────────────────────► **Refute**

Explain your judgement.

Bennett (1976) found that, in general, children taught via formal methods performed better in reading, maths and English. This implies that when acquiring these skills, formal methods may be more effective than allowing the child to discover and understanding things for themselves.

Support ◄─────────────────────────────────────► **Refute**

Explain your judgement.

Sinclair-de-Zwart (1969) found non-conservers used absolute terms such as 'big' and single terms for different dimensions, e.g. 'small' used for 'short', 'thin' or 'few'. Children who could conserve showed greater vocabulary, e.g. 'larger'. However, when such words were taught to non-conservers 90% were still unable to conserve.

Support ◄─────────────────────────────────────► **Refute**

Explain your judgement.

► Lesson notes p.44

Sort it out

Piaget proposed intellectual development occurred in stages, with each stage being linked to a specific age. As such, this aspect of Piaget's theory is sometimes referred to as an 'ages and stages' theory. Cut out each strip and arrange the information to reflect the four stages of intellectual development Piaget identified.

Stage 1: 0 to 2 years of age
Stage 2: 2 to 7 years of age
Stage 3: 7 to 11 years of age
Stage 4: 11 years +

Formal operational stage
Sensorimotor stage
Pre-operational stage
Concrete operational stage

Children can now solve abstract problems.
Children acquire the basis of logical reasoning.
Children learn to coordinate sensory input with motor actions.
Due to a lack of logical thinking, children rely on appearance rather than reality.
Children can think like a scientist - developing hypotheses and testing them.
Children cannot identify smaller groups contained in a larger category (class inclusion).
Children can engage in idealistic thinking – they can imagine an ideal world.
Children come to realise that objects out of sight still exist (object permanence).
Egocentric thinking prevents children taking the doll's perspective in the three mountains task.
Conservation is the most important achievement at this stage.
Children are able to use logical thinking to solve conservation tasks.
'Circular reactions' describes the repetition of actions to test sensorimotor relationships.

▶ Lesson notes p.45

Testing intellectual development

Piaget devised a number of tasks to test the intellectual abilities of young children. However, others suggest the design of these experiments may have confused children leading them to appear less capable that they actually are. Use your knowledge of Piaget's tasks and subsequent research to complete this handout.

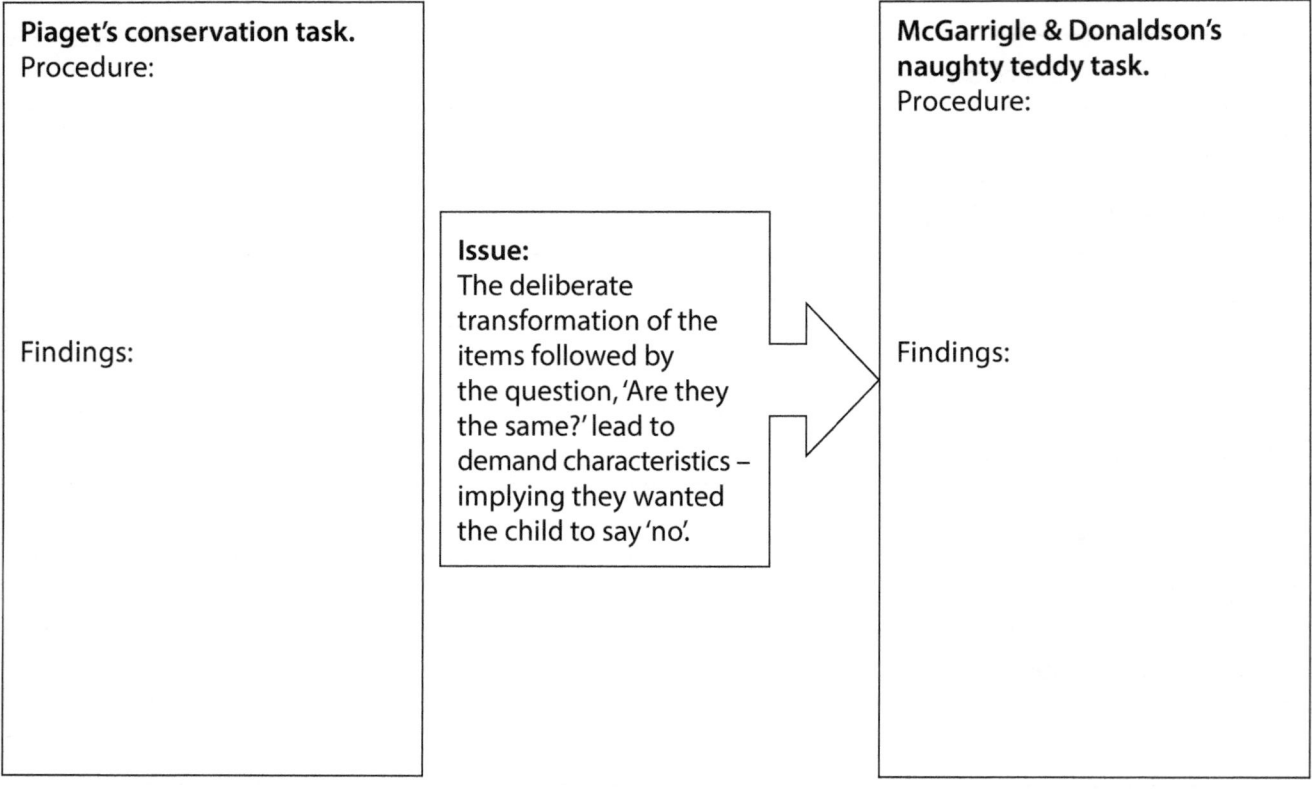

Piaget's conservation task.
Procedure:

Findings:

Issue:
The deliberate transformation of the items followed by the question, 'Are they the same?' lead to demand characteristics – implying they wanted the child to say 'no'.

McGarrigle & Donaldson's naughty teddy task.
Procedure:

Findings:

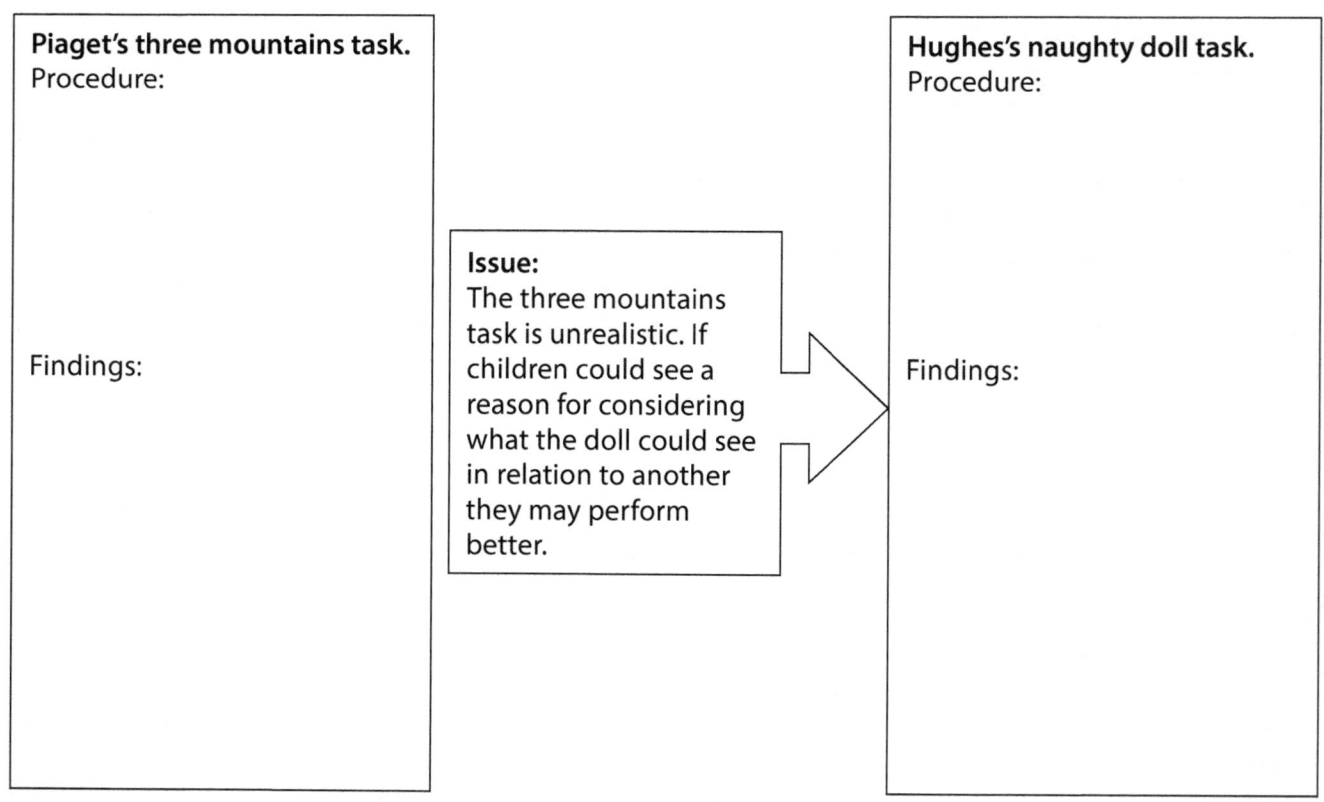

Piaget's three mountains task.
Procedure:

Findings:

Issue:
The three mountains task is unrealistic. If children could see a reason for considering what the doll could see in relation to another they may perform better.

Hughes's naughty doll task.
Procedure:

Findings:

▶ Lesson notes p.45

Explain the image

The role of others: experts

Zone of proximal development

The role of language

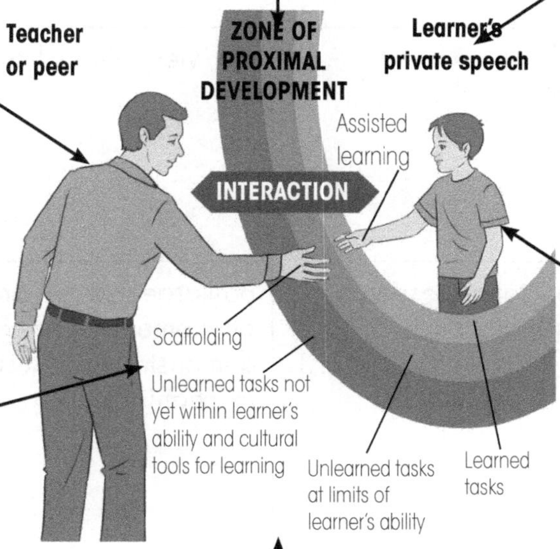

Teacher or peer

ZONE OF PROXIMAL DEVELOPMENT

Learner's private speech

Assisted learning

INTERACTION

Scaffolding

Scaffolding

Unlearned tasks not yet within learner's ability and cultural tools for learning

Unlearned tasks at limits of learner's ability

Learned tasks

Elementary functions

Higher mental functions

The social and individual level

Stretch question:

What similarities and differences can be identified between Vygotsky's and Piaget's theories of cognitive development?

▶ Lesson notes p.46

Baillargeon reading record

Baillargeon was interested in the cognitive abilities of newborns and infants. Her research suggests that very young children are capable of much more than Piaget suggested. Complete the sections below to create a record of Baillargeon's research in relation to Piaget's view of cognitive development.

Baillargeon claims that object permanence develops earlier than proposed by Piaget. Baillargeon suggested that the reason object permanence was not demonstrated by infants was because they cannot plan and execute the motor skills needed to search for objects hidden out of sight.	Baillargeon believes infants are born with innate mechanisms such as a primary reasoning system (PRS) to help the infant interpret and learn from experience.
Baillargeon's argument was that object permanence is not demonstrated earlier because...	Her view differs from Piaget's theory because...
Baillargeon's violation of expectation research demonstrated infant's object permanence abilities...	Baillargeon's research into the unveiling phenomenon (the covering principle) demonstrates the use of innate learning mechanisms...

Baillargeon applied the concept to innate learning mechanisms to an infant's understanding of the psychological world.
Song and Baillargeon (2008) used the violation of expectation methodology to test false beliefs in infants...

Violation of expectation

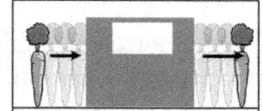

Baillargeon and DeVos (1991) designed a research methodology based on the principle that an infant would show surprise when they see an unexpected event.

Procedure. Infants saw a row of carrots passing along a track. At one point the carrots pass behind a screen with a large window cut out. Small carrots would pass below the window so no carrot tops could be seen (expected event). In contrast, carrot tops should show in the window as the large carrots pass by, however, the carrot tops do not appear (unexpected event).

Findings. Infants as young as three months old showed surprise when observing the unexpected event. They looked longer at the large carrots, presumably because they had object permanence and so expected the carrot tops to be visible in the screen's window – they understood the principle of occlusion (the view of the carrots was obstructed by the screen).

Consider the following controls the researchers used when carrying out their procedure. Can you explain why each one was implemented?

Control	Reason for implementation
Birth announcements in the local newspaper were used to gather participants.	
During the procedure parents were instructed to keep their eyes closed and not interact with their child who was sitting on their parent's lap.	
A double blind design was employed. Two observers, who did not know whether the infant was observing an expected or unexpected event, noted the level of interest infants showed.	

► Lesson notes p.47

Who said what and why?

Selman gave children a series of dilemmas to explore their reasoning skills when facing problems that required them to consider different people's perspectives. Use your knowledge of Selman's findings to match the responses shown below to the stage (rectangular box) and reasoning (dashed boxes) at that age. Why not use different colours for the boxes?

> Holly is an eight-year-old girl who likes to climb trees. She is the best tree climber in the neighbourhood. One day while climbing a tree, she falls off the bottom branch but does not hurt herself. Her father sees her fall, and he is upset. He asks her to promise not to climb trees any more, and Holly promises.
>
> Later that day, Holly and her friends meet Sean. Sean's kitten is caught up a tree and cannot get down. Something has to be done right away or the kitten may fall. Holly is the only one who climbs trees well enough to reach the kitten and get it down, but she remembers her promise to her father.
>
> (Selman, 1976)

Holly's dad would be mad but when she shows him the kitten he will change his mind.

Holly's father will understand why she saved the kitten and so he will not be angry with her.

Holly's dad will not be angry because Holly will feel Ok about climbing the tree. He will feel the same as Holly.

Holly's dad will understand that taking care of animals is more important and so will not be angry with her for breaking her promise and climbing the tree.

Holly will not be in trouble with her dad because he can understand why Holly broke her promise on this occasion and she understands why he made her promise originally.

Stage 0. Undifferentiated perspective taking. Age 3–6 years.	Stage 1. Social-informational perspective taking. Age 6–8 years.	Stage 2. Self-reflective perspective taking. Age 8–10 years.	Stage 3. Mutual perspective taking. Age 10–12 years.	Stage 4. Societal perspective taking. Age 12–15+ years.

Personal decisions are now made with reference to social conventions.

Children can distinguish between self and others but are largely influenced by their own perspective.

Children can now view their own thoughts and feeling from someone else's perspective and understand that others can do the same.

Children are aware of perspectives that are different to their own but assume this is because others have different information.

Children can step outside a two-person situation and imagine how the self and others are viewed from a third, impartial party. They can also consider two points of view simultaneously.

▶ Lesson notes p.47

Theory of mind exam answers

> Briefly outline theory of mind as an explanation for autism. (2 marks)

Selina's answer.
People with autism find it difficult to understand the mental states of other people and to predict and adjust to the behaviour of others. This is because autism is the result of 'mindblindness' the term used to explain the absence of a theory of mind.

Alan's answer.
Simon Baron-Cohen was interested in the concept of theory of mind as an explanation for the childhood disorder of autism. Autistic individuals find social interaction difficult and this can lead to social isolation if other people do not understand the condition.

> Explain **two** limitations of theory of mind as an explanation for autism. (6 marks)

Selina's answer.
Baron-Cohen et al.'s eyes-task may not have been measuring theory of mind. In the eyes task adults with and without autism were shown pictures of people's eyes and asked to identify the emotion represented from two options, for example attraction/ repulsion or interested/disinterested. Baron-Cohen et al. found that autistic adults had a mean score of 16.3 which was lower than the mean score of adults without autism (20.3 – out of a maximum of 25). Baron-Cohen claimed this test measured mindreading. However, some critics argue this mindreading may not be the same as theory of mind in everyday life. Therefore, the eyes-task has low internal validity as it does not ability to understand how others experience the world.

Alan's answer.
It is difficult to identify a causal relationship between lack of theory of mind and autism. For example, abnormal language development and lack of social skills may prevent children communicating and engaging with others. Therefore, a lack of appropriate experiences prevent theory of mind being acquired rather than a lack of theory of mind causing poor social interaction.

A second limitation is that if a lack of theory of mind was a central aspect of autism then we would expect all autistic children to show an inability to see the world from another person's perspective. However, research only shows that some individuals lack this ability while other autistic participants demonstrate a theory of mind.

Mark scheme for 6 mark question in Handout 71:

Level	Marks	Description
3	5–6	Two limitations are explained in a clear and effective manner. The answer is coherent and well organised. Specialist terminology is used effectively.
2	3–4	Two limitations are given, but one or both may lack explanation. The majority of the answer is clear and organised with appropriate use of specialist terminology. **OR**, one limitation is given at top of level 3.
1	1–2	At least one limitation is given but explanation lacks detail, is vague or muddled. Specialist terminology is used inappropriately or is absent. **OR**, one limitation is explained at the top of level 2.

▶ Lesson notes p.48

If this is the answer...
...what is the question?

A mirror neuron encodes the activity of another individual as if the observer were acting out the same activity. This can explain how, at the most basic level, humans and animals are able to imitate others.

Recordings of the neural activity in the motor cortex of macaque monkeys revealed that certain neurons in the F5 area of the premotor cortex became active when the monkey was inactive but watching another (monkey or researcher) perform an action. The same neurons became active when the monkey imitated the action.

1. It is important in the acquisition of skilled behaviours. Through copying the actions of others we are developing our range of behaviours.

2. It is the beginning of the development of social cognition.

Usually, watching another's actions does not lead to automatic imitation of that action. The mirror neuron response is said to be generally 'off-line' as the observer is inactive at the time of exposure.

If a person did copy the behaviour they observe simultaneously to it being performed by another, we would refer to this as 'on-line' as the person is active.

Mirror neurons in the interior frontal cortex are most active when performing this task.

Mirror neurons may be seen as the mechanism by which we are able to take the perspective of others as they enable us to experience someone else's actions as our own.

Another aspect of social development that may rely on mirror neurons is that of language acquisition. For example, the imitation of speech sounds when learning to talk. Furthermore, mirror neurons have been identified in Broca's area, an area involved in speech production.

The complexity of human social behaviour suggests mirror neurons are especially developed in humans compared to other animals. The heightened development of mirror neurons have enabled us to excel at social relationships, more so than any other species.

▶ Lesson notes p.49

Develop the detail

The level 4 mark scheme for 16-mark questions states evaluations should be, 'thorough and effective' with, 'minor detail and/or expansion of argument sometimes lacking'. The following extract from a student's essay shows the AO3 content only. Read the essay and match each paragraph to a relevant development comment on the right to improve the evaluative content.

Discuss the role of the mirror neuron system in social cognition. (16 marks)

...In support of the concept of a mirror neuron system research is now beginning to provide evidence of individual neurons involved when observing and performing tasks. Mukamel et al. (2010) found recordings of neural activity in 21 epileptic patients showed certain neurons were active during task performance and task observation. These neurons were found in expected (premotor cortex) and unexpected (medial temporal cortex) areas of the brain.

Hickok (2009) suggests that research into the role of mirror neurons should not be solely focused on seeking patterns of increased neuronal activity when observing actions. For example, research into patients with damage to areas in the brain know to contain mirror neurons should reveal deficits in performance.

Mirror neurons are implicated in the ability to understand another individual's feelings (known as social sensitivity). It is often reported that females are more socially sensitive than males and so we would expect to see a gender difference in mirror neuron activity.

While critics of research into the role of mirror neurons accept they exist they are more cautious when considering the importance of the mirror neuron system in social cognition with some arguing mirror neurons are the result of experience rather than an innate as Ramachandran suggested.

A

For example, when watching a moving dot (an action that does not involve social sensitivity) EEG activity was the same for both genders. However, when watching hand actions female participants showed a significantly stronger response.

B

Researchers also recorded neurons with *anti-mirror* properties. Anti-mirror neurons are inhibited when the individual observes actions but respond when the action is performed. These neurons have an important role - allowing us to think about the actions of another person without actually performing the action ourselves.

C

Research has shown that disruption of mirror neuron areas does indeed result in deficits. Tranel et al. (2003) found damage to the left premotor area resulted in patients being able to identify pictures of motor actions but being unable to access words for the actions.

D

Heyes (2009) suggests mirror neurons are the result of experience. She explains that neurons become paired when they are excited the same time or when one regularly precedes the other. Therefore, mirror neurons are the outcome of associative learning (classical conditioning) not an evolutionary adaptation.

▶ Lesson notes p.49

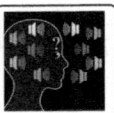

Matching clinical key terms

Delusions	For a significant portion of the time since the onset of the disturbance, one or more major areas of functioning such as work, interpersonal relations, or self-care are markedly below the level achieved prior to the onset.
Disorganised thinking	The reduction of, or inability and persistance in goal-directed behaviour (for example, sitting in the house for hours every day, doing nothing).
Affective flattening	These are unreal perceptions of the environment that are usually auditory, (e.g. hearing voices) but may also be visual (see lights, objects or faces), olfactory (smelling things) or tactile, (e.g. feeling that bugs are crawling on or under the skin).
Alogia (poverty of speech)	This refers to bizarre and abnormal motor movements. For example, holding the body in a rigid stance, moving in a frenzied way, peculiar facial movements, copying movements of others.
Social/ Occupational dysfunction	Bizarre beliefs that seem real to the person with schizophrenia, but they are not real. Sometimes these beliefs can be paranoid, (i.e. persecutory) and sometimes involves themselves, e.g. inflated belief about their own importance.
Avolition	This is characterised by the lessening of speech fluency and productivity; this is thought to reflect slowing or blocked thoughts.
Hallucinations	A reduction in the range and intensity of emotional expression, including facial expression, voice tone, eye contact, and body language.
Catatonic behaviour	The feeling that thoughts have been inserted or withdrawn from the mind. In some cases the person may believe their thoughts are being broadcast so that others can hear them.
Anhedonia	A loss of interest or pleasure in almost all activities, or lack of reactivity to normally pleasurable stimuli.

Tasks:

- Match the schizophrenic clinical key terms to the definitions on the right.
- Highlight which of the characteristics you think are positive symptoms of schizophrenia in one colour, and the negative symptoms in a different colour.

▶ Lesson notes p.50

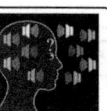

It's not as clear-cut as you think...

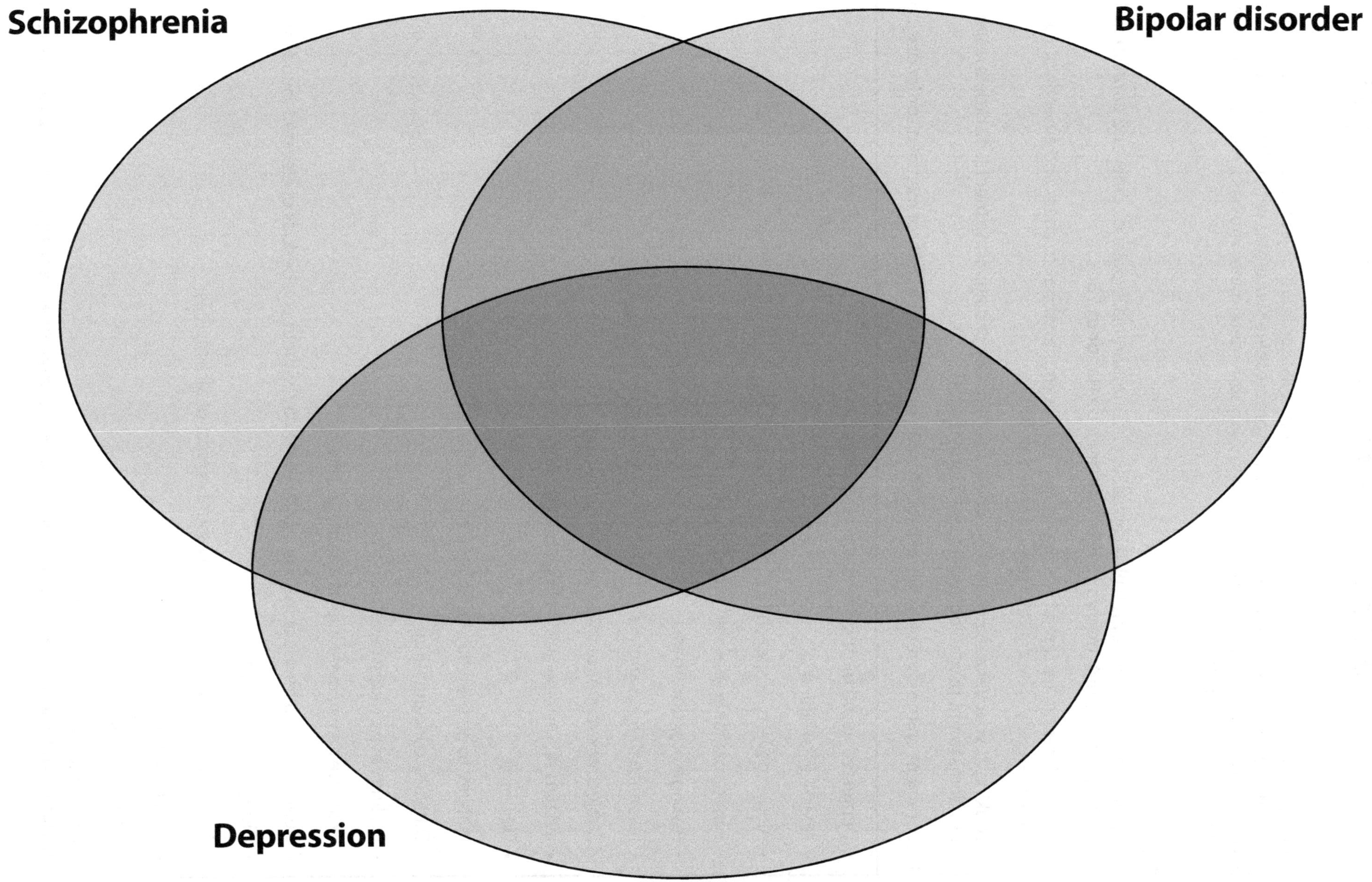

Bipolar disorder

Schizophrenia

Depression

▶ Lesson notes p.51

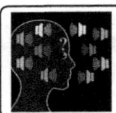

It's not as clear-cut as you think...

There is a tendency to think that the diagnosis of mental disorders is objective, clear-cut and relatively simple. However, this is far from the case. Many disorders share symptoms with other disorders which makes it very difficult for psychiatrists and psychologists to determine who has a mental disorder and which mental disorder they have.

Tasks:

1. Below is a list of symptoms which can occur in schizophrenia, bipolar disorder and depression. Write each of these symptoms into the Venn diagram on **Handout 75**.

2. Use the internet (be careful which sites you use) or your textbook to check and amend your answers. Were there any answers you were surprised about?

3. Looking at your Venn diagram, think about the difficulty of diagnosing mental disorders *reliably*. What problems might psychologists and psychiatrists face?

4. Comment on the issues this Venn diagram might raise for the *validity* of mental disorder diagnosis.

- Depressed mood most of the day, nearly every day

- Affective flattening

- Alogia (poverty of speech)

- Periods of mania (elevated mood)

- Psychomotor disturbances

- Insomnia or hypersomnia

- Subjective experience that thoughts are racing

- Inflated self-esteem and feelings/beliefs of grandiosity

- Delusions

- Inability to do everyday tasks

- Difficulty concentrating

- Feelings of worthlessness

- Excessive involvement in pleasurable activities

- Depressed mood most of the day, nearly every day without any periods of elevated mood (mania)

- Disorganised speech

- Anhedonia – loss of interest or pleasure in most or all activities

- Hallucinations

- Significant weight loss or weight gain

- Recurrent thoughts of suicide

▶ Lesson notes p.51

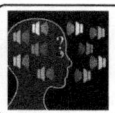

Understanding twin studies

There are two types of twin... (draw stick people versions of them here...)

Twin type: **Twin type:**

    AKA: **AKA:**

  Genes   **Genes**
 shared: **shared:**

Dave is one half of a MZ twin pairing. He suffers from schizophrenia.

Assuming schizophrenia is *completely genetic*, what are the chances of his identical twin Arnold developing the disorder? Explain your answer.

....

....

....

....

....

Arnold does NOT suffer from schizophrenia. Are Dave and Arnold concordant? What is meant by a concordance rate?

....

....

....

....

It is assumed that MZ and DZ twins share 'equally similar environments'. What does this mean?

....

....

....

....

▶ Lesson notes p.52

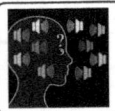

Writing about twin studies

Outline and evaluate one biological explanation for schizophrenia. (8 marks)

AO1. Twin study. Joseph (2004) reported a mean concordance rate of 40.4% for MZ twins and only an 7.4% rate for DZ twins. This suggests ....

....

....

....

This is because (explain MZ/DZ difference + relate to concordance rates, genes and schizophrenia)........

....

....

....

In addition, the difference in concordance rates cannot be explained by the environment because.........

....

....

....

Therefore… (brief conclusion linked to essay)...

....

....

....

▶ Lesson notes p.53

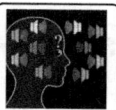

Writing about twin studies

Outline and evaluate one biological explanation for schizophrenia. (8 marks)

AO3. There could be a flaw in the argument that MZ and DZ twins share equally similar environments because... (explain one or two of the reasons, e.g. male/female, how treated)..

....

....

....

....

This is a problem for the conclusions drawn from the study (refer to the difference in concordance rates)..

....

....

....

....

....

Therefore (conclusion, link back to essay)..

....

....

....

....

▶ Lesson notes p.53

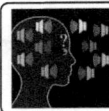

Feedforward marking

Evaluate the family dysfunction explanation of schizophrenia.
(10 marks)

Bateson et al. (1956) suggest that children who frequently receive contradictory messages from their parents are more likely to develop schizophrenia. These interactions prevent the development of an internally coherent construction of reality.

A: Look at the exam question. Why should you NOT include these two paragraphs?

Another family variable associated with schizophrenia is a negative emotional climate or, more generally, a high degree of expressed emotions. It appears that the negative emotional climate in these families arouses the patient and leads to stress beyond his or her already impaired coping mechanisms, thus triggering a schizophrenic episode.

The importance of family relationships in the development of schizophrenia can be seen in an adoption study by Tienari et al. (1994). In this study those adopted children who had schizophrenic biological parents were more likely to become ill themselves than those children with non-schizophrenic biological parents.

B: This evaluation is muddled. It appears to support the genetic explanation NOT the family dysfunction explanation. What did Tienari et al. also find in this study that does suggest family dysfunction is involved?

Berger (1965) found that schizophrenics reported a higher recall of double blind statements by their mothers than non-schizophrenics. However, this evidence may not be reliable as patients' recall may be affected by their schizophrenia.

C: Write a clear AO3/ evaluation signpost sentence. Make it clear to the examiner what this paragraph will be about and how it is an evaluation of the family dysfunction hypothesis.

Liem (1974) measured patterns of parental communication in families with a schizophrenic child and found no difference when compared to normal families. Hall and Levin (1980) analysed data from various previous studies and found no difference between families with and without a schizophrenic member in the degree to which verbal and non-verbal communication were in agreement.

D: Again, this needs a signpost so that it is clear you are evaluating. This is worth no evaluation marks at the moment. Try to link to the previous paragraph as well.

Not all patients who live in high EE families relapse, and not all patients who live in low EE homes avoid relapse. Research has found individual differences in stress response to high EE-like behaviours. Altorfer et al. (1998) found that one quarter of the patients they studied showed no physiological responses to stressful comments from their relatives. Vulnerability to the influences of high EE may also be psychologically based. For example, research by Lebell et al. (1993) suggests that how patients appraise the behaviour of their relatives is important. In cases where high EE behaviours are not perceived as being negative or stressful, they can do well regardless of how the family environment is objectively rated.

E: Not previously mentioned, what is EE?

F: What does this evidence/ paragraph show? Why is the point EE important? Why is EE relevant? Write a brief concluding sentence to summarise the point.

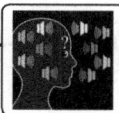

Feedforward marking

Teacher Comments:

> *This answer does need some work in order to achieve a higher level. Ensure that you read the exam question carefully and solely focus on what is required. In some cases you have included relevant material but have not made it clear how/why it is related to the <u>evaluation</u> of the family dysfunction explanation. Your job is to convince the examiner how/why the evidence you have included is relevant. You need to read over Tienari et al.'s study again as you've missed their most important finding in the context of this explanation.*

Improvements/Amendments/Responses:

A:

....

B:

....

C:

....

D:

....

E:

....

F:

....

▶ Lesson notes p.54

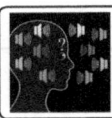

Choose the right word

Drugs that are effective in treating the most disturbing forms of psychotic illness, such as schizophrenia and **[unipolar / bipolar]** depression, are called antipsychotics. All antipsychotics work by **[increasing / maintaining / reducing]** the action of the neurotransmitter dopamine in areas of the brain associated with the symptoms of schizophrenia.

Typical antipsychotics

Typical antipsychotics (such as **[chlorpromazine / clozapine]**) were developed in the 1950s. The basic mechanism of typical antipsychotic drugs is to reduce the **[causes / effects]** of dopamine and so reduce the symptoms of schizophrenia. Typical antipsychotics are dopamine *antagonists* in that they bind to but do not stimulate dopamine receptors (particularly the **[D1 / D2 / D3 / D4]** receptors in the **[mesolimbic / mesocortical]** dopamine pathway), thus blocking their action. By reducing stimulation of the dopamine system in the mesolimbic pathway, antipsychotic drugs eliminate the hallucinations and delusions experienced by people with schizophrenia. Hallucinations and delusions usually diminish within a few **[hours / days / weeks]** of beginning medication, although other symptoms may take several **[days / weeks /months]** before a significant improvement is noted. Kapur et al. (2000) estimate that between 60% and 75% of **[D1 / D2 / D3 / D4]** receptors in the **[mesolimbic / mesocortical]** dopamine pathway must be blocked for these drugs to be effective. Unfortunately, in order to do this, a similar number of **[D1 / D2 / D3 / D4]** receptors in other areas of the brain must also be blocked, leading to undesirable side effects. This problem has been addressed by development of the *atypical* antipsychotic drugs.

Atypical antipsychotics

Atypical antipsychotic were so called because of three main differences to the first-generation typical antipsychotics. They carry a **[lower / higher]** risk of side effects, have a beneficial effect on **[positive / negative /positive and negative]** symptoms and cognitive impairment, and are suitable for treatment-resistant patients. As with the typical antipsychotics, these drugs also act on the dopamine system by blocking **[D1 / D2 / D3 / D4]** receptors. However, they only temporarily occupy the **[D1 / D2 / D3 / D4]** receptors and then rapidly **[associate / dissociate]** to allow normal dopamine transmission. It is this characteristic, (i.e. 'rapid **[association / dissociation]**') of atypical antipsychotics that is thought to be responsible for the **[lower / higher]** levels of side effects found with these drugs compared to conventional antipsychotics. Because atypical antipsychotics have very little effect on the dopamine systems that control **[movement / perception]**, they tend not to cause the **[movement / perception]** problems found with the typical antipsychotics. Atypical antipsychotics have a stronger affinity for **[serotonin / noradrenaline]** receptors (particularly the 5-HT2A receptors) and a lower affinity for **[D1 / D2 / D3 / D4]** receptors. It is this characteristic that explains the different effects of atypical compared to typical antipsychotics.

▶ Lesson notes p.54

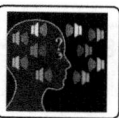

Better in 10: Make CBTp relevant to schizophrenia

The basic assumption of CBTp is that people[*1] often have distorted beliefs, which influence their feelings and behaviours in maladaptive ways[*2]. The aim of CBTp when used in this context is to help people establish links between their thoughts, feelings or actions and their symptoms and general level of functioning.

In CBTp,[*3] patients are encouraged to trace back the origins of their symptoms in order to get a better idea of how they might have developed[*4]. Patients might also be set behavioural assignments so that they might improve their general level of functioning. The learning of maladaptive responses to life's problems is often the result of distorted thinking or mistakes in assessing cause and effect[*5]. CBTp usually proceeds through the following phases:

- **Assessment** – the patient expresses his or her thoughts about their experiences to the therapist. Realistic goals for therapy are discussed[*6], using the patient's current distress as motivation for change.

- **Engagement** – the therapist empathises with the patient's perspective and their feelings of distress, and stresses that explanations for their distress can be developed together.

- **The ABC model** – the patient gives their explanation of the activating events (A) that appear to cause their emotional and behavioural (B) consequences (C). The patient's own beliefs, which are actually the cause of C, can then be rationalised, disputed and changed[*7].

- **Normalisation** – information that many people experience their symptoms helps the patient feel less isolated[*8].

- **Critical collaborative analysis** – the therapist uses gentle questioning to help the patient understand illogical deductions and conclusions[*9].

- **Developing alternative explanations** – the patient develops their own alternative explanations for their previously unhealthy assumptions[*10]. These healthier explanations might have been temporarily weakened by their dysfunctional thinking patterns. If the patient is not forthcoming with alternative explanations, new ideas can be constructed in cooperation with the therapist.

*1	
*2	
*3	
*4	
*5	
*6	
*7	
*8	
*9	
*10	

▶ Lesson notes p.56

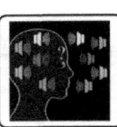

Family therapy: Evaluation elaboration

Your A Level exam essays are marked out of 16 and evaluation will be judged as part of the marking process. Many students miss out on evaluation marks because they do not elaborate their evaluations in sufficient detail to get the full marks. Here are the general marking descriptors for evaluation: (*Level 1 = Evaluation/Discussion is limited*), (*Level 2 = Evaluation/Discussion is partly effective*), (*Level 3 = Evaluation/Discussion is mostly effective*), (*Level 4 = Evaluation is thorough/effective*).

Obviously, the higher the level of evaluation, the more marks you are likely to be awarded. Your task here is to match up the evaluation points for the differential association explanation of family therapy from the left, further and further to the right in order to increase your evaluation marks.

▶ Lesson notes p.57

Level 1 ....

Level 1	Level 2	Level 3	Level 4!
Research evidence suggests that family therapy can be effective in improving clinical outcomes.	Pharoah et al's meta-analysis identified the problem of random allocation. A large number of studies were from China. Evidence has emerged that in many Chinese studies, random allocation had been stated as having been used, yet was not (Wu, 2006).	However, the authors suggest that the main reason for its effectiveness may have less to do with the interventions themselves and more to do with that fact that it increases medication compliance.	The issues with the evidence mean that conclusions on the effectiveness of family therapy are difficult to determine.
There are a number of methodological issues in research into family therapy.	Garety et al. (2008) failed to show any better outcomes for patients given family therapy compared to those that simply had carers.	The extra cost of family therapy is offset by a reduction in costs of hospitalisation because of the lower relapse rates.	However, the researchers also concluded that the methodological quality of the studies was poor, making it difficult to distinguish effective from ineffective interventions in terms of family members.
An advantage of this therapy is the considerable economic benefits.	For example, Pharoah et al. (2010) reviewed 53 studies published and found that patients showed some improvement in social functioning and mental state. Patients were also less likely to relapse.	Individuals in both groups were found to have low relapse rates compared to the no therapy/carer control group. The researchers also found that the carers displayed low rates of expressed emotion.	This suggests that family intervention may not improve outcomes further than a good standard (carers with low expressed emotion) of treatment as usual.
Family therapy has an additional advantage in having a positive impact on family members.	The NICE review of family therapy studies demonstrated that it was associated with significant costs savings when offered to patients *alongside* the standard care.	In some studies, the observers were not 'blinded' to the condition (family therapy or standard care) which increases the possibility of observer bias.	There is also evidence that relapse rates are lower after the completion of the intervention – which suggests that the savings could be even higher.
Some of the evidence questions the worthiness and value of family therapy.	Lobban et al. (2013) analysed the results of 50 family therapy studies than had included an intervention to help relatives.	60% of these studies reported a significant positive impact on at least one outcome category for relatives, e.g. coping, relationship quality, problem-solving skills.	As such, this undermines the evidence. It suggests that the beneficial effects are NOT the result of family therapy itself, but because family therapy means patients are more likely to take their drugs (which are effective).

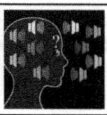

Brief summaries: Token economy

Making notes on the **token economy** in these 'briefs' will force you to summarise the information. Use your textbook, (e.g. page 152 of *Complete Companion*) to help you. Try and include the key words written beneath the 'briefs' in your summaries.

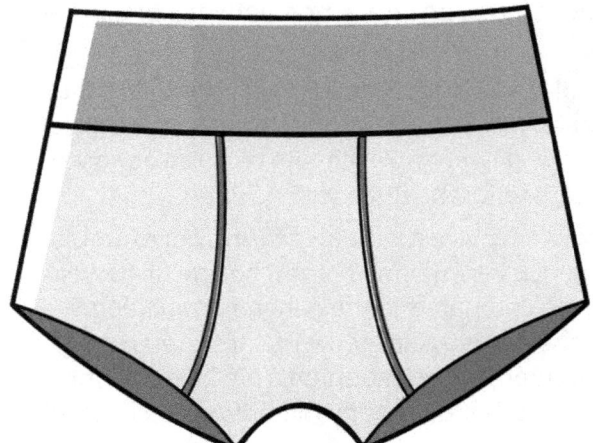

A TOKEN ECONOMY
Behavioural therapy, desirable behaviours, tokens, exchange

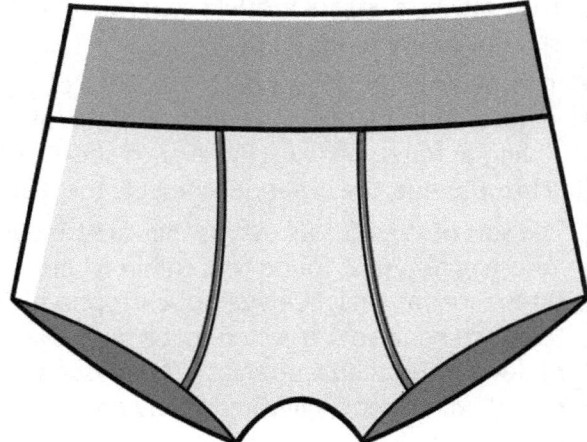

HOW IT WORKS
Operant conditioning, primary reinforcer, secondary reinforcer, immediate

TOKEN VALUES
Repeatedly presented, neutral tokens behaviour, classical conditioning

REINFORCEMENT & TRADE
Exchanged, privileges and rewards, variety of items, frequency

▶ Lesson notes p.58

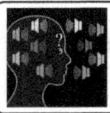

Moving up the levels

Imagine that you have been set the following examination question:

- Outline the diathesis-stress model for explaining schizophrenia. (6 marks)

The answer below is accurate but may not gain full marks because it lacks some detail in places. Use the table below to make *additions* to this answer that take it up to a 'level 4' maximum mark answer.

The **diathesis–stress model** sees schizophrenia as the result of an interaction between biological*[1] and environmental*[2] influences.

In terms of biology, support for the idea of a genetic role for schizophrenia is the finding that the identical twin of a person with schizophrenia is at greater risk of developing schizophrenia than a sibling or fraternal twin. However, in about 50% of identical twins in which one twin is diagnosed with schizophrenia, the other never meets the diagnostic criteria for the disorder.*[3]

The sort of stressful life events that can trigger schizophrenia take a variety of forms. For example, Varese et al. (2012) found that children who experienced severe trauma before the age of 16 were three times as likely to develop schizophrenia in later life compared to the general population*[4]. Research has also suggested that a high level of urbanisation is associated with increased risk of developing schizophrenia*[5]. The reason why urbanisation and schizophrenia are linked is not clear*[6]. Many people live in densely populated urban areas, but only a tiny minority actually develop schizophrenia*[7].

The idea of additivity is that diathesis and stress add together in some way to produce the disorder.*[8]

*1	
*2	
*3	
*4	
*5	
*6	
*7	
*8	

► Lesson notes p.59

Eating past and present

Use your knowledge of evolutionary explanations and experiences of modern society to answer the following questions about food preferences.

How accessible was food for hunter-gatherers in the EEA?

How accessible is food in today's society?

Why was meat an important food source?

How can veganism be explained in today's society?

Why was a preference for sweet tasting food an adaptive advantage?

Why might preference for sweetness be maladaptive?

How does taste aversion increase survival?

How is taste aversion expressed in modern society?

How would food neophobia be an important survival strategy?

Can experiences in modern society reduce dislike of new foods?

▶ Lesson notes p.60

Data - - - - Analysis

To create effective evaluations, it is important you consider what research findings (the data) tell us about evolutionary explanations for food preferences (the analysis). Match the relevant commentary (on the right) to each study (on the left).

Preference for sweetness.

Grill and Norgren (1978) found newborn infants show an acceptance response (sucking, licking upper lip, slight smile) the first time they taste sweet substances.

The illness resulting from the treatment has been paired with consumption of the food leading to an aversive response to the novel taste. These findings lead to the development of the 'scapegoat technique'.

Taste aversion.

Bernstein and Webster (1980) reported how chemotherapy patients given a novel-tasting ice cream prior to their treatment showed a later aversion to the novel taste.

The data suggest a strong genetic component for neophobia. Food neophobia evolved among humans as it held the adaptive advantage of protecting individuals from potentially harmful foods.

Heritability of neophobia.

Knaapila et al. (2007) estimated heritability for food neophobia, as measured by the Food Neophobia Scale Questionnaire, was 67% (about 2/3rds of variation in food neophilia is genetically determined).

It seems food neophobia can be reduced in situations where a reluctance to consume new or unfamiliar foods would be maladaptive. For example, when restricted diets could lead to poor nutrition or reduced health benefits.

Food neophobia.

Birch et al. (1987) found that repeated taste exposure without visual and olfactory cues increased preference for initially novel foods.

Sucking implies attempts to ingest the substance. This suggests an innate preference for this taste rather than preference being learnt over time through experience.

▶ Lesson notes p.60

Reading between the (head)lines

For each headline, rate the validity of the story: 1 = invalid, 10 = valid.
Be sure to include at least one piece of research evidence to support your judgement.

Parenting Periodical.

Mummy and Daddy's diet dictates junior's snacking, eating motivations and body dissatisfaction.

Related study.

Validity of headline: 1   2   3   4   5   6   7   8   9   10

Reason for judgement made:

Cultural Chronical.

Media influences food preferences as well as eating habits: the rise of the TV dinner.

Related study.

Validity of headline: 1   2   3   4   5   6   7   8   9   10

Reason for judgement made:

▶ Lesson notes p.60

Neural & hormonal mechanisms

Leptin

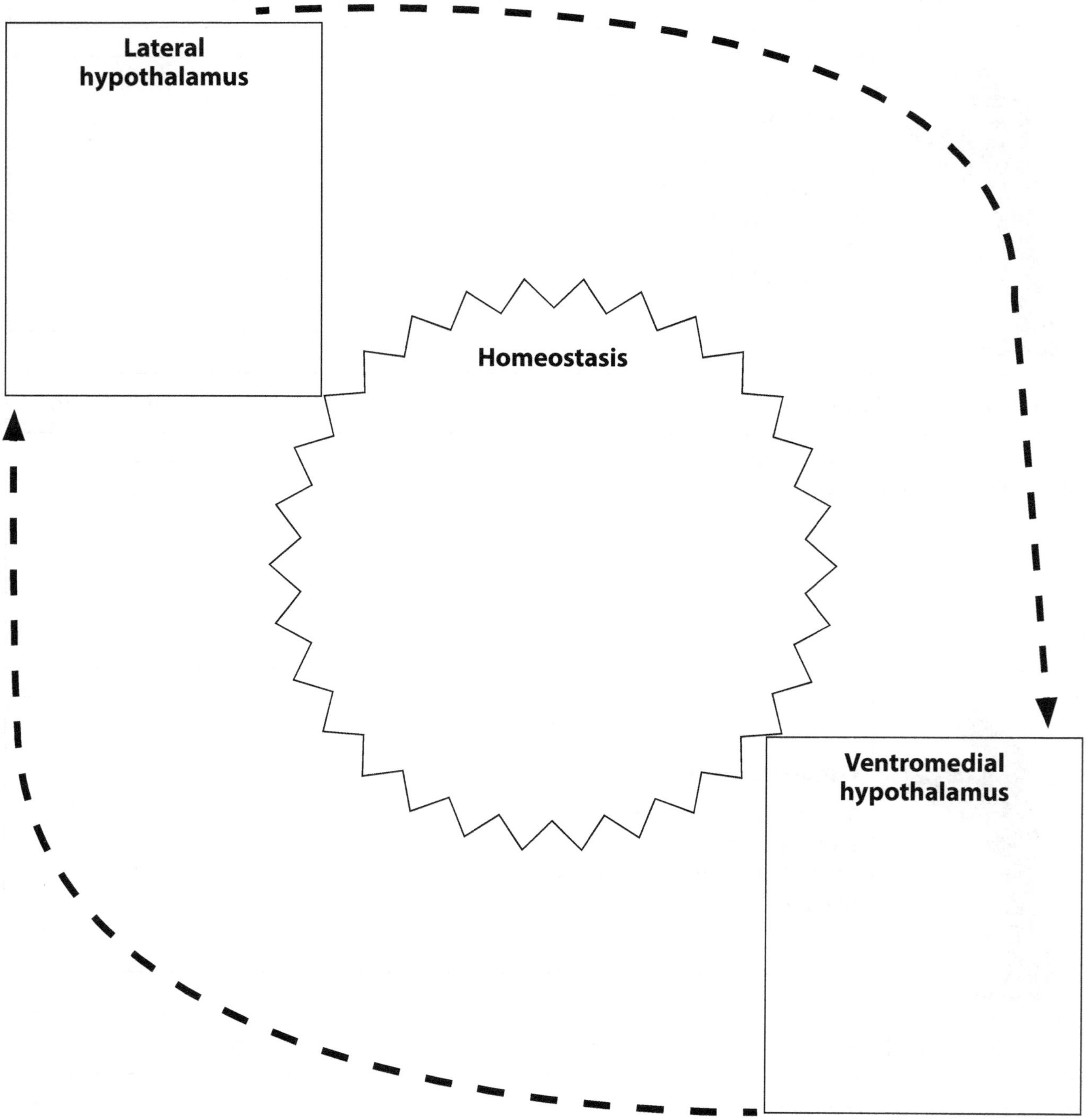

Lateral hypothalamus

Homeostasis

Ventromedial hypothalamus

Ghrelin

▶ Lesson notes p.61

Constructing a critique

Damage to the lateral hypothalamus of rats resulted in a condition called aphagia (an absence of eating). However, other research has shown damage also causes deficits in other areas of behaviour such as thirst and sex. This suggests the lateral hypothalamus is not just the brain's 'eating centre'.

In a number of different species, including humans, damage to the ventromedial hypothalamus resulted in obesity and so the VMH became known as the 'satiety centre'. Gold (1973) proposed damage to the PNV alone causes hyperphagia but later research has failed to replicate Gold's findings.

Wren et al. (2001) reported that healthy volunteers who received ghrelin intravenously for one week showed a significant increase in food consumption compared to when they were given intravenous saline for one week. A mean difference of 28% was recorded between the two conditions.

Some people develop resistance to the hormone leptin making weight loss difficult. This resistance is often found in overweight and obese people. Heymsfield et al. (1999) found that doses of leptin up to 20 to 30 times more than that normally seen produced significant weight loss in obese adults.

How can research into neural and hormonal control of eating be used to comment on free will and determinism when considering eating and weight gain/loss?

How useful is research using non-human animals into developing our understanding of the control of eating?

What real-life applications can be made from research into neural and hormonal control of eating?

▶ Lesson notes p.62

Magic numbers

Genetic explanations have used family, twin and adoptive studies to determine whether anorexia nervosa is an inherited condition. Match the numbers shown below to each type of study then use the data to create a summary of findings from each type of study.

Family studies ☐
Strober et al. (2000)

Twin studies ☐
Wade (2000)

Adoption studies ☐
Klump et al. (2009)

1st

28-78%

10x

123

50%

59-82%

2000

56

58%

Family studies	Twin studies	Adoption studies

Exploded outline

When outlining family systems theory as an explanation for anorexia nervosa, you should ensure you make reference to a number of key components relating to the 'psychosomatic' family.

Psychosomatic family

Psychological factors, dysfunctional, physiological vulnerability

Enmeshment

proximity, intensity, over-involved

Autonomy

freedom, independence, transaction

Control

over-protective, high degree of concern

Rigidity

flexibility, exploration of alternatives

Conflict resolution

low tolerance, unresolved conflict, façade

▶ Lesson notes p.63

Developed evaluations

When evaluating explanations, in this case family systems theory, you should aim to create concise, well-structured evaluations if you wish to access the higher mark bands. Using PEEL is a useful way of ensuring ideas are well-developed and clearly explained.

> (*Point*) Gremillion (2003) claims there is gender bias in family systems theory (*Evidence*) because it focuses almost exclusively on the mother-daughter relationship. (*Expansion*) Despite the fact that fathers also contribute to the enmeshment process, enmeshment is mostly seen as maternal in origin (*Link*) which means that the father's role in the development of AN is often overlooked.

Using the example above as a guide, identify the Point, Evidence, Expansion and Link in the following paragraph.

> Tests for characteristics specific to families in which a member has AN have been generally disappointing. For example, Kog & Vandereycken (1989) failed to find the characteristics predicted by the psychosomatic family model in families of AN sufferers. There is growing evidence that families in which someone has an eating disorder are a diverse group meaning general statements about the nature of family relationships, emotional climate and patters of family interaction cannot be made.

Now create two PEEL paragraphs of your own evaluating family systems theory of anorexia nervosa.

_____
_____
_____
_____
_____
_____
_____
_____
_____
_____
_____
_____
_____
_____
_____
_____
_____
_____
_____
_____

▶ Lesson notes p.63

Complete the critique

Discuss social learning theory as an explanation for anorexia nervosa. (8 marks)

Although the question doesn't state it, AO1 (knowledge) is worth 3 marks, AO3 (evaluation) is worth 5 marks. Use your understanding of the strengths and limitations of social learning theory to complete the AO3 critique.

Social learning occurs when a model's behaviour, such as a parent or peer, is observed and imitated. In terms of AN it has been suggested that mothers 'model' weight concerns for their daughters, for example dieting behaviours are observed and imitated by the daughter as she identifies with her mother. Others' responses to this imitation can be reinforcing. Comments such as, 'You are so slim, you look great' makes the individual feel better about themselves and so dieting continues. The media's positive portrayal of thin models can lead to body dissatisfaction with individuals who have low self-esteem being more likely to compare themselves to the idealised images the media promotes.

However, research into the role of mothers as models for disordered eating is inconsistent…

_____

_____

_____

_____

_____

_____

_____

Studies of societies where Western television has been introduced have supported the role of the media in development of body dissatisfaction…

_____

_____

_____

_____

_____

_____

_____

However, not all forms of media have the same effect…

_____

_____

_____

_____

_____

_____

_____

▶ Lesson notes p.64

A cognitive behavioural model

Garner and Bemis (1982) proposed a model of the development of AN.

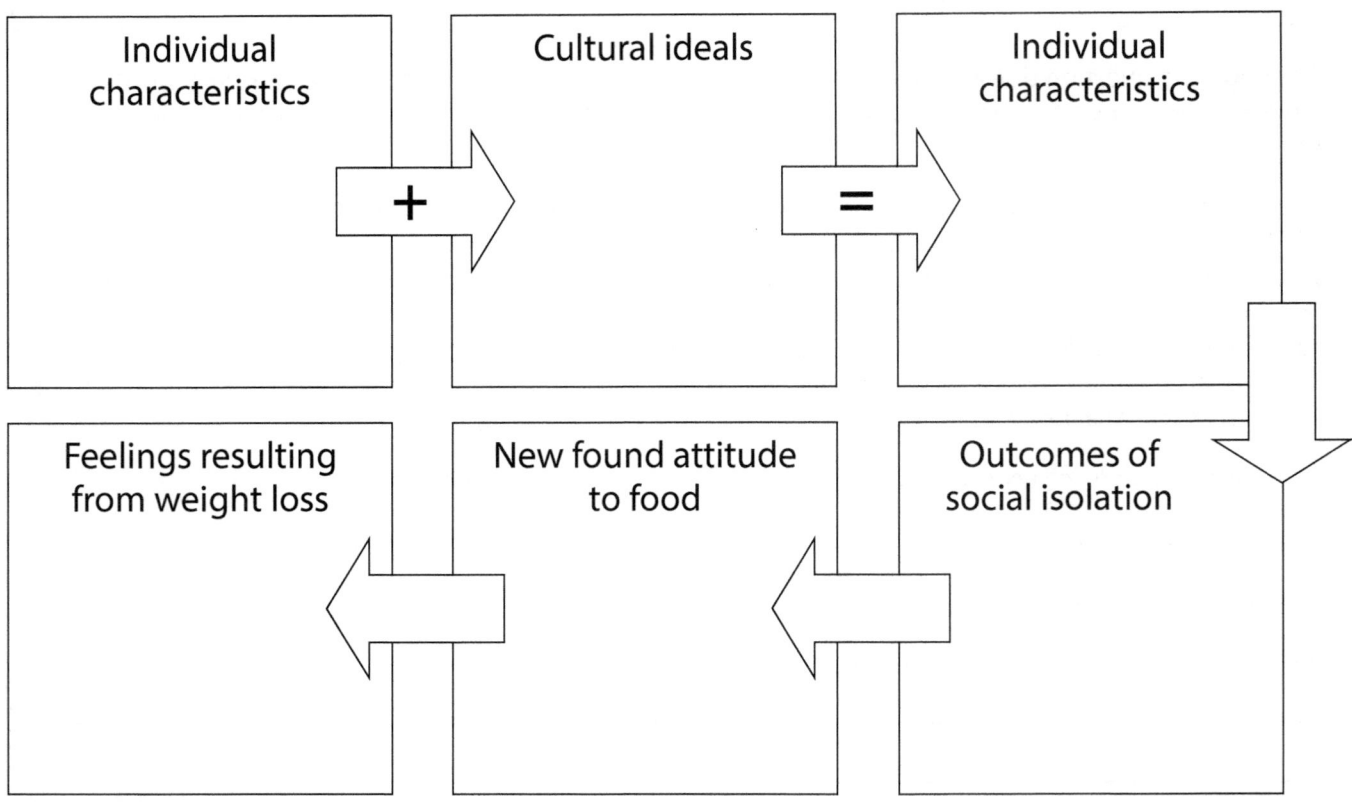

Despite performing well at school, Jessie is full of self-doubt. While her teachers praise her achievements and her parents boast to their friends that she is a perfectionist, Jessie worries that she cannot keep up with these high standards. She believes that if she is able to lose weight and look more like the celebrities she sees on TV and in magazines, she will feel better and be more attractive to others. She has already lost a few pounds and has received positive comments from her peers. For a while things seemed to be looking up, but she has now become worried around meal times and has begun making excuses not to eat with her family.

How might cognitive explanations of anorexia nervosa be applied to Jessie's case? (4 marks)

_____

_____

_____

_____

_____

_____

_____

_____

_____

_____

▶ Lesson notes p.64

Cognitive chit-chat

Read the information in your textbook (page 176 in *Complete Companion*). Make brief notes to summarise evaluative comments relating to the cognitive explanation of anorexia nervosa. Move round the room chatting to others to help you complete all the speech bubbles on this handout.

_____ summarised the main problem with cognitive explanations as _____

_____

_____

_____

_____

_____

_____ feels an important issue is _____

_____

_____

_____

_____ thought _____

_____

_____

_____

_____ feels the cognitive theory is supported by _____

_____

_____

_____

_____

_____ explained that the success of cognitive behavioural therapy suggests _____

_____

_____

_____

_____

_____

In conclusion…

▶ Lesson notes p.65

Exam marking

Two candidates have attempted the exam question shown below.
For each response, consider how well the candidate has addressed the question (explanation and criticism)
before using the mark scheme to award a mark.

> Briefly explain and give **one** criticism of neural explanations of obesity. (6 marks)

Candidate 1

Obesity is when an individual has an excess of body fat usually defined by their BMI and waist circumference. Recent reports show a sharp increase in obesity in the last 20 years. Some neurons in the hypothalamus monitor sugar levels in the body and act when energy levels are low producing the desire to eat. A malfunction in this area can lead to eating when the body does not need food. This explanation implies obesity is out of the person's control and so reduces blame unlike psychological explanations which highlight personal failings.

Mark awarded.

Justification.

Candidate 2

The hormone leptin is secreted by fat cells and has the effect of decreasing food intake by acting on receptors in the appetite control centres in the brain. For example, leptin inhibits the appetite-stimulating hormone neuropeptide Y. Disruption of leptin signalling in the hypothalamus leads to obesity. Research has supported the role of leptin in regulating appetite. For example, treatment of an obese child with leptin injections showed beneficial effects on appetite, metabolism and weight.

Mark awarded.

Justification.

Level	Outline	Evaluate	Construction	Specialist terms
Level 3 5–6 marks	Accurate and generally detailed.	Effective, only minor expansion is lacking.	Clear, coherent and focused on the question.	Terms used effectively.
Level 2 3–4 marks	Evident but may have occasional inaccuracies.	Some effective evaluation seen.	Mostly clear, coherent and focused.	Most terms used effectively.
Level 1 1–2 marks	Limited detail.	Limited evaluations, mainly descriptive.	Poorly focused and organised, lacks clarity.	Absent or used inaccurately.
0 marks.	No relevant comments.			

▶ Lesson notes p.65

Dangers of dieting

The Daily News

Dangers of dieting: Psychologists suggest attempts to restrict food intake can actually lead to over eating increasing the risk of obesity.

In 2015 the UK government reported a sharp increase in obesity rates in the last 20 years. In 1993, 13% of males were classified as obese, this had risen to 36% by 2013.

Psychologists have suggested this rise must be the result of environmental factors and have laid the blame at the door of diets. They claim rigid attempts to reduce the amount eaten or avoid certain food groups leads to a 'what the hell' effect where individuals who have broken their diet boundary continue to eat to the point of satiation and in some cases beyond this limit.

Use your psychological knowledge to expand the explanation in this news story. Make sure you include the terms *restraint theory, the boundary model (Herman and Polivy, 1984)* and *disinhibition* in your answer.

_____

_____

_____

_____

_____

_____

_____

_____

_____

_____

_____

_____

_____

_____

_____

_____

_____

_____

_____

_____

_____

_____

_____

_____

▶ Lesson notes p.66

Exploring the evidence

Herman and Mack (1975) requested that 45 female participants ate nothing for several hours before randomly assigning them to one of three groups:

- 15 participants consumed no milkshake
- 15 participants consumed one milkshake
- 15 participants consumed two milkshakes.

They were then given three flavours of ice cream to taste, being told that this was to determine whether the flavour of the milkshake affected their sensory experience of the ice cream.

Participants also completed a questionnaire to assess their level of restrained eating.

Those who reported not being on a diet (non-restrained eaters) ate less ice cream if they had previously consumed the 'preload' milkshake (whether one or two milkshakes).

Restrained eaters reacted differently. Those who had not received the milkshake showed high restraint when tasting the ice cream. However, those who had already had a milkshake ate more ice cream. The greater the pre-load the more ice cream consumed.

Why might this study be gender biased?

What ethical issues might have arisen?

Why should self-reports of eating behaviour be treated with caution?

Wardle and Beales (1988) randomly assigned 27 obese women to either a diet group (restrained eating), an exercise group or a non-treatment group for seven weeks. At week four all participants were given a preload snack (a small chocolate bar) with food intake and appetite being assessed before and after the snack. At week six, food intake was assessed under stressful conditions.

Results showed that at both assessment sessions, women in the diet condition ate more than women engaging in exercise and those receiving no treatment.

What experimental design was used?

Why were participants randomly assigned to each condition?

What do findings suggest about treating obesity?

▶ Lesson notes p.66

Daisy's diet club

Daisy runs a diet club. Each Monday her members weigh themselves after a week of restricted eating.

She finds a lot of her members struggle to stick to their eating programmes (she doesn't like to call them diets).

To help her members stick to their eating regimes and adopt a healthier eating lifestyle she designed a leaflet.

To help Daisy everyone should choose two statements from the leaflet and explain the psychology behind the diet tip given.

Some of you should choose two statements to explain the psychology behind the tips and add research findings.

You may wish to challenge yourself by explaining different psychological explanations and evidence behind three of Daisy's diet tips.

Hello ladies and gents, welcome to new members and warm embraces for long-standing clients. We all know how hard it is to be sticking to our eating regimes, so I thought I'd gather together some handy tips to help you stay on the straight and narrow avoiding any temptations. I've based each tip on psychological research to give you a brainy boost to eating healthily and losing weight safely.

Reduce eating boredom by concentrating on the details of your dinner. Monday = Rocket salad (rather than just 'salad'), Tuesday = Three bean salad (rather than just thinking, 'salad again'), Wednesday = pear and walnut salad.

If you really want chocolate, don't deny yourself, just take a little nip occasionally. Try freezing fun size versions of your favourite bars – they take a little longer to eat but have less calories than a full-sized bar.

Remember, there are other pleasures in life than just food. Arrange a healthy dinner party and enjoy spending the evening with friends and family.

Avoid tempting triggers! Take the long way through town to avoid walking past the cake shop to reduce the risk of the shop window triggering pleasurable thoughts of food.

Remember, there are no forbidden foods, just limited portions. Denying yourself chips means you spend all your day thinking chips, chips, CHIPS!

► Lesson notes p.67

Discussing diets writing frame

Write a brief summary of reasons for diet success and/or failure here.

Evidence for the theory of ironic processes of mental control.

Evidence for the hedonic theory.

Limitations of ironic process theory.

Limitations of anecdotal evidence.

Real-world application: Anti-dieting programmes.

Free will or determinism?

▶ Lesson notes p.67

General adaptation syndrome (GAS)

Use your knowledge of the general adaptation syndrome to match each stage with associated physiological changes and the subsequent effects an individual would experience.

Stage	Physiological changes	Effects experienced
Stage 1 Alarm reaction. Threat or stressor is recognised.	Biochemical substances constantly manufactured by the body such as sugars, neurotransmitters, proteins and hormones are gradually depleted and the immune system becomes less effective.	Symptoms of the stress response may reappear; the person experiences sweating, raised heart rate. Stress-related illnesses may be experienced such as depression, ulcers and cardiovascular problems.
Stage 2 Resistance. Body adapts to the stressor.	Previous over-activity of the adrenal glands can lead them to become damaged. The immune system may not be able to cope as production of proteins necessary for functioning has been reduced.	Fight or flight response is experienced: heart beats faster, muscles tense ready for action and sweating increases.
Stage 3 Exhaustion. The body cannot maintain normal functioning.	The hypothalamus triggers production of adrenaline / noradrenaline from the adrenal glands.	The body appears to be coping; heart rate reduces and muscles relax.

Once you have correctly identified the changes and effects for each stage apply the GAS to the following case:

Tom received a call at work from a local hospital informing him that his elderly father had fallen in the carpark of a nearby supermarket. Tom grabbed his car keys and raced to the hospital where he learned his father needed an emergency operation as he had broken his hip. After the initial shock Tom felt he adapted well to visiting his father in hospital. He arranged with his boss to work around hospital visiting times which meant he had to use weekends to catch up on any missed work. Now Tom's father has returned home and Tom spends as much time as possible at his father's home caring for him. Recently Tom has been suffering from a lingering cold and feels he cannot cope for much longer working full time and being his father's main carer.

Using your knowledge of the general adaptation syndrome, explain why Tom feels the way he does.

▶ Lesson notes p.68

Evaluating the GAS

TASK: Complete the evaluation by adding the missing words.

rats	doctrine	human	general	appetite

Selye's research with humans and rats supported his '_____ of non-specificity' – the notion that

the body responds in the same way to any stressor. In his observation of _____ patients, he

noticed how they all presented with a similar set of symptoms (aches and pains, loss of _____)

regardless of what was actually the problem. When he exposed _____ to surgical injury, excessive

muscular exercise or injected them with sublethal doses of a range of drugs the rats all showed a similar

response. It seems the GAS is a '_____' response as the same outcomes are seen regardless of the

stressor.

TASK: Now create a second evaluative paragraph using the words shown below.

Depleted resources	Sugars, proteins	Exhaustion phase	Hormone activity	Cortisol levels

_____

_____

_____

_____

_____

_____

_____

_____

_____

_____

_____

_____

_____

_____

_____

▶ Lesson notes p.68

Developing the detail

Describe **one** study into the role of stress in cardiovascular disorder. In your answer explain what the researcher(s) did and what was found. (4 marks)

Identify the correct data in the answer below to create an accurate and detailed description.

Williams et al. (2000) surveyed about **1300 / 13,000 / 130,000** people using an anger questionnaire consisting of **10 / 20 / 30** questions such as whether they were hot-headed and if they felt like hitting someone when angry. **Three / six / nine** years later, it was found **85 / 170 / 256** participants had experienced heart attacks. Those who scored highest on the anger scale were over **two / three / four and a half** times more likely to have a heart attack than those with the lowest anger ratings. People with moderate anger ratings were **3% / 15% / 35%** likely to suffer a coronary event than those with lower ratings.

Describe **one** study into the role of stress on immune suppression. In your answer, explain what the researcher(s) did and what was found. (4 marks)

Use the items listed below to create an accurate and detailed description of the Kiecolt-Glaser's et al. (1984) study.

Natural experiment

75 medical students

Blood samples

Low / high stress periods

Exams

SRRS

Life stressors

Loneliness scale

Interpersonal contacts

NK cell activity

_____

_____

_____

_____

_____

_____

_____

_____

_____

_____

_____

_____

_____

_____

_____

▶ Lesson notes p.69

Life changes: true or false?

Decide whether each statement is true or false. If false, write the correct statement in the space provided.
Extension: for correct statements add further details to develop the point.

Holmes and Rahe proposed that adapting to life changes requires psychic energy.	True	False
Extension / correction (circle)		

The SRRS consisted of 40 negative life events.	True	False
Extension / correction (circle)		

Death of a spouse is assigned 100 life change units (LCU).	True	False
Extension / correction (circle)		

Rahe et al. (1970) investigated the relationship between LCU score and illness.	True	False
Extension / correction (circle)		

Participants completed the SRRS for events experienced in the previous two years.	True	False
Extension / correction (circle)		

A record of illness was kept during the 6–8 month tour of duty.	True	False
Extension / correction (circle)		

A negative correlation was found between LCU score and illness score.	True	False
Extension / correction (circle)		

Stretch: Other research has supported a link between life changes and illness.

▶ Lesson notes p.70

Creating concise evaluations

To create a 'thorough and effective' discussion of life changes you should aim for five evaluative points with each one explained in around 50 words.

When creating concise evaluations from your textbook and/or class notes use the following strategies:

1. Read the passage and make sure you understand what you have read.
2. Define any words you are unsure of.
2. Highlight the key words.
3. Underline the central point of the passage.

You are now ready to create a summary of the text in your own words.

Individual differences.

The life change approach ignores the fact that life events will inevitably have different significance for different people. For example, the untimely death of a much-loved spouse will undoubtedly have a devastating effect on the surviving partner, but the death of an elderly spouse after a long and painful illness may not be quite so stressful for the survivor. Similarly, what are relatively minor stressors for some people, such as a son or daughter leaving home or even a particularly busy Christmas, would be major stressors for other people.

Word count: 89 words

Untimely = sudden

Life events will not affect everyone in the same way. For example, unexpectedly losing a partner to a sudden illness or accident may require more readjustment than experiencing the death of a partner after suffering from a terminal illness for an extended period of time.

Word count: 45 words

Daily hassles may be more significant.

Lazarus (1990) suggested major life events are relatively rare in the lives of most people. It is minor daily stressors, (i.e. hassles) that are the more significant source of stress for most people. For example, DeLongis et al. (1988) studied stress in 75 married couples. They gave the participants a life events questionnaire and a Hassles and Uplifts Scale. They found no relationship between life events and health, but did find a significant positive correlation of +.59 between hassles and next-day health problems such as flu, sore throats, headaches and backaches.

Word count: 91 words

_____
_____
_____
_____
_____
_____
_____
_____
_____
_____
_____
_____

Word count: 45 words

▶ Lesson notes p.70

The six hats

Edward de Bono's six hats is a way of looking at an issue from a number of different perspectives. Use this technique to consider the view that daily hassles play a significant role in psychological well-being.

White hat:	What data is available regarding daily hassles as a source of stress?
Red hat:	What do you feel about the suggestion 'daily hassles cause stress'? How do you feel when experiencing hassles and uplifts?
Black hat:	What problems does the theory face? Who disagrees that daily hassles cause stress? Are there any weaknesses to the explanation?
Yellow hat:	What are the strengths of the theory? Who supports the suggestion that 'stress results from daily hassles'?
Green hat:	How can this theory be applied to the real world to improve people's psychological well-being?
Blue hat:	How would this theory be viewed by Holmes and Rahe?

▶ Lesson notes p.71

Apply your understanding

Natasha has a high pressured job working for a large retail company. She is unable to plan her day as she often receives a call from head office asking her to visit various stores in a 50-mile radius. As such, her job involves a lot of travelling and she often needs to work over the weekend to make up for the time she has lost while supporting other stores.

Using your knowledge of workplace stress, explain why Natasha may be experiencing stress-related symptoms. (4 marks)

Assess the two exam responses using the mark scheme provided. Justify the marks you have awarded.

Candidate 1.

Natasha's case demonstrates the job-strain model of workplace stress. This model proposes that a high workload, which Natasha has, creates greater job demand which, along with low job control can lead to stress as there is a lack of predictability in her job. This model is supported by Kivimäki et al. (2002) who found that workers with 'job strain' were 2.2 times more likely to die from CHD than those with low workload and high control.

Mark awarded and justification.

Candidate 2.

Natasha may well experience stress-related symptoms as she has little control over her work because head office sends her to different stores meaning she is not able to plan her day as she wishes. Furthermore, because of extensive travelling she is unable to get her own work done during the week so she has to catch up on work at the weekend which could be seen as work overload. However, Natasha may have a hardy personality which means she may feel in control of the situation and see work as a challenge she is committed to.

Mark awarded and justification.

Level	Marks	Description
2	3–4	Knowledge of the effects of high workload and low control is clearly identified and mostly accurate. The material is used appropriately to explain Natasha's work experiences. The answer is coherent with effective use of terminology.
1	1–2	Some knowledge of the effects of workload and control is evident. Links made to Natasha's case are not always effective. The answer may lack accuracy and detail. Use of terminology is absent or inappropriate.
0	0	No relevant content given.

▶ Lesson notes p.71

Improving the answer

Below is an extract from an answer to the question, **'Describe and evaluate research into workplace stress. Include the effects of workload and control in your answer.' (16 marks)** Use the teacher comments to improve the answer.

…Marmot et al. (1997) followed the health of civil servants working in Whitehall, London for eleven years. They found those who experienced the most job strain (high workload and low control) suffered more ill health. These tended to be the younger, lower grade workers.

> Relevant study for AO1 but further detail could be added.

Marmot's study is further supported by Kivimäki et al. (2002) who found that in a sample of 800 Finnish workers those with job strain were 2.2 times more likely to die from CHD than those who felt they had a high level of control and low workload. However, it was the combination of the two factors that seemed problematic as workload or control alone did not have an effect.

> Detailed evidence but candidate could make reference to factors associated with each occupational group that could be influential.

Questionnaires are often used to gather information in workplace stress questionnaires. However, this may not produce valid data. Participants may give socially desirable answers, overexaggerate some items and deliberately ignore others. Therefore, it may be better to interview workers as a way of assessing the impact of workplace stress.

> This criticism could apply to questionnaires used to investigate a range of topics. Consider issues specific to asking questions about stress.

Both Marmot and Kivimäki focused on work overload but work underload has also been associated with stress-related illness. Work underload occurs when people are given tasks beneath their abilities that lack creativity or do not stimulate them mentally. Research into work underload suggests the job-strain model is too simple.

> 'Research' is implied but not explained. Include Shultz's et al. (2010) European data.

Individual differences should be considered when discussing the effect of workplace stress. Lazarus (1995) proposed the transactional approach which suggests the person's perception of their ability to cope will have a large influence over the degree of workplace stress experienced. For example, some workers are less stressed by having no control.

> Consider adding a little more detail for Schaubroeck's et al. (2001) study (measured saliva to assess immune function).

In conclusion, there is research to support the job-strain model but methodologies used to investigate stress may reduce validity. Furthermore, the job-strain model may be an oversimplification as it does not consider the effects of work underload.

> The conclusion is a repetition of previous material. Make a new point, e.g. changing nature of the workplace.

▶ Lesson notes p.72

Measuring stress is difficult!

Provide a brief summary of the different methods used to measure stress.
Then match the evaluative comments shown to each method.

Self-report scales		Physiological measures	
Social Readjustment Rating Scale (SRRS)	Hassles and Uplifts Scale (HSUP)	Skin conductance response	Other physiological measures

People who lack emotional responsiveness, such as psychopaths, can lie without any associated physical response and so this measurement may not be as useful as previously thought when trying to detect deception.

Events have different meanings for different people, e.g. a divorce may be less stressful if the marriage was unhappy. Therefore, assigning a fixed score for each event may not represent the degree of stress experienced.

This measurement can be used to investigate stress in groups for which questionnaires would be unsuitable or impossible to use, for example, when studying stress in children or non-human animals.

The scale is only applicable to adults, e.g. death of spouse (100 LCU). A scale for young people has been developed which assigns the most LCUs to pregnancy.

Items relating to physical well-being (medication side effects, low energy levels) would increase the likelihood of a correlation with illness so were removed from the scale to improve validity.

Stress is not just a physiological response. We also need to understand how the perception of stress can have an effect on people.

Ratings scales remain popular in stress research with either the original versions or adaptations of the scales being used.

Having to consider over 250 items may have led respondents to lose focus when completing the scale which would reduce validity. Test-retest correlations show +.48 for severity ratings of hassles and +.60 for frequency ratings of uplifts.

Increased sweating and skin conductance could result from experiencing a range of emotions such as fear and surprise. Temperature and humidity can also effect the response recorded.

▶ Lesson notes p.72

Reading race response sheet

Compete against your fellow students to reach the finishing line. Remember, your answers need to be accurate and detailed for you to receive the next question.

Question 8.   Accurate. Detailed.

Question 7.   Accurate. Detailed.

Question 5.   Accurate. Detailed.

Question 6.   Accurate. Detailed.

Question 4.   Accurate. Detailed.

Question 3.   Accurate. Detailed.

Question 1.   Accurate. Detailed.

Question 2.   Accurate. Detailed.

Reading race Q and A

Questions and answers for reading race activity. Next question is available if previous answer is deemed to be accurate and detailed.

1. What characteristics did Friedman and Rosenman (1959) associate with the Type A personality?

- Competitiveness and achievement striving.
- Impatient and time urgent.
- Hostility and aggression.

2. Describe the sample Friedman and Rosenman gathered in their Western Collaborative Group Study.

- Approximately 3000.
- Californian males aged 35–59.
- Healthy (examined for signs of CHD, those who were ill were excluded).

3. How was personality assessed?

- Structured interview.
- Questions designed to assess how participants would respond to everyday pressures.
- Interviewer spoke slowly and hesitantly to illicit Type A behaviour.

4. Why does the collected data suggest a relationship between personality and CHD?

- 8 ½ years later Type A showed greater rate of heart attacks (12.8% compared to 6.0% for Type B).
- Twice as many Type As (2.7%) had died compared to Type Bs (1.1%).
- Recurring heart attacks showed As were more susceptible (2.6%) then Bs (0.8%).
- Type As also showed higher blood pressure and cholesterol, were more likely to smoke and have a family history of CHD.

5. Which seems to be a greater contributing factor to CHD; personality or lifestyle?

- 22 years later Ragland and Brand (1988) found 15% (214 men) had died of CHD.
- They confirmed the importance of CHD risk factors (age, smoking, high blood pressure) but found little relationship between Type A behaviours and mortality.
- This challenges the conclusion that Type A personality was a significant risk factor.

6. How can our understanding of the risk posed by aspects of the Type A personality be refined?

- Myrtek's (2001) meta-analysis of 35 Type A studies.
- Found relationship between one component of Type A (hostility) and CHD.
- This is only evidence of an association between Type A personality and CHD.

7. Why was Friedman and Rosenman's study gender biased?

- In the 1950s and 60s the concepts of competitiveness and assertiveness were deemed to be masculine behaviours.
- Their original sample consisted only of men.
- Friedman's later research found both men and women experience Type A behaviours.

8. What has research suggested about Type C personality?

- Morris et al. (1981) found women who suppressed their emotions (Type C) were more likely to suffer from cancerous breast lumps.
- However, Giraldi et al. (1997) found no association between psychosocial variables such as emotional suppression and cancer progression.
- Giraldi et al. did find an increase in stressful life events in the months preceding the cancer diagnosis.

▶ Lesson notes p.73

Critical questioning

Read about Kobasa's research into the hardy personality then complete the questions.

Identifying the facts: what happened in the study?	Personal response: how do you feel about the findings?	Evaluating: what methodological issues does hardiness research face?
Summarising: what is a hardy personality?	Kobasa contacted about 800 American male middle and upper level executives from a large US company. She asked them to identify life events experienced in the last three years and list any illnesses experienced during the same period of time. From this she was able to categorise people into high stress/low illness (n = 86) and high stress/high illness (n = 75). Three months later participants were assessed for control, commitment and challenge. Kobasa found individuals who were highly stressed but experienced low illness scored high on all three hardiness characteristics; supporting the view that hardiness defends against stress.	Wider research: do all components of hardiness hold equal importance?
Reasoning: how can hardiness reduce the likelihood of stress-related illness?	Real-life application: how could research help society?	Alternative views: how do other people view hardiness?

▶ Lesson notes p.74

Describing drug therapies

Order the statements below to form a coherent outline of benzodiazepines' mode of action.

Order	
	• The neurotransmitter GABA is a natural form of anxiety relief.
	• This boosts the action of GABA.
	• Activity of the postsynaptic neurone is slowed.
	• More chloride ions are able to enter the neurone increasing resistance to excitation.
	• About 40% of neurons respond to the quietening effect of this neurotransmitter.
	• BZs bind onto special sites on the GABA receptor.
	• As a result, the individual feels more relaxed and less anxious.
	• GABA locks onto receptors on the outside of the postsynaptic neurone.
	• It is now harder for other neurotransmitters to stimulate the neurone.
	• This leads to chloride ions flooding into channels that open on the postsynaptic membrane.
	• BZs enhance the action of GABA.
	• BZs also reduce any increased serotonin activity which reduces anxiety.

Complete the questions after each statement to explain the action of beta blockers on the body.

• Beta blockers reduce the physiological effects experienced as a result of the sympathomedullary response.

  a) What hormones are produced as a result of this response?

  b) What glands are these hormones released from?

• Beta blockers bind to beta-receptors in heart cells and other areas of the body.

  c) What effect do beta blockers have on the body's immediate response to stress?

  d) What other uses do beta blockers have?

  e) Why have the International Olympic Committee banned the use of beta blockers by competitors?

▶ Lesson notes p.74

Discussing drug therapies

Tanya visited her GP complaining of anxiety. She has an important exam coming up as part of her accountancy course and is worried she will not perform well. When revising or even just thinking about possible exam questions Tanya finds her heart races, breathing becomes shallow and she starts sweating.

Tanya's GP suggests a course of beta blockers will help her manage through the exam period. What could her GP tell her about the benefits of beta blockers as a stress management tool? (4 marks)

Skill	AO2: Application	Structure and specialist terminology
Level 2 3–4 marks	Suggestions provide an effective commentary on the benefits of beta-blockers.	Answer lacks clarity, accuracy and organisation in places. Specialist terminology used appropriately on occasion.
Level 1 1–2 marks	Suggestions regarding the benefits of beta-blockers are limited, poorly focused or absent.	The whole answer lacks clarity, shows many inaccuracies and is poorly organised. Specialist terminology is either absent or inappropriately used.

On being diagnosed with severe anxiety, Jay has been prescribed a short course of benzodiazepines. He understands how they work to increase the calming effect of chemicals in his brain but he would like to discuss the possible benefits and issues associated with their use before he begins taking them.

What does Jay need to consider before deciding whether to use BZs to manage his stress? (8 marks)

Skill	AO3: Evaluation	Structure and specialist terminology
Level 4 7–8 marks	Discussion is thorough and effective. Minor detail and/or expression of argument sometimes lacking.	Answer is clear, coherent and focused on the question. Effective use of specialist terminology.
Level 3 5–6 marks	Evaluation is apparent and mostly effective though there may be occasional inaccuracies.	Answer is mostly clear and organised but may lack focus in places. Specialist terminology mostly used effectively.
Level 2 3–4 marks	Evaluative comments have limited effectiveness.	Answer lacks clarity, accuracy and organisation in places. Specialist terminology used appropriately on occasion.
Level 1 1–2 marks	Evaluation is limited, poorly focused or absent.	The whole answer lacks clarity, shows many inaccuracies and is poorly organised. Specialist terminology is either absent or inappropriately used.

▶ Lesson notes p.74

SIT revision record

Conceptualisation

collaborative process, maladaptive strategies, perceived threats

SIT has been shown to be effective in a variety of situations

SIT helps prepare for future stressors

Skills acquisition

coping skills, coping self-statements, rehearsal: imagining, modelling, imitating, role-playing

The hello-goodbye effect makes it difficult to evaluate SIT's effectiveness

Application

Applying skills, follow-through

SIT may be unnecessarily complex, it is time consuming and requires the client to be highly motivated

▶ Lesson notes p.75

Biofeedback: fill in the blanks

noradrenaline	muscle	parasympathetic	parasympathetic
real world	relaxation	unconsciously	feedback
sympathetic	electrical	operant	(EEG)
rewarding	(EMG)	blood pressure	heart rate

Explain how a therapist might use biofeedback to treat a person with stress. (6 marks)

First the client is taught _____ to reduce the activity of the _____

nervous system (SNS) and activating the _____ nervous system. This should reduce

heart rate and _____ as adrenaline and _____ are no longer produced.

Once this technique has been mastered the client is attached to machines which provide

_____ about autonomic nervous system activity. For example, an electromyograph

_____ measures _____ activity and an electro-encephalograph

_____ measures _____ activity in the brain. When a client sees or

hears a change in feedback they activate a _____ response by practicing relaxation.

_____ conditioning occurs as the experience of reducing the _____

is _____ which increases the likelihood of the same behaviour being repeated. This

learning occurs _____ .

The client finally learns to transfer skills learnt in biofeedback to the _____ .

EXTENSION: Explain **one** criticism of using biofeedback as a method of managing and coping
with stress. (3 marks)

_____

_____

_____

_____

_____

_____

▶ Lesson notes p.75

Reading record: Gender differences

Gender	Physiological explanations	Psychological explanations
	Fight-or-flight. Role of testosterone.	Problem-focused. Tackling stressor.
	Tend-and-befriend. Role of oxytocin.	Emotion-focused. Reduce stress response.
	The type of stressor experienced may determine the type of response seen.	
Exam practice: Explain **one** gender difference in coping with stress. (4 marks)		

▶ Lesson notes p.75

Creating commentaries

When evaluating gender differences in coping with stress it is not enough just to state evidence, you need to USE the research to address the exam question. Effective evaluations analyse research, consider implications of findings and look at wider psychological issues.

Everyone should complete the bold boxes.

Stretch yourself by completing the dashed boxes.

Challenge yourself by completing the dotted boxes.

Taylor et al. explains that while females, in general, are less aggressive than men there are situations where an aggressive 'fight' response is called for.

What situations may elicit an aggressive response from females?

What does research suggest about expression of the 'flight' response?

The claim that men engage in problem-focused coping while females have a tendency to use emotion-focused coping has not been upheld by many research studies.

Explain one study that has found no gender differences in coping.

Why should research into gender differences from earlier decades be treated with caution?

Research into gender differences faces a number of methodological problems such as confounding variables, social desirability bias and issues with retrospective recall when completing self-report scales.

Identify one factor that may act as a confounding variable in research into stress and gender.

Other than self-report scales, how could researchers investigate gender differences?

▶ Lesson notes p.76

Social support scenarios

Read the scenarios shown below and identify the different kinds of social support available to each individual.

Brenda recently broke her leg in a car crash and while she is on the way to a full recovery, she has been finding it very stressful managing on a day-to-day basis. Luckily her friends have stepped in to help out; offering her lifts to the doctor, showing her how to order her weekly food shop online and stopping by on their way to work to walk her dog.

Type of social support experienced.

Definition of this type of social support.

Raj is worrying about his A Level studies. He recently received low marks for two assessments in different subjects. Deep down he knows he could have performed better if he had taken more time to prepare but he feels like A Levels are not for him. His friends have reminded him how well he has performed in other assessments and pointed out areas of his assessments that were successful.

Type of social support experienced.

Definition of this type of social support.

Liam has had a horrible day at work. He had two difficult meetings with unhappy customers, his team doesn't seem able to work co-operatively and he is concerned they will not reach this month's sales targets. On arriving home his partner gives him a hug and makes him a cup of tea. Then listens while he complains about work and offers to run him a bath to help him relax.

Type of social support experienced.

Definition of this type of social support.

Stretch: What gender differences may exist in the extent to which men and women benefit from social supporting in coping with stress?

▶ Lesson notes p.76

Aggression quintuplets

1. Low levels	2. Increased susceptibility to impulsive behaviour	3. Long-term memories	4. Men are generally more aggressive than women
5. Compare current threats with past experiences	6. Causes the amygdala to become more active when stimulated	7. Evaluating importance of sensory information	8. Peak in young males
9. Includes the hippocampus	10. Violent criminals have higher levels than non-violent criminals	11. Injections increase aggressive behaviour	12. Dexfenfluramine
13. Calming, inhibitory effect on neural firing	14. Includes the amygdala	15. Appears to increase amygdala reactivity	

The limbic system

Group A: ____ ____ ____ ____ ____ **Title of Group:** ....

Brief Summary: ....

....

....

....

....

Group B: ____ ____ ____ ____ ____ **Title of Group:** ....

Brief Summary: ....

....

....

....

....

Group C: ____ ____ ____ ____ ____ **Title of Group:** ....

Brief Summary: ....

....

....

....

....

▶ Lesson notes p.77

Genetic factors – key details

Twin studies

MZ twins genes shared ....

DZ twins genes shared ....

Aggression variance ....

Adoption studies

Positive correlation = genetic effect ....

Positive correlation = adoption effect ....

14,000 ....

Significant number ....

Meta-analyses

24 ....

50% ....

Age differences ....

51 ....

Other factors ....

MAOA

MAOA ....

Metabolism ....

Dutch Family ....

MAOA-H ....

MAOA-L ....

Maltreated children ....

One third ....

Hot and spicy sauce ....

► Lesson notes p.77

Ethological spot the mistakes

Fixed action patterns and innate releasing mechanisms

The ethological explanation states that all members of the same species, (i.e. conspecifics) have a repertoire of stereotyped behaviours which occur in specific conditions and which require learning, i.e. are innate. Ethologist Niko Tinbergen called these innate behaviours flexible action patterns (FAPs). FAPs are produced by a neural mechanism known as an innate releasing mechanism (IRM) and are triggered by a very specific stimulus known as a sign stimulus. The IRM receives its input from sensory recognition circuits that are stimulated by the presence of the sign stimulus. The IRM then communicates with motor control circuits to prevent the FAP associated with that sign stimulus. Tinbergen's research with sticklebacks showed that a male stickleback fish will produce a fixed sequence of mating actions when another male enters its territory. The sign stimulus in this case is not the presence of the other male, but the sight of its distinctive red underbelly that acts as the sign stimulus. If this is covered up, the intruder is not attacked (Tinbergen, 1951).

The 'hydraulic model'

Each FAP has a reservoir of 'action-specific-energy' (ASE) that builds up over time. The appropriate sign stimulus causes the IRM to create this energy and the animal then performs the FAP. After performing the FAP, the reservoir of ASE is empty and the behaviour cannot be repeated until the ASE has built up again. This is sometimes called the hypothetical model of instinctive behaviour (Lorenz, 1950). Lorenz's model provides a way of visualising how these various hypothetical systems might work together to organise an animal's response to its internal and external environment. In the model, FAP is represented by fluid in a reservoir that, as it builds up, places pressure on a spring (the IRM), which is also being pulled by weights (the sign stimulus). Together these lead to the release of the FAP when ASE is

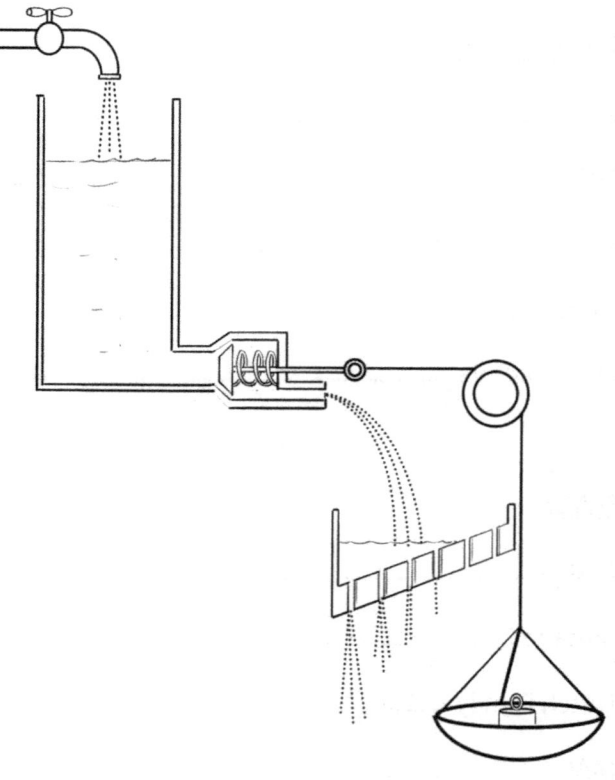

high enough and the appropriate sign stimulus is present. However, the ASE may also be produced in the absence of the sign stimulus if the level of ASE is sufficiently high, i.e. a behaviour can occur spontaneously.

▶ Lesson notes p.79

Ethological AO3: Brief summaries

Making notes on the **evaluations of the ethological explanation of aggression** in these 'briefs' will force you to summarise the information. Use your textbook, (e.g. page 232 of *Complete Companion*) to help you. Try and include the key words written beneath the 'briefs' in your summaries.

CRITICISMS OF INSTINCTIVE VIEW

Environmental factors, interact, 'behaviour patterns', subtle variations

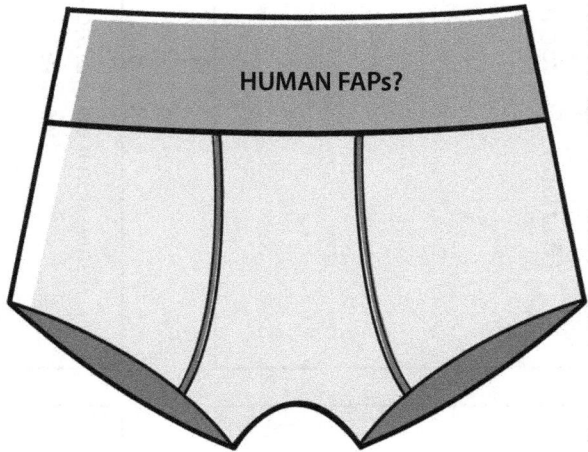

HUMAN FAPs?

Smiling, no longer adaptive, flexible, less predictable

HYDRAULIC MODEL PROBLEM

Feedback, critical point, reduction in biological energy

BENEFITS OF RITUALISED AGGRESSION

Prevents escalation, chest pounding, preventing injury

▶ Lesson notes p.79

Evolution, aggression & now...

(Warfare) – Environment, EEA:	Aggression is an evolved adaptation because…	Has the environment now changed for humans? Is aggression still adaptive? (Genome lag)
(Sexual jealousy) – Environment, EEA:	Aggression is an evolved adaptation because…	Has the environment now changed for humans? Is aggression still adaptive? (Genome lag)
(Sexual competition) – Environment, EEA:	Aggression is an evolved adaptation because…	Has the environment now changed for humans? Is aggression still adaptive? (Genome lag)

▶ Lesson notes p.80

Feedforward marking

Evaluate the frustration-aggression hypothesis. (10 marks)

Social learning theorists, (e.g. Bandura, 1973) have argued that aggressive behaviour is only one possible response to frustration. They claim that frustration produces only generalised arousal in the individual, and that social learning determines how that arousal will influence an individual's behaviour. A limitation of the frustration-aggression hypothesis is that aggression is not an automatic consequence of frustration.

A: *This needs to be explained. Why does social learning determine the behaviour? Why is this a criticism of the frustration-aggression hypothesis?*

Some researchers, (e.g. Bushman, 2002) have found that behaving aggressively is likely to lead to more rather than less aggression in the future. Bushman found that aggressive behaviour kept aggressive thoughts and angry feelings active in memory and made people more angry and more aggressive, directly contradicting the claims that catharsis reduces aggression.

B: *Write a clear AO3 signpost sentence. Make it clear to the examiner what this paragraph will be about and how it is an evaluation of the hypothesis.*

A problem for the frustration-aggression hypothesis is that not all aggression arises from frustration. For example, in a study of baseball games in the US, Reifman et al. (1991) found that as temperatures increased, so did the likelihood that pitchers would display aggressive behaviour toward the batters, with balls often thrown at 90mph direct at the batter's head.

C: *How could this evidence be used to revise the frustration-aggression hypothesis?*

The frustration-aggression hypothesis has been used as an explanation of mass killing. Staub (1996) suggests that mass killings are often rooted in the frustration caused by social and economic difficulties within a society. These frustrations typically lead to scapegoating, (i.e. finding someone to blame) and then discrimination and aggression against this group.

D: *Can you include an example to support your point?*

Priks (2010) studied violent behaviour among Swedish football fans. He used teams' changed position in the league as a measure of frustration and the number of objects (missiles, fireworks etc.) thrown as a measure of aggression. The study showed that when a team performed worse than their fans expected, its supporters threw more things onto the pitch. A one-position drop in the league led to a 5% increase in such unruly behaviour.

E: *At the moment, this paragraph is just a description of a study, it has not been used as a way to evaluate the hypothesis. Write an AO3 signpost to make the evaluation obvious.*

F: *Briefly explain how and why the study supports the hypothesis.*

▶ Lesson notes p.81

Feedforward marking

Teacher Comments:

> *This is a good attempt at evaluating the frustration-aggression hypothesis. You've selected relevant material and there is a clear attempt to structure the answer into five separate points. Occasionally it is unclear that the paragraph is an evaluation. Make sure you 'signpost' your evaluations with a sentence at the start of the paragraph which introduces the point that you are trying to make. In addition, try to ensure that the concluding sentence of each paragraph concisely summarises the argument for/against the hypothesis. Write answers/responses to my A, B, C, D, E, F questions/tasks in order to make improvements.*

Improvements/Amendments/Responses:

A:

....

B:

....

C:

....

D:

....

E:

....

F:

....

▶ Lesson notes p.81

Making it relevant

Bandura and Walters (1963) believed that aggression could not be explained using traditional learning theory. Social learning theory (SLT) suggests that we also learn by observing others. We learn the specifics of *1 behaviour, (e.g. the forms it takes, how often it is enacted, the situations that produce it and the targets towards which it is directed).

Children primarily learn their *2 responses through observation – watching the behaviour of role models and then imitating that behaviour *3. Whereas Skinner's operant conditioning theory claimed that learning takes place through direct reinforcement, Bandura suggested that children learn just by observing role models with whom they identify.

Children also observe and learn about the consequences of *4 behaviour by watching others being reinforced or punished. This is called indirect or vicarious reinforcement. Children witness many examples of *5 behaviour at home and at school, as well as on television and in films. By observing the consequences of *6 behaviour for those who use it, a child gradually learns something about what is considered appropriate (and effective) conduct in the world around them. Thus they learn the behaviours (through observation) and they also learn whether and when such behaviours are worth repeating (through vicarious reinforcement). *7

Bandura (1986) claimed that in order for social learning to take place, the child must form mental representations of events in their social environment. The child must also represent possible rewards and punishments for their *8 behaviour in terms of expectancies of future outcomes. When appropriate opportunities arise in the future, the child will display the learned behaviour as long as the expectation of reward is greater than the expectation of punishment. To accommodate this focus on mental representation, social learning theory has been extended to include the idea of a particular kind of cognitive schema – the script. Children learn rules of conduct from those around them, *9. These rules then become internalised.

If a child is rewarded, (i.e. gets what he wants or is praised by others) for a behaviour, he or she is likely to repeat the same action in similar situations in the future. *10

In addition to forming expectancies of the likely outcomes of their *11 behaviour, children also develop confidence in their ability to carry out the necessary *12 actions. Children for whom this form of behaviour has been particularly disastrous in the past *13 have less confidence (lower sense of self-efficacy) in their ability to use it successfully.

*1	
*2	
*3	
*4	
*5	
*6	
*7	
*8	
*9	
*10	
*11	
*12	
*13	

▶ Lesson notes p.82

Links – Turning study evaluation into theory evaluation

- Very often, the essays will ask you to discuss **theories** but NOT **studies**. In an essay on Social Learning Theory, students often make the mistake of focusing too much on the outline and evaluation of the Bobo doll studies. The Bobo doll study **can** be used in this essay, but only as a way to evaluate the theory. You can use the burger technique in order to help you do that (see **Handout 10**).

- What about evaluating the **Bobo** doll study? Is that relevant? … It could be. In order to gain the evaluation marks you have to evaluate the studies you have used to evaluate the theories!

- What does that mean?! This means that you need to **link** (hence the graphic below!) your evaluation of a study, back to the evaluation of the theory in order to make it relevant to the essay – and get the marks!

🎧 Use the framework below to help you make these links!

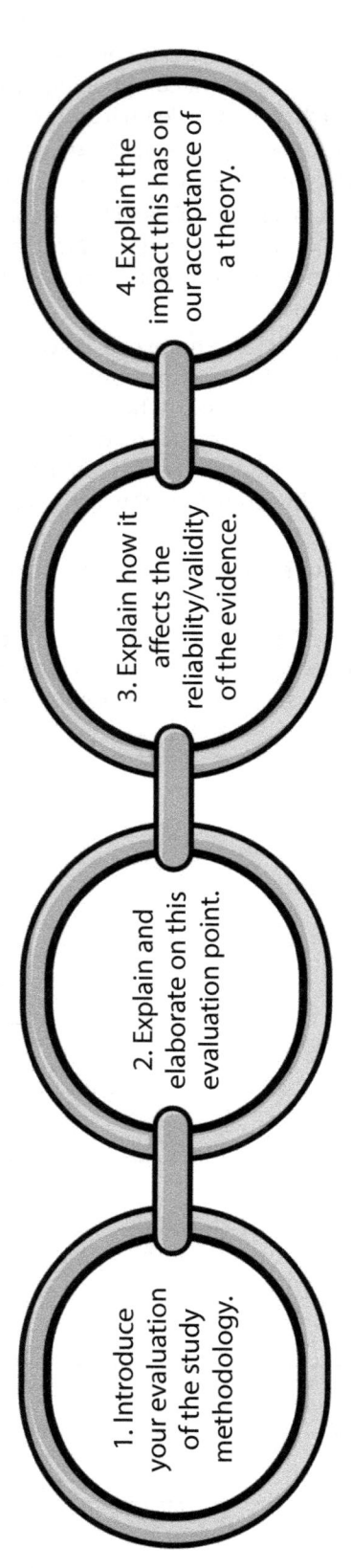

1. Introduce your evaluation of the study methodology.

e.g. One problem with Bandura's study is ecological validity…

2. Explain and elaborate on this evaluation point.

…This is because the children only hit an inflatable doll, rather than a real person who might hit back.

3. Explain how it affects the reliability/validity of the evidence.

…This means the results may not generalise to other settings where children may be given the opportunity to engage in aggressive acts against humans.

4. Explain the impact this has on our acceptance of a theory.

…As such, we cannot be sure from this study that social learning theory and vicarious reinforcement can explain the performance of aggressive acts against other humans.

Links – Turning study evaluation into theory evaluation

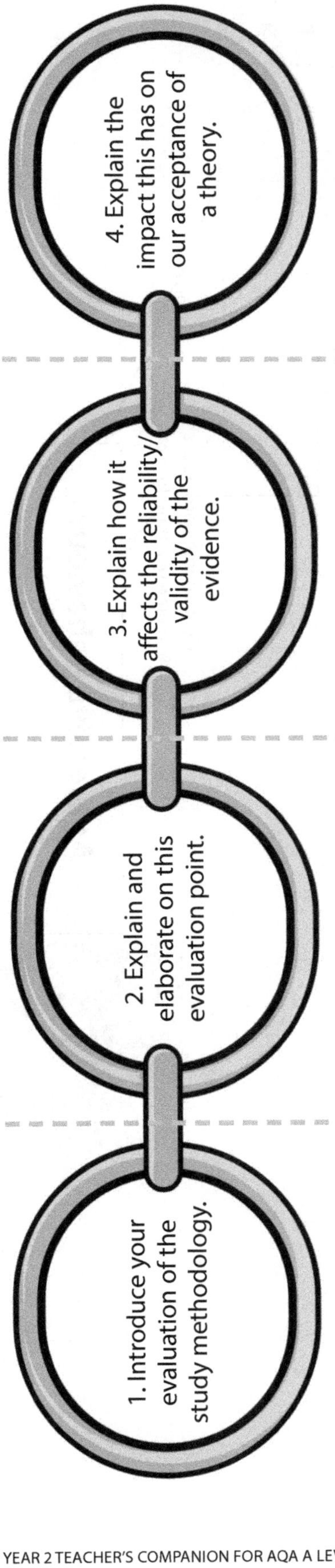

4. Explain the impact this has on our acceptance of a theory.

3. Explain how it affects the reliability/validity of the evidence.

2. Explain and elaborate on this evaluation point.

1. Introduce your evaluation of the study methodology.

Try using this framework yourself using the evaluation below.

Remember, the fourth link is the MOST important and makes the evaluation relevant to the essay.

One problem with Bandura's study is that it only measures short-term effects.

▶ Lesson notes p.82

Linking crowds to aggression

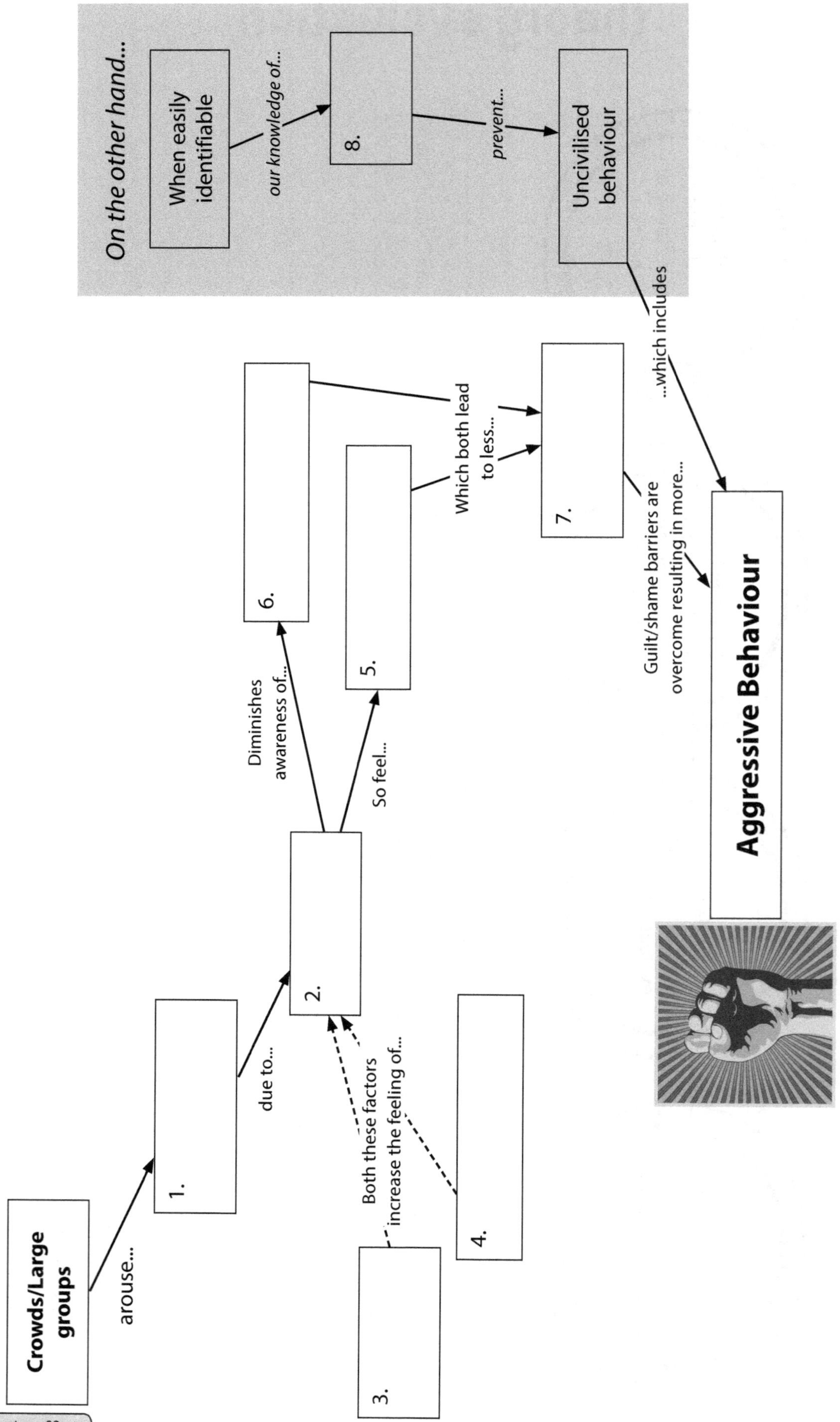

On the other hand...

When easily identifiable → *our knowledge of...* → 8. → *prevent...* → Uncivilised behaviour

...which includes →

Crowds/Large groups → *arouse...* → 1. → *due to...* → 2.

Both these factors increase the feeling of... ⇢ 2.

3. ⇢

4. ⇢

2. → *Diminishes awareness of...* → 6.

2. → *So feel...* → 5.

6. → *Which both lead to less...* → 7.

5. → 7.

7. → Guilt/shame barriers are overcome resulting in more... →

Aggressive Behaviour

▶ Lesson notes p.83

Burger evaluation skills

This technique ensures that you use research studies to evaluate explanations of institutional aggression, rather than just *describe* the research. Your job is to explain how and why the study supports or contradicts the explanations.

Top of the burger: Here you write a simple sentence that introduces the evaluation to the examiner. Try and be specific about which element the dispositional/situational explanation of institutional aggression you are evaluating.

Middle of the burger: Write a brief summary of the research. Only write what is necessary to your evaluation, procedural details can be left out if they are not required to make your general evaluative point. For example, the sampling technique is probably not relevant to the evaluation point you want to make and so it is not necessary to include it.

Bottom of the burger: Here is where you show off your understanding. How and why does this support or contradict the explanation? What would that explanation have predicted? Why? How do these results correspond with those predictions?

> A study that contradicts the importation model explanation is…

> Describe findings of study (and procedure if it is necessary).

> This contradicts the importation model because…

Use these studies and Handout 10 to evaluate the importation and deprivation explanations of institutional aggression.

Mears et al. (2013)

Mears et al. (2013) measured the street code belief system and prison experiences of inmates. They found that a 'code of the street' belief system affects inmate violence and that this effect is particularly pronounced among those inmates who lack family support and are involved in gangs prior to incarceration.

DeLisi et al. (2004)

DeLisi et al. (2004) found that inmates with prior street gang involvement were no more likely than other inmates to engage in prison violence. (Although this may be explained by the fact that violent gang members tend to be isolated from the general inmate population.)

Poole and Regoli (1983)

Poole and Regoli (1983) found that the best indicator of violence among juvenile offenders was pre-institutional violence regardless of any environmental factors in the institution.

McCorkle et al. (1995)

McCorkle et al. (1995), in a major study of 371 US prisons, found that overcrowding, lack of privacy and the lack of meaningful activity all significantly influenced inmate on inmate assaults and inmate on staff assaults.

Harer and Steffensmeier (1996)

Harer and Steffensmeier (1996) collected data from more than 24,000 inmates from 58 prisons across the US. They included variables such as race, criminal history, staff to prisoner ratio and security level and tested which of these variables predicted the individual likelihood of aggressive behaviour while in prison. Race, age and criminal history were the only significant predictors of prison violence.

▶ Lesson notes p.84

Elaboration ladders

Why does that matter?

How would that affect the results/validity?

Can I explain my point with an example?

Have I got evidence?

How could it be improved?

Have I got a counter argument?

How does this affect the main argument?

Use the prompts above to help you elaborate the evaluative arguments on the bottom rung of the ladders.

The more you elaborate your points (without repeating yourself), the more marks you get – hence the smiley face at the top!

Hint: Why does any of this matter? Why is it an issue for the research and our understanding of the topic? Extra: Why is it necessary to measure aggression in artificial ways?

Hint: Why is this a problem? What doesn't it reflect? How might the results be different if aggression was measured differently?

Hint: Explain what this means with examples.

Another issue with much of the research is the operationalisation of 'aggression' is artificial.

Hint: Why does any of this matter? Why is it an issue for the research and our understanding of the topic? Extra: Why not study long-term effects in the lab?

Hint: Explain scenarios the results cannot be generalised to.

Hint: Explain what this means in the context of the research you are evaluating.

However, a weakness of lab experiments on the influence of media/video games on aggression is that they only measure short-term effects.

Hint: Ultimately, why is this useful/interesting for this topic?

Hint: Put this into context. What specific cause/effect relationships have been determined in the research you are evaluating?

Hint: Explain why they can. Use your research methods knowledge.

One of the strengths of lab/field experiments on the influence of media/video games on aggression is that they can determine cause/effect relationships.

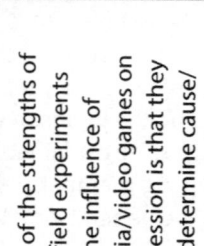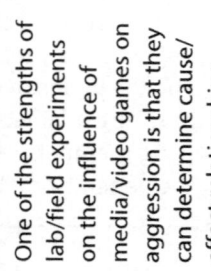

▶ Lesson notes p.84

Application skills

- Students often find application questions difficult to answer and do not receive full marks. When attempting to answer these types of questions, you should remember that the examiner is actually looking for two elements:

  – Selection of appropriate **KNOWLEDGE**

  – That the knowledge has been *APPLIED* appropriately

- One way to ensure that you include both elements is to write your answer using the 'two-sentence' technique.
- This means writing one **KNOWLEDGE** sentence from your textbook or revision that you feel is relevant to the question…
- And then, writing one *APPLIED* sentence where you explain how that knowledge is relevant to the question.
- You can do this several times until you think you have fully answered the question.

Example application question:

Zak spends most of his spare time either playing computer games or video arcade games. His favourite games are the 'shoot-em-up' games, where he tries to kill as many people as possible. His parents start to notice a change in their son's behaviour. Zak's parents are particularly concerned when they find him firing his BB gun at next door's cat and laughing at the poor animal's distress.

Explain the change in Zak's behaviour using your knowledge of explanations of media influence on aggression. *(4 marks)*

Example application answer:

KNOWLEDGE	*Desensitisation assumes that under normal conditions, anxiety about violence inhibits its use. Playing violent video games, however, may lead to aggression by removing this anxiety.*
APPLIED	*Zak has been playing violent video games in most of his spare time and therefore may have become less anxious about violence which means he is more able commit acts of violence such as firing his BB gun.*
KNOWLEDGE	*Desensitised individuals often have a change in their affective reactions, for example, they are less likely to feel sympathy for the victims of violence.*
APPLIED	*This can be seen in the way that Zak laughs at the animal's distress.*

▶ Lesson notes p.85

Application skills

Use **Handout 135** to help you complete this application examination-style question.

> Will spends most of his spare time either playing computer games or video arcade games. His favourite games are the 'shoot-em-up' games, where he tries to kill as many people as possible. His parents start to notice a change in their son's behaviour. When Will has been playing computer games he gets into more fights with his brothers who he believes are 'getting at him'.
>
> Explain Will's behaviour using your knowledge of explanations of media influence on aggression. *(4 marks)*

KNOWLEDGE	*Cognitive priming suggests that…*
APPLIED	
KNOWLEDGE	
APPLIED	

▶ Lesson notes p.85

Defining and measuring crime: True/False

1. Behaviours deemed as wrong by society become 'crimes'.	T	F

Extension / correction (circle)

2. Crimes vary from country to country, from decade to decade.	T	F

Extension / correction (circle)

3. Crime is a social construction.	T	F

Extension / correction (circle)

4. The Government publishes official statistics on crime every 10 years.	T	F

Extension / correction (circle)

5. Only crimes are recorded in the official statistics (National Crime Reporting Standard, NCRS).	T	F

Extension / correction (circle)

► Lesson notes p.86

Defining and measuring crime: True/False

6. The Crime Survey for England and Wales (CSEW) asks a sample of people to identify crimes that have been committed against them (victim surveys).	T	F

Extension / correction (circle)

7. The CSEW selects a random sample from the Royal Mail's list of addresses.	T	F

Extension / correction (circle)

8. The CSEW consists of a questionnaire with the questions tailored towards the participant.	T	F

Extension / correction (circle)

9. The Offending, Crime and Justice Survey (OCJS) was carried out annually.	T	F

Extension / correction (circle)

10. Official statistics are a more objective way of measuring crime compared to self-report methods.	T	F

Extension / correction (circle)

▶ Lesson notes p.86

Offender Profiling: Top-down flow chart

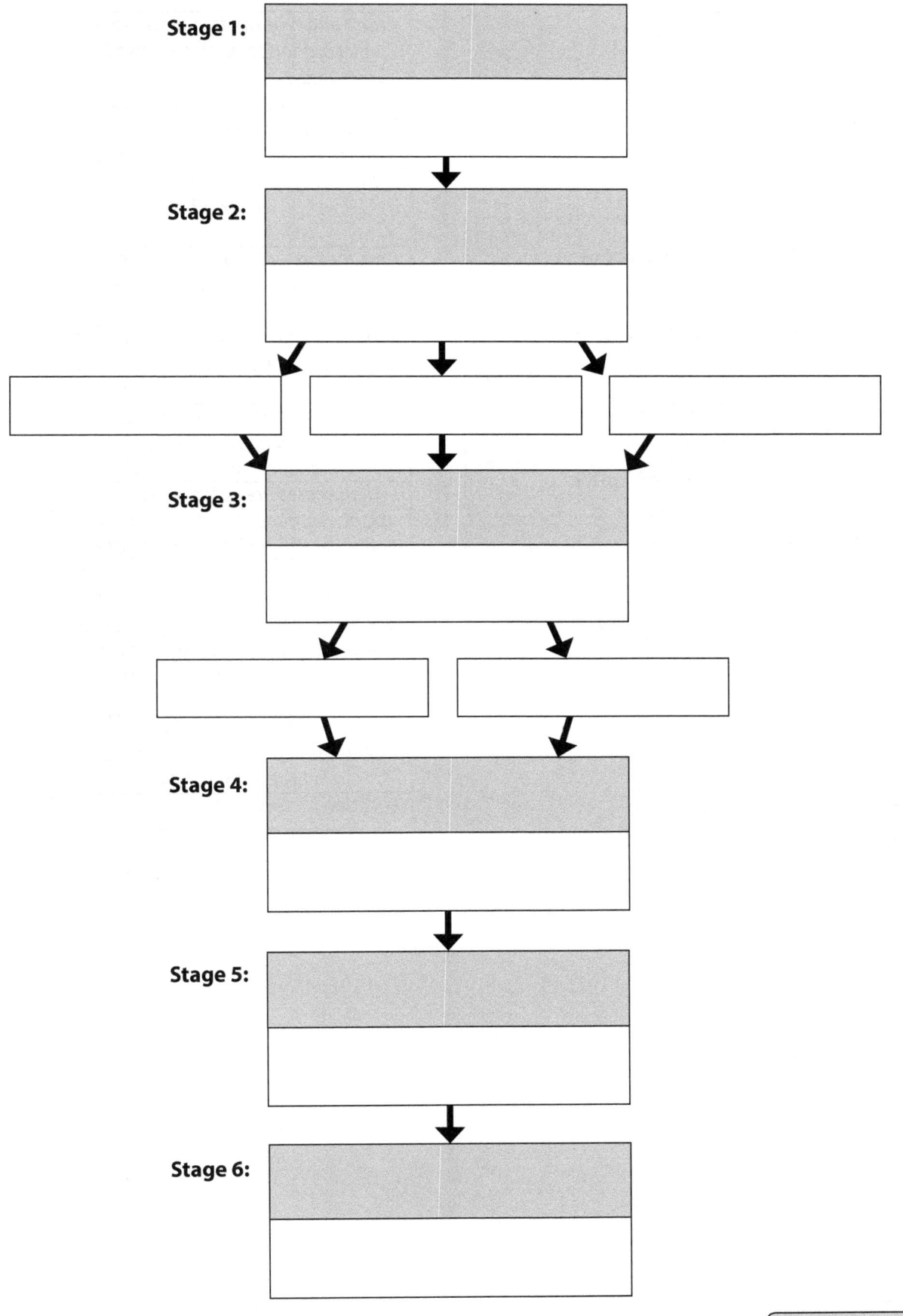

Stage 1:

Stage 2:

Stage 3:

Stage 4:

Stage 5:

Stage 6:

▶ Lesson notes p.87

Offender Profiling: Top-down flow chart

	Crime and type of offender is classified as organised or disorganised. Organised… Disorganised…
	Written report is given to the investigation agency and persons matching the profile are evaluated.
	Murder type – mass murder, spree or serial?
Crime Assessment	Time factors – did the crime take a long time, short time? Night or day?
Apprehension	Crime is unplanned, random victim, little engagement with victim. Crime scene contain clues, e.g. blood, semen.
Crime Assessment Part 2	Data collected on the crime scene, background info on the victim and details of the crime itself.
Criminal Profile	Hypotheses are constructed about the background, habits and beliefs of offender. This informs investigation.
Decision Process Models	Crime is planned, victim targeted, body transported, weapon hidden. Offender intelligent, competent, lives with partner.
Profiling Inputs	The profiler starts to organise the data into meaningful patterns
	If suspect is arrested, the profile-generating process is reviewed and checked for validity.
	Location factors – was the crime scene the same as the murder scene?

▶ Lesson notes p.87

Bottom-up approach:
Spot the deliberate mistakes

In the bottom-up approach, the profiles are driven from the judgements of the profiler rather than from 'above' by the actual data.

Approach 1: Investigative Psychology

Canter proposed that profiling can and should be based on psychological theory and research.

- **Interpersonal coherence:** People are inconsistent in their behaviour therefore there will be links (correlations) with elements of the crime and how people behave in everyday life. At the same time, people's behaviour remains stable over time and therefore looking at the differences in crimes over a four-year period might offer further clues.

- **Finger awareness:** Certain behaviours may reveal an awareness of particular police techniques and past experience, for example Davies et al. (1997) found that rapists who conceal fingerprints often had a previous conviction for burglary.

- **Smallest space analysis:** Data about many crime scenes and offender characteristics are correlated so that the most common connections can be identified. For example, Salfati and Canter (1999) analysed the co-occurrence of 48 crime scene and offender characteristics taken from 82 UK murder cases where the victim was a stranger. They identified three underlying themes:
  - *Instrumental opportunistic* – 'opportunistic' refers to using murder to obtain something or accomplish a goal, 'instrumental' means that the offender took the easiest chances.
  - *Instrumental cognitive* – a concern about being detected and therefore more unplanned.
  - *Expressive impulsive* – controlled, in the heat of strong emotions, feel provoked by victim.

Approach 2: Geographical profiling

Canter has also proposed that criminals reveal themselves through the locations they choose. Geographical profilers are concerned with who rather than where. Offenders are more likely to commit a crime near where they live or where they habitually travel because it involves less effort.

- **Circle theory** Canter and Larkin (1993) proposed that most offenders have a spatial mindset – they commit their crimes within a kind of imagined circle.
  - *Commuter* – offender's home is within the geographical area where crimes are committed.
  - *Marauder* – offender travels to another geographical area and commits crimes within a defined space around which a circle can be drawn.
- **Criminal geographic targeting (CGT)** This is a computerised system developed by Kim Rossmo. It produces a two-dimensional map displaying spatial data related to time, distance and movement to and from crime scenes. The map is called a *jeopardy surface*.

▶ Lesson notes p.88

Historical approach crossword

ACROSS

2. Body type most likely to commit crimes of violence.

5. The idea that certain individuals are born with a criminal personality which is a throwback to earlier evolutionary primate forms. [Two words]

10. 'Asymmetry of the _____' (a characteristic historically associated with criminality).

11. 'Excessive _____ of the jaw and cheekbones' (a characteristic historically associated with criminality).

12. Term used to describe inborn features and characteristics.

13. The number of 'types of criminals' Lombroso identified in his 1897 book.

DOWN

1. One of the main sources of Lombroso's empirical evidence.

3. In later years, Lombroso recognised that other factors and influences would contribute to criminality.

4. Type of crimes said to be committed by 'Pyknic' body type.

5. 'Excessive length of _____' (a characteristic historically associated with criminality).

6. Historical approach to criminality based on body shape.

7. Criminologist in 1876 who suggested that offenders possessed characteristics similar to lower primates.

8. '_____ of unusual size' (a characteristic historically associated with criminality).

9. Criminals suffering from mental illness.

▶ Lesson notes p.90

Biological explanations – key details

Genetic explanations

52% ....

21% ....

28 ....

MAOA ....

900 ....

CHH13 ....

5–10% ....

1000 ....

12% ....

44% ....

Neural explanations

60% ....

Prefrontal cortex ....

71 ....

Limbic system ....

NGRI ....

Amygdala ....

Serotonin ....

Dopamine ....

Noradrenaline ....

▶ Lesson notes p.90

Eysenck: Evaluation 'signposts'

'Level 4' evaluation includes the 'effective use of evidence' and is 'coherent, clear and focused'. One of the most important opportunities to show this is at the start of every evaluation paragraph. The sentence or two at the start of the paragraph sets out your *clear and coherent* line of argument, it ensures that the paragraph is *focused,* it ensures that you use the evidence *effectively*.

Perhaps even more importantly, it screams to the examiner 'I AM NOW DOING SOME EVALUATION!' Use words like 'supports', 'contradicts', 'strength', 'weakness', 'practical application', 'on the other hand' etc. Make it clear in the signpost what argument will be made in that paragraph.

Add signposts to the following evaluation paragraphs:

> Zuckerman (1987) found +.52 correlation for identical (MZ) twins on neuroticism compared with .24 for non-identical (DZ) twins, showing a large genetic component. For extraversion the figures were +.51 and +.12 respectively. Zuckerman (1989) provided similar data for psychoticism. However, even though this shows there is a considerable genetic component, it is not as high as Eysenck had claimed – a +.50 correlation means that about 40% of the variance in these traits is due to genes.

> A number of psychologists suggest that people may be consistent in similar situations but not across situations. For example, someone may be relaxed and calm at home but quite neurotic at work. Walter Mischel has supported his situational theory with research. Mischel and Peake (1982) asked family, friends and strangers to rate 63 students in a variety of situations and found almost no correlation between traits displayed. Any regularity of behaviour is likely to be due to the fact they we tend to often be in similar situations. This means that the notion of a criminal personality is flawed as people don't simply have 'one' personality.

> When a person answers the EPQ they are responding to the demands of a questionnaire – they are asked to select traits that apply to them but their responses may not represent 'reality'. For example, consider the question 'Are you rather lively?' For most people the answer is probably 'sometimes', but the questionnaire forces them to say yes or no. In addition people may tend towards a socially desirable answer and thus their answers are not truthful. This is countered by the use of lie scales in such questionnaires. This is a set of questions such as, 'Are all your habits good and desirable?' A person who says 'yes' consistently to lie scale items is probably being 'dishonest' through the questionnaire and their data are discarded.

> Dunlop et al. (2012) found that both extraversion and psychoticism were good predictors of delinquency. However, the participants were all students and their friends (15–75 years) and delinquency was an assessment of minor offences in the previous 12 months, (e.g. theft, traffic offences – though armed robbery was included).

> The three traits are good predictors of delinquency, but not good enough as a means of detecting who is likely to become an offender. On the other hand, it may provide some useful ideas of how to treat offenders, for example by modifying the socialisation experiences of children who may have the potential to become offenders.

▶ Lesson notes p.92

Feedforward marking

Outline the cognitive explanation of offending behaviour. (6 marks)

The cognitive explanation of offending behaviour ~~includes~~ the idea of cognitive distortions.

A: Can you give a quick definition of what a 'cognitive distortion' is and why they might be relevant to offending behaviour?

For example, one relevant cognitive distortion is 'hostile attribution bias'. 'Attribution' refers to what we do when we observe someone's actions and draw an inference about what it means. A hostile attribution bias is when someone has a leaning towards always thinking the worst. Such negative interpretations then lead to more aggressive behaviour. In terms of criminal behaviour, hostile attribution bias is most likely to be linked to increased levels of aggression.

B: Can you give an example of a 'hostile attribution bias' to show your understanding?

C: What are these types of distortions called?

Another distortion is where the consequences of a situation are either over or under exaggerated. ~~In the case~~ of criminal behaviour, under exaggeration can explain how an offender may reduce any negative interpretation of their behaviour before or after a crime has been committed. For example, a burglar might think, when planning a crime, that stealing a few things from a wealthy family really has very little effect on their lives. Thus the burglar doesn't feel as bad about committing the crime and it doesn't really effect their conscience.

D: What is the difference between 'effect' and 'affect'? Write yourself a short guide on how to use them in a sentence.

Another cognitive explanation of offending behaviour is Kohlberg's (1969) theory of moral reasoning. Kohlberg interviewed boys and men about the reasons for their moral decisions and constructed a stage theory of moral development. Each stage represents a person becoming more mature.

E: This sentence is a bit simplistic. Rewrite the sentence. <u>How</u> do they become more morally mature?

Most criminals are likely to be at the pre-conventional level (Hollin et al., 2002) which fits with the idea of an 'age of criminal responsibility'.

F: What does that level mean? How does it explain offending behaviour?

One major issue is that Kohlberg's theory concerns moral thinking rather than behaviour. Krebs and Denton (2005) suggest that moral principles are only one factor in moral behaviour and may be overridden by more practical factors, such as making personal financial gains. In fact, Krebs and Denton found, when analysing real-life moral decisions, that moral principles were used to justify behaviour after it had been performed.

G: This is a well-argued and interesting point. But why should it NOT be in your answer?

▶ Lesson notes p.92

Feedforward marking

Teacher Comments:

> You have included an excellent level of detail on the cognitive approach for explaining offending behaviour. It is accurate and there are no major errors. In most topics you have also included specialist terminology (although there are a couple of additions you could make). The main area for improvement is on proving that you understand the cognitive approach – this can be done by including more relevant examples and by explaining the relevance of key terms. Also be careful to ensure that all of the material included is relevant to the question.

Improvements/Amendments/Responses:

A:

....

B:

....

C:

....

D:

....

E:

....

F:

....

G:

► Lesson notes p.92

Differential association – Evaluation elaboration

Your A Level exam essays are marked out of 16 and evaluation will be judged as part of the marking process. Many students miss out on evaluation marks because they do not *elaborate* their evaluations in sufficient detail to get the full marks. Here are the general marking descriptors for evaluation: *(Level 1 = Evaluation/Discussion is limited), (Level 2 = Evaluation/Discussion is partly effective), (Level 3 = Evaluation/Discussion is mostly effective), (Level 4 = Evaluation is thorough/effective).*

Obviously, the higher the level of evaluation, the more marks you are likely to be awarded. Your task here is to match up the evaluation points for the differential association explanation of offending behaviour from the left, further and further to the right in order to increase your evaluation marks.

Level 1.. Level 2.. Level 3 .... Level 4!

The major strength of the differential association explanation of offending is that it changed people's views about the origins of criminal behaviour.	This is because it is largely based on correlational analysis.	This evidence suggests that criminality appears to run in families and that therefore suggests that criminal behaviours and attitudes are the result of social learning.	In terms of peer influences, it could be that offenders seek out other offenders and this would explain why offenders are likely to have peers who are offenders.

	Social learning influences are probably confined to 'smaller' crimes rather than violent and impulsive ones such as rape and murder.		

Differential association theory is supported by evidence.	The theory marked an important shift from 'blaming' individual factors to pointing to social factors. The theory suggested that crime did not have to be explained in terms of personality (mad or bad).	Predisposing factors may be innate genetic ones or early experiences such as maltreatment.	Sutherland also shifted the emphasis away from 'bad' individuals by highlighting white-collar crime which is often committed by those otherwise seen as 'respectable'.

There are methodological issues with this theory.		On the other hand, in England and Wales in 2014 there were 500 murders and 400,000 burglaries; so the theory is able to explain a large proportion of the crime.	A related criticism is that differential association also can't explain why most offences are committed by people under 21.

The absence of biological factors from this account is a drawback.	Osborne and West (1982) found that, where there is a father with a criminal conviction, 40% of the sons had committed a crime by the age of 18 compared to 13% of sons of non-criminal fathers.	The problem with this type of data is that it is not possible to determine the cause from the effect.	Indeed, attachment research suggests that emotional problems in childhood make a child vulnerable to deviant peer influences later in life. As such, the social approach on its own may be an insufficient explanation.

The differential association explanation struggles to account for all kinds of crime.	The diathesis-stress model may offer a better account by combining social factors with vulnerability factors.	Such an approach has important real-world implications because learning environments can be changed.	

			On the other hand, it could also be argued that the evidence could be explained in terms of genetic inheritance as well.

► Lesson notes p.93

Building the bigger picture

Id:

Ego:

Superego:

Phallic stage:

Offending behaviour:

Electra complex:

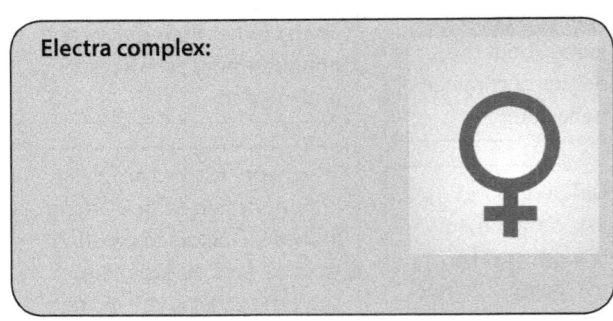

Oedipus complex:

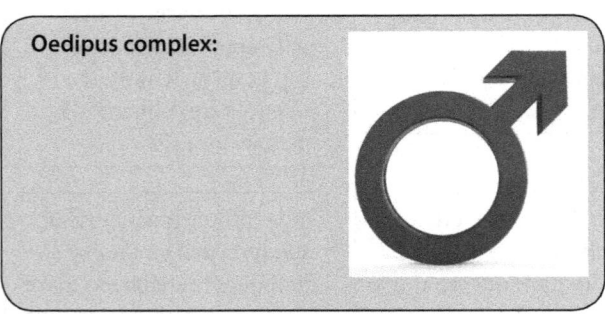

Underdeveloped:

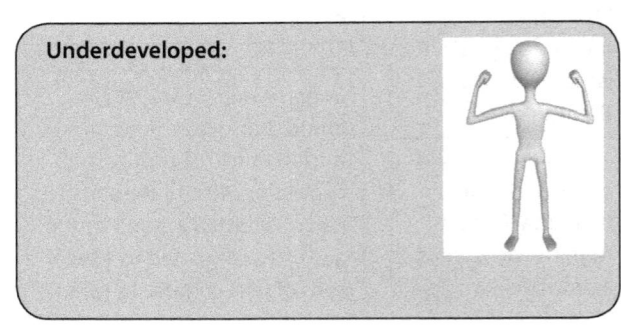

Parents:

Overdeveloped:

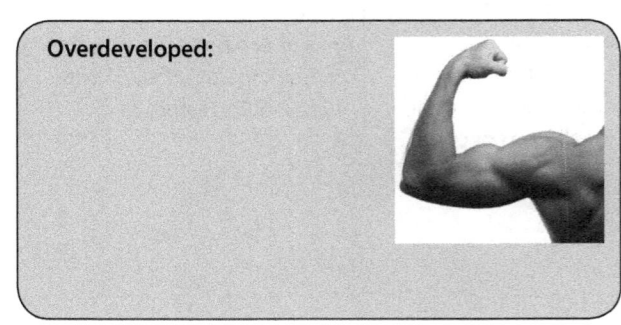

▶ Lesson notes p.94

Considering the evidence

In the UK in 2015 there were about 80,000 men and 4000 women in prison. This population has almost doubled from 20 years ago. Do you think that this increase in custodial sentencing is worthwhile and justified? Or do you think that fewer offences should receive a prison sentence?

Tasks:

1. **Cut out the arguments/evidence/data fragments below.**
2. **Sort the fragments into arguments for and against the increase in custodial sentences.**
3. **Rate each of the arguments from 1 (very weak argument) to 5 (very strong argument).**
4. **Review the arguments/evidence and write a brief conclusion.**

In the US, murder rates are not lower in the states where there is the death penalty, despite the fact that the punishment is higher.

Deterrent. Prison sentences discourage the general population from committing crime. We learn indirectly from the consequences of others' behaviour.

Recidivism. Punishing the behaviour decreases the likelihood of offenders repeating the behaviour in the future.

The majority of offenders are not dangerous, (i.e. violent, rapists, murderers etc).

Prisons may increase the likelihood of reoffending because they are 'a training ground for crime'.

Recent data suggests that 25% of prisoners are in overcrowded accommodation. Calhourn (1962) showed that rats in overcrowded conditions became aggressive, stressed, ill and 'hyper-sexed'.

There are alternative ways to achieve retribution, e.g. restorative justice… where offenders make amends to their victims in some way.

Klein et al. (1977) found that offenders sentenced to community rehabilitation were less likely to reoffend.

Deindividuation. Prison guards and uniforms may lead to a loss of individual identity which is associated with increased aggression.

The Howard League for prison reform reported 10,000 incidents of self-harm in 2008.

Incapacitation. To protect the public from violent offenders and psychopaths.

Retribution. The victim and their family/friends wish to feel that a sense of justice has been done… that the offender has paid for their crime.

Rehabilitation. Prison offers the ability to educate the offender and/or treat them for mental health issues.

Depression. Lack of control, a new and frightening experience and anxiety about the future lead to feelings of hopelessness and helplessness.

Custodial sentences for parents may lead to separation anxiety, attachment issues and financial issues for the family.

50% of the prison population go on to reoffend.

▶ Lesson notes p.95

Hobbs and Holt (1976)

What potential threat is there to the external validity of this study?

What was the independent variable in this study?

What was the dependent variable in this study?

What is observer bias and why is it a threat to this study?

How did the researchers attempt to minimise observer bias?

What experimental design was used in this study?

What is the potential problem with that design?

How did the researchers attempt to account for this in the results?

Hobbs and Holt observed a token economy in use at Alabama Boys Industrial School, a state training school for adolescent delinquents (aged 12–15 years). The aim was to reduce inappropriate social behaviour.

The staff at the centre were given extensive training: 3 x four hours and then twice weekly over three months. In total, 125 delinquent males were observed living in four cottages. One cottage was a control group where the boys did not received tokens. Baseline data, before tokens, were collected for all groups.

Two supervisors recorded what each boy did in a number of categories. For example:

- Following cottage rules, (e.g. no smoking during games).
- Before dinner: following rules of group games, completing assigned chores (sweeping, taking out rubbish).
- After dinner: interacting with peers 30–50% of the time (defined as being less than 3 feet way, talking and looking at peer, and body facing peer).

Boys were told the target criteria and told how many tokens they could earn in each category. Each day the boys were told how many tokens they had earned. They were taken to a token economy store once a week where they could buy drinks, sweets, toys, cigarettes. They could also save tokens and use them for more expensive off-campus activities such as baseball games or a visit home.

The baseline mean percentages for social behaviours before the boys were given tokens were 66%, 47% and 73% for each of the three cottages. These increased post-tokens to 91%, 81% and 94%, an average increase of 27%. The control group showed no increase in the same time period.

What type of experiment is this?

What is the strength of that type of experiment?

▶ Lesson notes p.95

Moving up the levels

Imagine that you have been set the following examination question:

- Outline anger management as a method for dealing with offending behaviour. (6 marks)

The answer below is accurate but may not gain full marks because it lacks detail. Use the table below to make *small additions* to this answer that take it up to a 'level 4' maximum mark answer.

Anger management programmes use a cognitive approach*1. Novaco (2011) has identified three key aims for any anger management programme:

- Aim 1*2 – greater self-awareness.
- Aim 2*3 – learning to control the physiological state.
- Aim 3*4 – learning problem solving skills, strategic withdrawal and assertiveness.

Most anger management programmes used with offenders are based on work by Novaco 's stress inoculation approach.*5 The three key steps are:

- **Cognitive preparation:** In the initial phase clients learn about anger generally.*6
- **Skill acquisition:** In the second phase clients are taught various skills to help manage their anger*7 and taught better communication skills.*8
- **Application training:** Clients apply the skills initially in controlled situations*9, receive extensive feedback and later clients can try out their skills in real world settings.*10

---

*1	
*2	
*3	
*4	
*5	
*6	
*7	
*8	
*9	
*10	

▶ Lesson notes p.96

Plenary Questions

In two years, when your memory of this lesson has decayed, what fact are you most likely to remember?

How would you describe restorative justice to a victim of crime? Would you recommend it?

What are the three most important key words from this lesson and what do they mean?

Define restorative justice in less than 16 words.

Bullet point three key aims of restorative justice.

Summarise in one sentence what a 'peace circle' is.

Compare restorative justice to custodial sentencing in less than 16 words.

If your parents ask about today's psychology lesson, what are you likely to tell them?

What was the most difficult part of this lesson to understand? Why?

Pick one aspect of restorative justice that might be a problem.

How does this lesson fit in the overall forensic psychology topic?

▶ Lesson notes p.97

Tolerance & withdrawal

Read the outline below of tolerance in relation to addictive behaviour.

Identify 8 key terms in the outline below that you would be sure to include if you were asked to produce an outline of tolerance.

When using drugs for a long time, tolerance can develop. This means that increasingly larger doses are needed to experience the same effects as the body no longer responds in the same way to the drug.

Metabolic tolerance occurs when enzymes become more effective at metabolising the drug resulting in reduced concentrations in the blood and at the sites of drug action. This means the effect experienced is weaker than before and so the user takes higher doses.

Prolonged drug use can also lead to changes in receptor density which reduces the response to the normal dose of the drug.

Finally, learned tolerance refers to the way users will become accustomed to functioning normally when under the influence of the drug and so higher doses are needed to experience an effect.

Give a brief outline of withdrawal syndromes associated with addiction.

Use as many of the following key terms and phrases as possible.

discontinued	wears off
negative impact	acute
physical dependence	post-acute
cessation	symptoms

_____

_____

_____

_____

_____

_____

_____

_____

_____

_____

_____

_____

_____

_____

_____

_____

_____

_____

_____

_____

_____

_____

_____

▶ Lesson notes p.98

Apply your addiction knowledge

Terrance hurt his back in a car crash and found it uncomfortable to sit and stand due to the whiplash he experienced. He was prescribed a course of painkillers and advised to take one tablet twice a day. After a few weeks, Terrance decided to increase this dose to four tablets a day as he was worried the pain would return. He was finding he needed a larger dose to experience the same effect as those first few weeks using the medication.

When he realised his course would shortly run out he began to feel anxious. He returned to his GP complaining of severe backache to ensure he would receive a second prescription. He quickly used up this second course as he was taking larger and larger doses and so was soon back at the doctor's surgery. His GP realised Terrance had been misusing his medication and refused to prescribe a third course.

Without the medication in his system, Terrance no longer felt 'normal'. He experienced increased anxiety, shakiness and experienced terrible headaches. In the first few weeks without the painkillers he had strong physical cravings. Months later, Terrance was still reporting periods of emotional turmoil.

Use your knowledge of physical and psychological dependence, tolerance and withdrawal to explain Terrance's experiences.

▶ Lesson notes p.98

Single-sentence summary

For each risk factor create a single-sentence summary. It's a tricky task to produce a summary in just one sentence; you need to think really carefully about the central point for each risk factor. The first one has been done for you.

Biological factors

Generic vulnerability	Twin studies suggest an inherited predisposition making addictive habits more likely.
Dopamine	

Stress

Self-medication	
Traumatic stress	

Personality

Key traits	
Addiction-prone	
Personality disorder	

Apply your knowledge

Lottie's family regularly spend £5 to £10 on scratch cards in the hope of winning a large cash prize. She is in a lottery syndicate with her work colleagues, as well as buying her own lottery tickets when it is a rollover weekend. She is often short of money before payday as she often logs on to online bingo sites.

Briefly explain risk factors relevant to Lottie's gambling addiction. (4 marks)

▶ Lesson notes p.99

Social risk factors match up

Students may miss out on evaluation marks because they do not elaborate their comments and evaluations sufficiently to access the higher mark bands. Your discussion of the social risk factors related to the development of addiction needs to be 'effective'. Match the evaluative points from left to right in order to increase the effectiveness of the evaluation.

Rudimentary ⇨ ⇨ ⇨ ⇨   Basic ⇨ ⇨ ⇨ ⇨   Reasonable ⇨ ⇨ ⇨ ⇨   Effective ⇨ ⇨ ⇨ ⇨

Bahr et al. (2005) supports the importance of family influences on substance abuse.	Stattin & Kerr (2000) suggest an absence of parental monitoring may result in adolescents revealing too much about their substance abuse to their parents.	Adolescents with tolerant parents were also more likely to interact with peers who smoked, drank or took drugs.	Therefore, peer influences as a risk factor for development of addictive behaviour may be overstated.
Drug and alcohol abuse may result from a withdrawal of parental involvement rather than parental tolerance of addictive behaviour.	Litt & Stock (2011) found teenagers who viewed peers' Facebook profiles that portrayed alcohol use were more likely to drink themselves.	Parent's inability to deal with this over-sharing may lead to them view their child as out of control and so stop monitoring their child's behaviour.	This research suggests exposure to social media alters adolescents' normative perceptions and other alcohol-related risk cognitions.
Social media research supports the claim that peers are an importance influence on addictive behaviours.	They found tolerant parental attitudes and sibling substance abuse were strongly associated with increased prevalence of binge drinking, smoking and drug use.	Their study found parental rather than peer influence was a stronger predictor of smoking adoption.	This lack of monitoring and control enables the adolescent to continue abusing substances and increases their vulnerability to peer influences.
De Vries et al. (2006) challenge the claim that peer influence is an important part of the development of addictive behaviour.	They suggest smoking behaviour is more likely a consequence of friendship – smokers befriend other smokers rather than encourage non-smokers to take up the habit.	Teens reported exposure to Facebook profiles led to a greater willingness to drink alcohol, more positive feelings towards drinking and lowered perceptions of negative consequences.	This suggests tolerant parental attitudes make it more likely adolescents will seek the company of others who endorse substance abuse.

STRETCH: Create your own effective evaluation discussing real-world applications of research into social risk factors.

▶ Lesson notes p.100

Detailed descriptions

Use your textbook to develop the detail in the description of brain neurochemistry as an explanation for nicotine addiction.

Nicotine can have a range of different effects.

The nicotine paradox describes how smoking can have both a stimulating and relaxing effect.

Nicotine attaches to neurones that release dopamine in nearby brain receptors.

Nicotine also has an effect on other neuro-transmitters and enzymes in the brain.

The short lasting effects of nicotine creates a continual need.

Key terms to include: Dopamine, ventral tegmental area (VTA), nucleus accumbens (NAc), glutamate, GABA, monoamine oxidase (MAO).

▶ Lesson notes p.100

Save or steal?

For each evaluative category create a brief summary of relevant evidence and suitable expansions.			
Research evidence supports the effect of nicotine on brain chemistry.	Research with Parkinson's sufferers supports the link between nicotine and dopamine.	Implications: the effect of nicotine addiction and negative mood.	Gender differences in the effect of nicotine on dopamine.
Now **steal** any further evaluative comments made by others in your class.			
Finally, **save** the most relevant points for each evaluation to create four 50-word summaries.			

▶ Lesson notes p.101

Examining evaluations

Students were asked to answer the following question by their teacher:

Give *two* criticisms of the learning theory of nicotine addiction. (3 + 3 marks)

Read the two candidates' answers to identify effective comments and areas needing improvement.

Candidate 1.

Research supports the claim that peers influence smoking behaviour. Karcher & Finn (2005) reported youths were 8 times more likely to smoke if their close friends did. This was greater than if their parents smoked (1.88 times more likely) or if their siblings smoked (2.64 times more likely). This suggests peers are the primary influence for adolescents who experimented with smoking.

Gender differences exist in smoking behaviour. Women are more likely than men to light up a cigarette when stressed and their dependence on nicotine is said to develop more rapidly than men's.

This answer is effective because…

However, the candidate could improve…

Candidate 2.

Cues have been shown to be classically conditioned. Heavy smokers showed a greater approach bias compared to ex and non-smokers. The greater the bias, the higher the craving score. Learning theory has led to the development of addiction therapies. Cue exposure therapy (CET) presents smokers with cues but denies them the opportunity to smoke. This extinguishes the association between the cue and smoking so reduces cravings that arise in the presence of the cue. CET's success has been reported by Unrod et al. (2014) who found 76 moderately dependent smokers showed a progressive decline in craving over six sessions.

This answer is effective because…

However, the candidate could improve…

▶ Lesson notes p.102

Slot machine addiction

Charlie enjoys playing slot machines in his local pub. His favourite machine once gave him a pay-out of £150, since then he always makes sure he plays this machine when he is in the pub. A few times he has nearly reached the top pay-out only to fail at the final hurdle. Every so often Charlie wins £5 or £10 which he feeds straight back into the machine. He recently visited a casino and loved the bright lights and sound of pound coins falling into the trays of the slot machines lined up in a row.

Use your knowledge of learning theory to explain Charlie's gambling.

Partial and variable reinforcement.

The 'big win' hypothesis.

The 'near miss'.

The gambling environment.

▶ Lesson notes p.102

Improve the evaluation

A student has written an evaluation of learning theory's explanation of gambling addiction below. However, while a range of evaluative points has been identified they are underdeveloped and the author has neglected to use paragraphs to produce a clear and coherent evaluation.

Use their answer to produce an improved 10-mark evaluation of learning theory's explanation of gambling.

One problem with learning theory is that it cannot explain all forms of gambling through the concept of operant conditioning. This is because gambling can have short-term or long-term intervals between action and outcome. The theory also fails to explain why only some people become addicted to gambling; not everyone who has one win goes on to develop an addiction. It has been found that high-frequency gamblers (those who play a lot) continue gambling when rewards occur occasionally compared to low-frequency gamblers. However, the suggestion of a 'big win' encouraging further gambling is supported when considering the role of irrational beliefs, e.g. the gambler overestimates their chance of winning. Individual differences should be considered. Some people may develop an addiction through imitating role models but others may gamble due to a mood disorder, poor coping skills or negative life events. These people use gambling to improve their emotional state.

To help you identify the different evaluative points, colour code the essay
(each colour should have been a discrete paragraph in the student's answer).

- ☐ Learning theory cannot explain all types of gambling.

- ☐ The theory cannot explain why only some people become addicted.

- ☐ There is support for the effect of partial reinforcement.

- ☐ Reinforcement schedules may lead to irrational beliefs.

- ☐ Different pathways exist to gambling addiction.

▶ Lesson notes p.102

Cognitive biases match up

Match the key term to the definition and gambler's thoughts.

The gambler's fallacy	Illusions of control	The 'near miss' bias	The recall bias

Almost winning gives the gambler a feeling of not constantly losing, rather, they are nearly winning so the gambling behaviour is maintained.

The belief that completely random events are somehow influenced by recent events.

The tendency to remember and overestimate wins while forgetting about or underestimating losses.

Performance of superstitious behaviours which the gambler believes helps them manipulate the event in their favour.

The last four roulette spins have all landed on a red number. It must be time for black to win.

When playing the lottery, I don't lose that often. In fact, I'll probably win at least £10 on the next draw.

The horse I bet on came in second so I almost won. Next time I'll pick the winner.

I only play slot machines from 6pm to 8pm in the pub as that is when they are most likely to pay out.

▶ Lesson notes p.103

Making links

Link the point to the conclusion using your knowledge of research into drug therapy as a treatment for addiction.

NRT trials are not truly 'blind' because patients receiving nicotine have a different experience than those given a placebo.

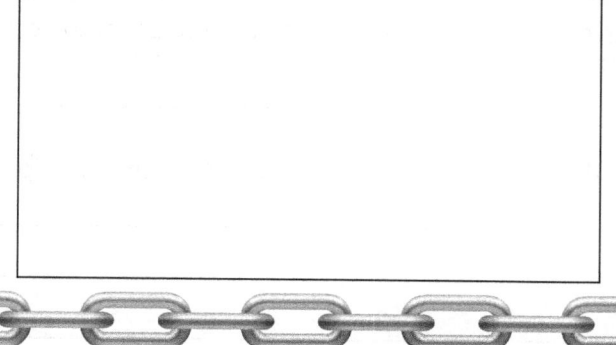

The lack of effective blinding in trials means conclusions about NRT therapy are more uncertain than previously claimed.

Opioid antagonists only offer a crude and general way of reducing the effect of the brain's reward system.

One side effect is that previously fun activities become 'uninspiring' which may lead to individual's discontinuing treatment.

Research into drug treatment faces a number of methodological problems.

These problems, along with co-morbidity issues, make it difficult to draw conclusions about the influence of drug therapies alone.

SSRIs raise serotonin levels in the brain. These drugs have been seen to reduce gambling behaviour.

Effects reported seem linked to the action of the drug rather than factors such as receiving attention or visiting their doctor's surgery.

▶ Lesson notes p.104

Behavioural interventions

Aversion therapy associates the performance of an addictive behaviour with an unpleasant or uncomfortable sensation in an attempt to reduce the undesired behaviour. For example, a small electronic device is placed on a gambler's wrist. When shown pictures of casinos, chips, online poker sites etc. the device emits a small shock. The duration and intensity of the shock are pre-planned to ensure the level of shock is aversive in order for the conditioning effect to occur.

Why can we conclude the theory is based on classical conditioning principles?
_____
_____

Other than an electric shock, what other aversive stimuli may be used?
_____
_____

How is covert sensitisation similar to aversion therapy?
_____
_____

Why might aversive therapy be considered unethical?
_____
_____

Are aversion therapy and covert sensitisation effective treatments?
_____
_____
_____

▶ Lesson notes p.104

CBT summary

- Typically, 10 one-hour sessions.
- Focuses on how the individual feels and thinks when engaging in addictive behaviour.
- Helps the individual develop more adaptive ways of thinking and behaving.
- Follow up sessions help prevent relapse.

The summary above is a generic outline of CBT which would receive few marks from the examiner. When outlining CBT you need to apply aspects of the therapy to the treatment of addictive behaviours.

Identify any correcting cognitive biases.

> What irrational thoughts may an addict report experiencing?

Changing behaviour.

> What behaviours might addicts be encouraged to engage in?

Relapse intervention.

> What triggers may addicts identify?

STRETCH: How might CBT be used to help someone quit smoking? Consider what irrational thoughts may need to be challenged, what behaviours are to be changed and how the risk of relapse may be reduced.

▶ Lesson notes p.105

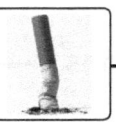

The theory of planned behaviour

Behavioural attitude

Subjective norms

Intention

Behaviour

Perceived behavioural control

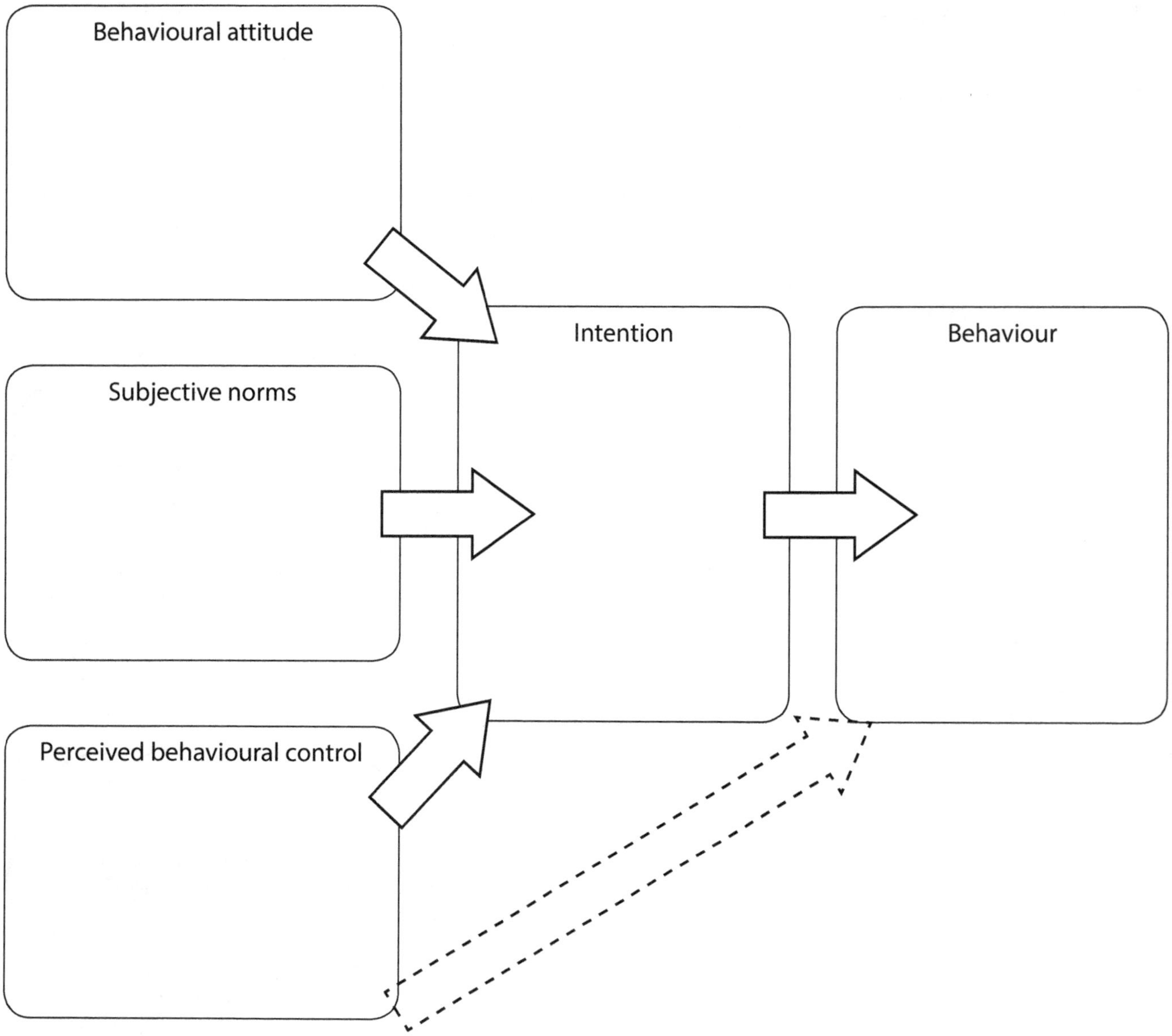

Lucy, by her own admission, is a chain smoker. Her first thought on waking is to have a cigarette and she schedules her work breaks and lunchtime around her nicotine cravings. On a night out she frequently leaves her friends inside pubs or restaurants so she can have another cigarette outside. When her friends suggest she tries to quit she explains she enjoys her habit and claims it helps her to relax. She promises them if she became sick she would give up but while she is young and healthy she cannot see the problem with having "one or two cigarettes". She argues lots of people smoke so she is no different from them and lists famous people who are regularly pictured with a cigarette. When Lucy is being honest with herself she doubts she would be able to reduce her intake let alone give up completely.

Explain how the theory of planned behaviour can be used to explain Lucy's current behaviour and suggest possible strategies to help her change her behaviour.

▶ Lesson notes p.105

Sort out the stages

Prochaska's six-stage model of behaviour change emphasises the gradual nature of behaviour change, assuming the addict moves through six discrete stages.

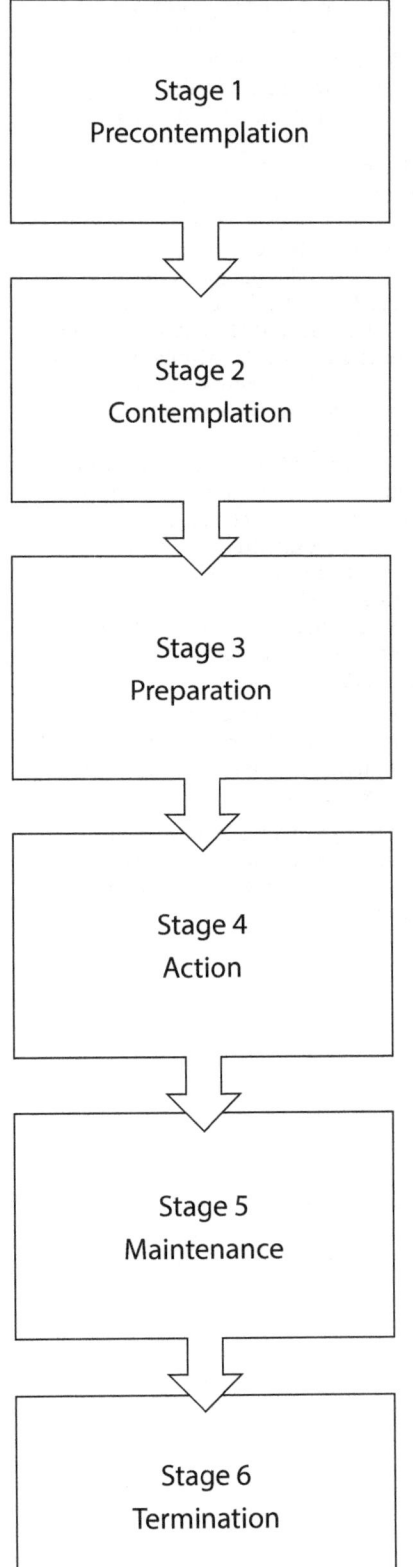

| Stage 1 Precontemplation |
| Stage 2 Contemplation |
| Stage 3 Preparation |
| Stage 4 Action |
| Stage 5 Maintenance |
| Stage 6 Termination |

The individual is no longer tempted to revert to the former behaviour and is confident they can maintain the change. Often people formulate new goals to achieve further success. Only 1 in 5 reach this stage.

Individuals now modify their behaviour to overcome problems. This stage involves the most overt behaviour changes and considerable commitment is needed to making a lasting change (up to six months).

The person may be aware a problem exists but have yet to make a commitment to change. The positive aspects of their addiction (the 'buzz') and effort needed to quit are barriers to change. This stage can last a long time.

The individual works to consolidate the gains attained during the previous stage and to prevent relapse. The individual is said to be in this stage once behaviour change has lasted over six months.

Individuals who currently have no intention to change their behaviour in the near future. They are unaware that their behaviour is becoming problematic and may only seek help because of pressure from others.

This combines intention to change with actual change. Small behavioural changes are reported. The person may have cut down but is not yet at a point of total abstinence.

▶ Lesson notes p.106

Great Clarendon Street, Oxford, OX2 6DP, United Kingdom

Oxford University Press is a department of the University of Oxford. It furthers the University's objective of excellence in research, scholarship, and education by publishing worldwide. Oxford is a registered trade mark of Oxford University Press in the UK and in certain other countries

© Oxford University Press 2016

The moral rights of the authors have been asserted

First published in 2016

All rights reserved. No part of this publication may be reproduced, stored in a retrieval system, or transmitted, in any form or by any means, without the prior permission in writing of Oxford University Press, or as expressly permitted by law, by licence or under terms agreed with the appropriate reprographics rights organization. Enquiries concerning reproduction outside the scope of the above should be sent to the Rights Department, Oxford University Press, at the address above.

You must not circulate this work in any other form and you must impose this same condition on any acquirer

British Library Cataloguing in Publication Data
Data available

ISBN 978-0-19-833869-7

10 9 8 7 6 5 4 3 2 1

Paper used in the production of this book is a natural, recyclable product made from wood grown in sustainable forests. The manufacturing process conforms to the environmental regulations of the country of origin.

Printed and Bound by CPI Group (UK) Ltd, Croydon, CR0 4YY

Dedications

Michael: Thanks to all at OUP for their support. Thank you to little Grace and Mummy Alana; both of you have been amazing in the last twelve months.

Rosalind: To Shawn, who continues to support me in everything I do. My friends and family who remind me there is life outside teaching. Finally, my wonderful students old and new.

Acknowledgements
Cover illustrations: Chris Cardwell

Credits
The publishers would like to thank the following for permissions to use copyright material:

Introduction icon (p1 onwards): xpixel/Shutterstock; **p3**: Author image; **p4**: Lukiyanova Natalia / frenta/Shutterstock; **Social Influence icon (p11 onwards)**: Qiun/Shutterstock; **p17**: With thanks to Adrian Frost; **Memory icon (p26 onwards)**: america365/Shutterstock; **Attachment icon (p36 onwards)**: Akinina Olena/Shutterstock; **Psychopathology icon (p49 onwards)**: Palto/Shutterstock; **Approaches in Psychology icon (p60 onwards)**: silvano audisio/Shutterstock; **Biopsychology icon (p69 onwards)**: fabioberti.it/Alamy; p71: (top) Christos Georghiou/Shutterstock; **Research Methods icon (p78 onwards)**: KlektaDarya/Shutterstock; **p101**: niderlander/Shutterstock; **p102**: niderlander/Shutterstock; **p110**: meaculpa_1/Shutterstock; **p113**: (top) © Don Troiani/Corbis; (middle) gielmichal/Shutterstock; (bottom) Stylus photo/Shutterstock; **p131**: vvoe/Shutterstock; **p163**: niderlander/Shutterstock; **p157**: (top) szefei/Shutterstock, (bottom) meunierd/Shutterstock; **p161**: KOUNADEAS IOANNHS/Shutterstock; **p172**: Kristina Stasiuliene/Shutterstock; **p183**: (data) scottlitt/Shutterstock, (feelings) f9photos/Shutterstock, (limitations) Eric Isselee/Shutterstock, (strengths) kungverylucky/Shutterstock, (creativity) 2happy/Shutterstock, (overview) Africa Studio/Shutterstock; **p186**: (top) Lightspring/Shutterstock, (bottom) Nicku/Shutterstock; **p196**: (tl, bl, br) PWT/Shutterstock, (tr) Fuse/Getty Images; **p210–211**: vasabii/Shutterstock; **p219**: (eye) Alexandru Cristian Ciobanu/Shutterstock, (light levels) monbibi/Shutterstock, (sleep/wake) Elena Tkachenko/Shutterstock; **p225**: A1Stock/Shutterstock; **p226**: Christophe BOISSON/Shutterstock; **p239**: cristi180884/Shutterstock; **p241**: (tl) leosapiens/Shutterstock, (tr) Yes Man/Shutterstock, (bl) Stephen Rees/Shutterstock

Although we have made every effort to trace and contact all copyright holders before publication this has not been possible in all cases. If notified, the publisher will rectify any errors or omissions at the earliest opportunity.

Links to third party websites are provided by Oxford in good faith and for information only. Oxford disclaims any responsibility for the materials contained in any third party website referenced in this work.